Court, Kirk, and Community

Scotland 1470 – 1625

Jenny Wormald

Edinburgh University Press

First published 1981 in The New History of Scotland series by Edward Arnold
(Publishers) Ltd and reprinted 1991 by
Edinburgh University Press
22 George Square, Edinburgh

Printed and bound in Great Britain by Billing & Son Ltd, Worcester

British Library Cataloguing in Publication Data
Wormald, Jenny
Court, kirk, and community. — (The new history of Scotland; 4)
1. Scotland — History — 15th century
2. Scotland — History — 16th century
I. Title II. Series
941.104 DA784

ISBN 0 7486 0276 3

Contents

Acknowledgements

Acknowledgements, like charity, begin at home. In the writing of this book, my greatest debt is to my husband, who metaphorically 'sewed buttons on my shirts', looked after the children, acted as reader and shared the typing, while leaving my conscience clear by managing to keep up his own work. I was also fortunate in my academic home, the University of Glasgow: to Dr Ian Cowan, Dr James Kirk, Dr John Durkan and Dr Rod Lyall, who all bore my questions with great patience, I express my considerable appreciation, for all their help and for being on the spot. And I thank Dr Simon Adams, my 'European' expert, also from Glasgow, even if in the 'rival' University of Strathclyde. Outside Glasgow, my demands on the friendship of Mrs Sheila Green, London, and Dr Henry Mayr-Harting, Oxford, included asking them to read the book to judge on general intelligibility, and got typically generous response. Dr Norman Macdougall, University of St Andrews, was also as generous with his time and advice as he has always been since we were research students; and Dr Sandy Grant, University of Lancaster, read the book with great promptness, and was trying to save me from errors even after the manuscript had gone to the printers. I am indebted to them, and to Dr Alasdair Stewart, University of Aberdeen, and Dr Emily Lyle, School of Scottish Studies, Edinburgh, whose immediate answer to a last-minute query about ballads prevented me from committing myself to an eighteenth-century text about a (possibly) thirteenth-century event, and elucidated one of the most problematic of all ballads. Above all, I thank my co-editors, Professor G.W.S. Barrow and Professor T.C. Smout, who combined the rôles of editors and historical advisors with a grace that made their suggestions seem immediately right. I also acknowledge a debt which gives particular pleasure. This book is the product of a course which I first taught in 1974–5. I would like to mention specifically my former pupil, Miss

Angela Galbraith, who read the manuscript, found that she could criticize the former critic, and did so to my considerable benefit. More generally, my ideas were developed as a result of discussion with students who, to my great good fortune, were interested in the subject and stimulating to teach. It is entirely correct to say that no one cited here is responsible for errors that remain; it is also entirely fitting to say that without their help, the errors would certainly be more numerous. Finally, to my parents, who first influenced my historical approach by encouraging me to realize that Protestants and Catholics should never by judged as 'right' or 'wrong', I dedicate this book.

Jenny Wormald
Glasgow
3 February 1981

I

Renaissance Scotland: The Reigns of James III, IV, and V

1

Politics and Government

James III began his personal rule in 1468–9, in the middle of a 'fallow' period in Scottish history. Apart from the short-lived crisis of Flodden, little happened in the two centuries between the end of the Wars of Independence and the Reformation to interrupt the prosaic and slow-moving pattern of events and make the blood of historians — and historical novelists — pulse quicker in their veins. It is the bread-and-butter period between two layers of jam. Until very recently it attracted little interest, and such attention as there was focused on the dreary power struggle between kings and magnates. Other European countries certainly suffered from such a struggle, but they at least provided the leavening of other themes, cultural, economic, and religious. In Scotland, the 'Waning of the Middle Ages' — to adopt the title of Huizinga's great book — contracted down to the waning of political relationships and the stagnation of everything else.

That picture is now becoming untenable, as modern scholars increasingly turn their attention to attitudes and aspects of the period ignored for five centuries. With the threat from England removed, the Scots could at last lift their heads and look beyond the consuming need for resistance to English imperialist aggression, and therefore look also beyond the military necessity of alliance with France. They had a breathing-space when, to an extent remarkable among European countries, they enjoyed, or were in some cases bored by, years of peace; there were few periods of war in these two centuries. Early-modern Scotland had a unique opportunity, such as had not existed before, and would not exist again after the union of the crowns in 1603, to act as a free and independent kingdom. It was an age of confidence and conscious determination to be 'European'. Nationalism, or perhaps more accurately, the growing awareness of Scotland as a nation-state, over which the king had 'ful Jurisdiction and fre Impyre', as parliament claimed in 1469, was no longer the defensive reaction to attack from without. It was pushy and self-assertive, fostered by the war of words which replaced the war of weapons, when chroniclers and poets developed and refined the origin myths that demonstrated Scottish independence and even Scottish superiority. The Scots knew well that the European mountain would not naturally come to the little Scottish Mohammed; had not that anxious father the duke of Milan turned down a marriage alliance with Scotland in 1474 on the grounds that no daughter of his should be banished to a place 'so far off as Scotland would be'? So they went to Europe.

From the unknown travellers who scribbled on the wall of the catacomb of San Callisto 'MCCCCLXVII quidam Scoti hic fuerunt' to the kings themselves, the same determination not to be ignored is clearly evident. The three universities founded in the fifteenth century remained, despite the intention of their founders, largely first-degree colleges, while students and academics went abroad to the great centres of learning on the continent, and to that cosmopolitan world contributed scholars of European distinction like Hector Boece, John Major, and George Buchanan. James IV attracted the services of Erasmus himself as tutor to his illegitimate sons. Even that most Scottish figure John Knox was a man of international reputation, with an influence far beyond his own country. Younger sons and soldiers-of-fortune, lacking opportunities at home, flocked abroad, some to Denmark, but most to join the French in the time-honoured sport of English-bashing; among the most successful was a cadet of the Stewart family, who was rewarded with an *entrée* into the French aristocracy as Lord d'Aubigny. The merchants looked far beyond the political confines of the Auld Alliance, and developed existing trading links with the Low Countries and the Baltic to the extent of setting up permanent communities in both. The monarchy also raised its sights; every king demanded a positive rôle in Europe, sometimes with grandiose lack of realism, such as James IV's passion to lead a European crusade against the Turks, but not always, as James V's hard-headed and successful diplomacy showed.

All this had its effect; foreign attitudes began to change. In the early fifteenth century, Aeneas Sylvius, the future Pope Pius II, came to Scotland and was immediately stricken with the rheumatism that afflicted him for the rest of his life, which added a particular venom to his literary annihilation of the country. But his description was of a kind that in the future would be increasingly restricted to the acid pens of English visitors. It stands in sharp contrast to the glowing account by Pedro d'Ayala, Spanish ambassador to the court of James IV; to the admission by two sixteenth-century scholars, Girolamo Aleandro, teacher of Greek and Hebrew at Paris, and the famous Milanese physician Girolamo Cardano, that where they had expected savagery, they had found humane and civilized qualities; even to Mary of Guise's praise of the palace of Linlithgow as the finest building she had seen outside the châteaux of the Loire, which may say more for her wifely tact than the extent of her travels or architectural accuracy, but still reflects the fact that James V's style of building, unlike the insular fantasies of Henry VIII, was consciously north-European.

This new approach was to provide a crucial context for the Reformation movement, among both supporters and opponents of the old church, and was the major factor in determining the new church's vision of itself as part of the church universal — with the additional belief in the Scottish part as 'one of the most pure kirks under heaven'. It underlay the political pride of late-sixteenth-century Scotland, a pride with which James VI was sufficiently imbued to upset his new English subjects badly when he became James I. In its worst form, assertiveness could topple over into arrogance, even into the gun-barrel vision of some of the leading Covenanters of the mid seventeenth century. But before it was so distorted, it enabled Scotland to play a part in European affairs greater than was justified by her economic position or political and military standing. For observers of this little society with large ideas, it presents a considerable paradox. At the time, men like Aleandro and Cardano began with a natural assumption of Scottish backwardness, and discovered that there was more to it than that. Modern commentators, with their equally natural preconceptions about what makes a primitive or a developed society, and their yardsticks dipped into the Burckhardtian concept of the Renaissance state, have the problem of reconciling the evidence of a country with the confidence to make successful contact with Europe and the fact of a country which was economically backward and possessed only undeveloped government institutions and a monarchy with few visible signs of control.

The crown's foreign policy began dramatically, with James III showing a marked taste for the kind of dynastic politics by which the greater powers of Europe extended their territories. The first effort was realistic, being close to home. His marriage to Margaret of Denmark in 1468 brought him Orkney and Shetland in pledge for part of her dowry; the king simply treated the islands as *de facto* part of Scotland, and followed this up by maintaining a relationship with Christian I which emphasized the power of the Scottish crown; in

1472, he master-minded the treaty between Christian and Louis XI, and James IV played a similar rôle when the alliance was renewed by Hans of Denmark and Louis XII. But James went further. Between 1471 and 1473 he proposed three campaigns, to annex part of Brittany, the county of Saintonge, and the duchy of Gueldres. Involvement in Europe was one thing; emulation of the great European rulers was another, and James's schemes were firmly rejected by parliament in 1473.

The attempt to maintain an independent position was the real theme of foreign policy. The monarchy was caught in a greater dilemma than it realized; the disaster of Flodden was the direct result of that dilemma, when James IV was finally unable to resolve Scotland's position in the maelstrom that was European politics. The problem was created by James III's attempt to push Scotland on to the road of alliance with England. Hindsight shows the wisdom of his decision. At the time, it seemed an appalling reversal of the natural belief in the English as the 'auld inemeis'; the 1470s was the decade that produced Blind Harry's *Wallace*, the second great epic on the Wars of Independence, under the patronage of landowners in southern Scotland. Yet James pursued his new policy tenaciously throughout the 1470s and 1480s, with a series of marriage alliances. The first of these, in 1474, arranged that his son James should marry Edward IV's daughter Cecilia when both grew up, but meanwhile brought James an annual pension of 2,000 merks as advance payment of a dowry of 20,000 merks. Counter-pressure from Louis XI produced ratification of the Auld Alliance in 1479. This ended the precarious new friendship and the pension; war was declared in 1480, although no English army crossed the border until the brief campaign of 1482, when having captured Berwick — its real objective — it went home again. Thereafter, James continued his original policy until his death.

James IV began by reversing the trend, renewing the Auld Alliance in 1492 and provoking the English by his ill-considered support for the Yorkist pretender Perkin Warbeck in 1496. He was lucky in that his would-be opponent was Henry VII, who refused to be distracted by this sword-rattling from the north, and continued to seek peace with Scotland, formalized by the Treaty of Perpetual Peace in 1502 and the marriage of his daughter Margaret to James in 1503. Credit for good sense seems to belong to Henry rather than James. But the spectacle of a Scottish king's favours being sought by an English king was extremely attractive, and did nothing but good for James's popularity. Yet this energetic king, pouring out correspondence with the chanceries of

Europe, was an unrealistic and ultimately pathetic figure, as events beyond his control overtook him. In 1508 the 'Warrior-pope' Julius II having used French help to overcome Venice, then allied with the Venetians to drive the French out of Italy. Three years later, under the utterly inappropriate title of the Holy League, Aragon, Venice, and England united, under the pope, in the attack on France, and Scotland was commanded to join in. James, whose relations with England had worsened with the accession of the bombastic Henry VIII in 1509, produced a different solution to the problems of a divided Europe. He demanded that Christendom should forget its internal difficulties and mount a crusade against the Turks. Undoutedly the Turks menaced eastern Europe; and in his vision of a re-united Christendom, James anticipated a much greater figure, the emperor Charles V. But Charles understood, as James did not, that the dream could never be realized. James bored the great powers of Europe with his insistence on crusade; only Louis XII, desperate for Scottish help, pretended to take him seriously. James was completely caught. The 1502 treaty, fatally as it turned out, had had papal confirmation. When James tried to break it, this devout son of the church, a former recipient of papal favours – including the blessed sword, which survives as one of the honours of Scotland – was excommunicated. In 1513 Henry invaded France. James, his options closed, declared war.

He had widespread support; the army that went to Flodden was drawn from all parts of Scotland. But it was a dramatic break in the pattern of years of peace; the last full-scale campaign had been the successful siege of Roxburgh in 1460. How unprepared the Scots were is seen in the individual disasters that made up the whole hideous débâcle. James sent his ships and gunners to France; at Flodden, the guns were fired by people who included his academic secretary and tutor to his sons, Patrick Paniter. His insistence on behaving impeccably according to the rules of war almost allowed Surrey, leader of the second-rank English army, to slip past him on the open road to Scotland. The expensive and prestigious 'white' – plate – armour worn by the Scots turned out to be a disastrous encumbrance in the Northumbrian mud. The governing class of Scotland – the king, 3 bishops, 11 earls, 15 lords – was wiped out, along with countless others. Paniter's violent translation from his study to death in battle sums up the utter futility of a battle that was fought in French interests, and should never have been fought at all.

The psychological shock of Flodden on the new ruling class, acting

for the infant James V, was vast. Panic produced immediate confirmation of the ties with France; in any case, the obvious choice of regent
was James's uncle, John duke of Albany, son of James III's exiled
brother who had died in France, leaving John to be brought up there.
But reaction set in. Determination never to be used by France again
produced a moment of enjoyable farce in 1523, when Albany, with a
French army of 5,000 and reluctant Scots trailing in its wake, crossed
the border and engaged with the English at Wark; the French and
English fought, and the Scots watched from the sidelines, as if at a
football match. Even in 1542, when Henry VIII was menacing Scotland, reviving the discredited claim of suzerainty and sending an army
north, reluctance to fight the English was strong enough to ensure that
the Scots lost the battle of Solway Moss.

Yet despite this failure, James V had astonishing success in his
foreign policy. Particularly for a minor power, success depends very
largely on circumstances, and James had advantages that his father
had lacked. The uneasy peace between Spain and her defeated enemy
France, acknowledged at the Peace of Cambrai in 1529, and French
alliance with England, seemed to leave Scotland with little bargaining
power. But other factors were involved. Henry VIII's Reformation
focused the eyes of pope and emperor on that other off-shore nation
which was still Catholic. Moreover, it was very much in Charles V's
interests to divide France and Scotland; hence he sought a marriage
alliance with James, initially suggesting no less a person than his sister
Mary of Hungary. That was useful for Scottish commercial negotiations with the Low Countries. But James's preference throughout was
for a French bride, long ago promised by the Treaty of Rouen in 1517.
Francis I, fearful of alienating his English ally, temporized with the
offer of Clement VII's kinswoman, Catherine de Medici, a marriage
whose consequences could have been remarkable. James's stated
interest in the dowry rather than the lady, and withdrawal of French
support, allowed the pope to save Catherine from life on the fringes of
Europe, while giving James a further lever against the papacy and the
freedom to continue his demand for marriage with Francis's daughter
Madeleine. His letters to the French king make marvellous reading;
signs of reluctance on Francis's part produced outpourings of grief
from the Scottish king that the alliance so long maintained between
their countries was now coming to an end, which brought return-of-
post replies begging James to do nothing rash. By 1535 negotiations for
James's marriage to Marie, daughter of the duke of Vendôme, were
well under way. In 1536 the combination of James's arrival in France,

and the breakdown of the English alliance and renewal of war with the emperor, made James's path straightforward; Marie was discarded, and James married Madeleine in January 1537, with a dowry of 100,000 livres, and annualrents from a further 125,000 livres.

Madeleine's death in July 1537 left him apparently saddened, but free to start afresh. He turned again to France, this time as the rival to his uncle Henry VIII, for the hand of Mary, daughter of the duke of Guise. The victory of a nephew and inferior king was a blow to Henry's pride which in part explains the violence of his policy and extremity of his claims towards Scotland, particularly after 1541 when James agreed to a personal meeting at York and committed the supreme insult of failing to turn up. Like his predecessors, James was not so central a figure in European politics as he thought. But a clear knowledge of what he wanted and a combination of circumstances brought him a great deal of money, two French brides, and recognition and advances from the great powers of Europe.

For a country whose leading figures in academic and economic life also sought a place in Europe, the rôle of the monarchy was both appropriate and prestigious. That in itself raises doubts about the weakness of the monarchy at home and its vulnerability in the face of an unusually lawless and boorish aristocracy, which have long been basic tenets of Scottish historiography. It is almost as if the Scots who went abroad and were received there as civilized beings, like William earl of Douglas in 1450 or Francis earl of Bothwell in the 1590s, 'troublemakers' both, changed their spots somewhere on the North Sea. But if relations between crown and nobility are considered in comparative terms, then it appears that the Scottish monarchy got off very lightly. Conflict between magnates and kings is a dominant theme of fifteenth-century Europe, a conflict resolved in favour of the crowns of England, France, and Aragon and Castile by the end of the century, leaving their power greater than it had been before, and opening the road to increasingly autocratic government in the sixteenth century. In his book *Imperial Spain*, J.H. Elliott has compellingly argued that it was the victory not of a 'new monarchy' so much as of 'old monarchy' using its powers in a new and impressively effective way. The problem is of course more complex than a simple 'crown—magnate' power-struggle, in European or Scottish terms; but the existence of tensions in other European countries reduces the Scottish situation to some kind of scale, putting into context the sporadic and individualistic clashes between kings and members of their nobility. There was no 'class' war; and Scottish nobles were not more violent, and not necessarily less civilized, than their European counterparts. Scotland suffered nothing like the six changes of ruling dynasty and numerous small rebellions of fifteenth-century England. Only one of the last three kings of pre-Reformation Scotland, James III, was significantly threatened, twice in a 20-year reign, and killed at the end of it not in battle against the massed ranks of an unruly nobility, but by a small minority, almost all individual victims of unusually arbitrary rule. But arbitrary treatment continued. The popular James IV and the impressive James V ruthlessly extorted money and, on occasion, imprisoned and executed their greatest subjects with an impunity more normally associated with Henry VII, Henry VIII, and Francis I.

The nature of James IV's government gives some support for the idea that the Scottish monarchy, like those of Europe, had triumphed after a century of struggle, with Stewarts, with Douglases, with the rebels of 1482 and 1488. After 1494 the practice of calling parliament almost annually ceased abruptly; for the remainder of the reign, only four parliaments met, with a significant gap between 1496 and 1503, and another between 1504–5 and the last parliament of the reign in 1509. This does suggest a parallel with the policy of other European rulers: the attempt to play down the rôle of the 'representative' assembly of estates, and build up more directly controllable conciliar government.

James's death in 1513 makes certainty on that point impossible. But there are other signs of the strength of royal power. In Scotland, as in any pre-industrial society, land was the decisive factor in determining a man's wealth and prestige. The man who increased his patrimony was the man of worldly success. Yet the monarchy was able to attack that most prized principle, the property rights of its subjects. Debtors had their lands apprised (valued) and assigned to their creditors; the crown forced 119 apprisings between 1488 and 1513. In strict and wholly financial interpretation of feudal law, those who alienated lands subject to wardship without the consent of the superior found that their lands were 'recognosced', and escheated. The earl of Angus was faced with a bill of £1,000 when the king pursued for 'non-entry' landowners whose entry dues had not been paid, by themselves or their ancestors. James V tightened the financial screw further. In 1537, when he issued the customary act of revocation, of all grants made during his minority, he made the usual regrants, but for the first time demanded large compositions for them. Not everyone had to pay up every penny. Some made bargains; for James V's secretary, Thomas

Erskine of Brechin, long service to the crown brought gentler treatment. But some did pay in full, like Lord Gray, who was finding the last instalment of his composition of 10,000 merks in 1543. And the king went to great lengths to protect his rights and his control over the landowners. Richard Maitland of Lethington's right to redeem the lands of Thirlestane from Alexander Forrester of Corstorphine, granted during the minority, was specifically revoked after the general act; the lands must stay with Forrester, because they were the only ones held by that family directly of the crown.

Any king who could revoke, wholesale, grants made in his name by a minority government because they might leave the crown 'grettumlie hurt' is not a weak king. The same can be said for the crown's other methods of raising money. D'Ayala's comment that 'the whole soil of Scotland belongs to the king' was not literally true, but it looked very like it to the many landowning families who offered the king any legal pretext to strike at their holdings. Yet these things are not so much evidence for the crown emerging as the winner of a long struggle, as evidence of Stewart ingenuity in finding new forms of expression of that characteristic which had been strikingly obvious in every king since James I, acquisitiveness, sometimes closely allied to vindictiveness. The act of revocation goes back to James II's reign, the earliest apprisings to James III's. More generally, the history of crown–magnate relations is strewn with victims of Stewart aggression against those who were vulnerable to the crown's thirst for land or those who could be regarded as political opponents. There was no real difference in the degree of royal power before and after the reign of James III. James IV and V simply extended and refined the methods used.

The ruthless exercise of power was taken to dangerous lengths by James III. He went beyond even the veneer of legality in withholding the earldom of Lennox from the rightful heir, and granting its lands in liferent to his chancellor, the illegitimate Andrew Lord Avandale; these lands were not in the royal gift, and his procuring of a legitimation for Avandale did nothing to make his sharp practice more respectable. More seriously, when in February 1488 he suddenly dismissed the earl of Argyll from the chancellorship which he had held since 1483, he ensured that Argyll would be one of the two earls who fought against him at Sauchieburn four months later, taking with him Drummond and Lord Oliphant, with whom he had marriage alliances. It was 20 years of such dealings that created the crises of James's reign, not the traditionally famous low-born favourites, who, if they existed at all, were of little significance.[1] The reasons for his downfall are a telling reminder that when kings and magnates did conflict, kings did not always have right on their side.

James III's style of kingship has something in common with that of the more able James V, probably the most unpleasant of all the Stewarts. James V's treatment of men he had formerly favoured was sensational to a degree, reaching its climax in the case of his master of works, James Hamilton of Finnart, whom royal patronage and favour had enriched far beyond the point of safety; in 1540 he was executed on the visibly trumped-up charge of communing with the Douglases and conspiring to kill the king. Failure of service, and even suspicion of potential failure, landed Argyll, Bothwell, and others in prison. Above all, the power of the Douglas earls of Angus was not proof against the unrelenting hatred of the king for a family unwise enough to seize his person, and with it control of government, during the minority. Angus himself, an exile in England throughout the reign, was reasonably safe. His kinsmen and associates were hounded by a king who regarded even intercommuning with the Douglases as a crime, for which he could forfeit or exact vast payments for remission. Moreover, James was the first king who did seem to want to edge the greatest laymen out of his government. He created no hereditary lords of parliament; his council was dominated by clerical lawyers. He did not share the fate of James III. Instead, he died in 1542 of what has been described as nervous exhaustion, five months short of his 31st birthday, and immediately after the humiliating defeat at Solway Moss.

The formidable power of kings who could thus attack the persons and properties of their magnates with no more than the occasional limited challenge can hardly be over-stated. It is the source of royal not magnate power that requires explanation. There were, after all, few formal props for their authority. They presided over a small kingdom, which was recognizably a social and political unit, but where the local community was still, for most people, the most important, even the only consideration, and where links between centre and locality were tenuous and sporadic. Their regular income was unimpressive: James III's £5,000 per annum was at best one-tenth of that of the English crown, and although James IV and V more than doubled it,

---

[1]This has been demonstrated beyond doubt by N.A.T. Macdougall, 'The source: a reappraisal of the legend', in *Scottish Society in the Fifteenth Century*, ed. Jennifer M. Brown (London, 1977), pp. 17–32.

the falling value of money meant that even in the best years it was never more than the income of an impoverished and second-string European king. Their government consisted of somewhat casual and ill-organized institutions at the centre, and local worthies in the localities whose position could depend on inheritance and local prestige rather than direct royal appointment. Moreover, early-modern government was still the king's government, personally directed by him. Like the monarchy of the eleventh to the thirteenth centuries, the house of Stewart was immensely fortunate in that it produced a line of highly able sovereigns, with the exception of the inept Mary. But if the motivating force could not function, because the king was a minor, the outlook was indeed grim; 'Woe unto thee, o land, when thy king is a child'. The Stewart monarchy was uniquely unfortunate in that from 1406 every ruler came to the throne as a child. Between 1460 and 1625 some 60 years were years of minority. That had an inevitable effect on the authority of the crown. The yardstick of a monarchy which directly controlled its kingdom through an impressive government machine, even the yardstick of a monarchy which was always there, simply do not apply to either the expectations or the realities of royal authority in early-modern Scotland. Yet in the weaknesses lay a source of immense strength, for these weaknesses brought expectations and reality into balance; the expectation of over-all control could never become the reality of oppression over a wide range of social groups or an extensive part of the country.

The minorities themselves provided a safety-valve. Had James V lived, for example, the history of the sixteenth-century monarchy might have more closely paralleled those of the English, French, and Spanish. His death removed the threat of growing autocracy. The faction-fighting of the minority which followed was exacerbated by religious dissent and diplomatic unheaval, as Scotland veered between alliances with England and France; but it was essentially no different from earlier minorities, where jockeying for power at the top had not significantly damaged the country at large. The repeated minorities did hamper developments in central government. They also temporarily reduced the crown's income, for those who controlled minority governments lacked the natural authority inherent in kingship, and had therefore to conciliate and buy support; between them, regent Albany and the queen mother, Margaret Tudor, succeeded in bringing royal revenues down from £30,000 Scots at the end of James IV's reign to £13,000 by 1526. But in a country where, for almost every aspect of every-day life, the important people were the local magnates and lairds, the king's absence was far more noticeable in his capital than in his country. Argyll and Huntly, the greatest magnates of western and northern Scotland, might take the chance offered by the death of James IV to fail to send the crown's rents to the exchequer. But they continued to hold courts, arbitrate in the quarrels of their followers, and generally oversee the running of their localities with exactly the same mixture of self-interest and responsibility to their dependants and tenants that any earl would show, according to his personality, at any time.

That exercise of local power was never significantly threatened, even by adult kings of considerable personal power. Most of his subjects never saw the king, and heard about his affairs only occasionally and belatedly; even those involved in government spent much of their time away from the capital and thus away from immediate royal influence. To many, not only the theory of kingship but also the person of the king was an ideal, and all the more powerful for that. As someone seen in the light of overseer of the affairs of the kingdom, rather than direct and ever-present ruler, the king provided an idealized focal point for society. But he should not be entirely remote. Kings whose reputation stood high were those who travelled through their country, holding justice ayres themselves as well as sending out their justiciars, descending in might against particular wrong-doers. Kingship was still peripatetic, not just throughout the royal palaces of the Home Counties, mainly for reasons of hygiene, as it had become in England, but in a very real sense. Edinburgh did not finally emerge as the capital of Scotland until the reign of James III; hitherto, Perth and Stirling had been equally important centres of government, while before the 1470s the supreme civil court, the Session, was a peripatetic court, intended to meet twice or three times a year in various parts of the country.

This adds another dimension to the unpopularity of James III. James's attempt to centralize government and even criminal as well as civil justice in Edinburgh – though not, surprisingly, the mint – was an unsatisfactory reversal of normal practice, particularly for a population whose main concentration was north of the Tay. In 1473 parliament counselled him to 'travel throw his Realme & put sic Justice and polycy in his awne realme that the brute & the fame of him mycht pas in utheris contreis'. James did not follow this classic advice. But his successors did. Very early in the reign of James IV, it was clear that an active king once again ruled, as he dragged his councillors about the country on justice ayres, and made a succession of increasingly punitive raids into the highlands in the 1490s. That pattern was maintained by James V, whose early raid into the borders in 1530, and dramatic execution of John Armstrong of Liddesdale, was the stuff of ballads and of strong kingship. More gently, James IV's regular pilgrimages, taking him from Whithorn in the south to Tain in the north, strengthened the impression of an active and interested king, and possibly even a human one, for one of the interests was Janet Kennedy, the king's mistress, conveniently installed at Darnaway on the Moray Firth and the road to Tain.

This style of kingship was all the more effective because it was not tarnished by repeated royal exactions. However the king forced up revenue, it was not by regular taxation. This was not a matter of weakness, but of commonsense. The normal reason for the introduction of regular taxation was war, and if, as in France, the war went on for long enough, it became a permanent feature. Among other European countries, Scotland stands out as being scarcely affected by war; while other kings might face enemies on several fronts, Scotland's only enemy was England, and even then, periods of fighting were rare. Thus the needs of the government were substantially reduced. In any case, the amount of taxation needed to finance an army of a size that would not look ridiculous when set against an English one would have imposed an intolerable burden on a population probably about one-fifth the size that of England. When kings needed troops, therefore, they relied on the leaders of the localities to turn out their men; like so much of Scottish government, it was done on a casual and personal basis, not a formal one. Occasionally money was raised for a particular campaign: about £1,500, for example, was levied under threat of English invasion in 1481, in stark contrast to the £13,000 paid by the English government when its army did invade in 1482. A royal marriage or an embassy might also produce taxation; James V got £6,000 in 1535 to pay for the embassy to negotiate his French marriage. But there was little taxation until the reign of James VI. The only partial exception to that was the savage taxation of the church by James V in the 1530s. But his onslaught on the wealthiest institution in Scotland, at a time when its wealth was under considerable attack, and its effect in forcing the church to feu its lands to the laity, were scarcely a matter for lay criticism.

Regular taxation encourages contact between government and governed; it was one reason for the interest of the English shire gentry in attending parliament, where those whose pockets were touched could make their voice heard. It also encourages more bureaucracy, for more officials become necessary. And it is unpopular. Its absence in Scotland meant that the governed remained less aware of the government, and certainly had no reason to see it as the oppressor, bearing down on its subjects with demands for money. That strengthened the idea of the king as paternalistic overseer, a view that gained further credence from the amount of legislation designed to help the 'pwr cowmonis' which king-in-parliament enacted. Even James V contributed his share, in a string of acts in 1535 and 1541, and in 1540, the rather touching insistence that 'the army of Scotland be unhorsit except greit baronis', partly because the horsemen got in the way of the infantry, but primarily because of the 'distructioun of Cornis medowis and hanyng of pure folkis'.

There was, therefore, little reason for general unrest, and such complaints as there were in the localities were more likely to be directed against the local landlord than against the king; apprizings, for example, were the direct consequence of an act of 1469 forbidding landlords to distrain their tenant's goods and holdings to pay their own debts. There was no groundswell of resentment against the crown on which discontented magnates could readily draw. In any case, not all the individual victims of Stewart greed or Stewart use of the law can be classed as opponents of the monarchy. When the king invoked the law to consolidate his position and gain or retain lands, he was only doing what any landowner would do in the interests of his inheritance and legal rights. That his cases were fought in *his* courts, by his advocate − an office created by James II − certainly gave the king an advantage, but that was not normally a reason for rebellion. And if his actions created resentment, they also brought him friends; it was the earl of Bothwell who gained in 1495 when the earl of Rothes' lands were apprized. Moreover, there is a considerable gulf between resentment and rebellion, and it was not easy to persuade people to cross it. Even James III had the majority of the nobility and gentry on his side in 1488; and some, like Huntly and Erroll, solved the dilemma created by a king who was hard to serve but was yet king by remaining neutral.

Ideologically, the *laissez-faire* monarchy of Scotland had much to offer. Its very existence provided the greatest source of stability within the country. Any who doubted that need only look south to England and the spectre of political upheaval, or back to the fate of those too-powerful families, the Stewarts and Douglases; indeed, the power of the last earl of Douglas was so thoroughly annihilated in the 1450s that in the late 1480s he was allowed to crawl back to Scotland to die. The nobles were not idealists, although it would be wrong to deny them any ideals. But they were at least realists. They were great lords; the decision to rebel against their own lord, the king, had to be weighed against the fact that it was in their own interests to uphold the principles of loyalty. They gained far more from co-operation with the king than the risky business of rebellion against him. A century later, that most articulate of kings, James VI, stated his intention of being a 'universal king'. It was not a new theory. The king alone could be above faction, control the balance of power within the state and prevent one magnate family gaining a monopoly of lands and offices in any region. Even the greatest families never reached the heights of the Douglases under James II. The Campbells and the Gordons, two of the most powerful families, began their rise to the top during the reconstruction of a badly depleted peerage in the mid fifteenth century, and for the next 150 years pursued a consistent policy of co-operation with the king, interrupted only by Argyll's rebellion in 1488, and two brief periods of trouble created by the Catholic earls of Huntly after the Reformation. Their service was rewarded by lands, wealth, and local offices; they were the king's lieutenants in the west and the north. But even they never became wholly dominant, for on a smaller scale there were many families, the Hays earls of Erroll, the Leslies, the Grants of Freuchy, and others, who also saw the wisdom of serving the crown, and benefited from it.

At the same time, there were limits to the king's patronage which themselves diffused a potential source of trouble. The crown did not possess enough to make those who sought enrichment turn too fixed and jealous an eye on it; royal patronage was one way for a family to get on in the world, but not the only way and not even necessarily the principal way. Moreover, in this localized society, local offices were important, but government offices were not prizes eagerly sought; on the whole, the problem was to persuade the great men of society to take part in central government, not to control the rush for places. The classic political struggle of the 'ins' and 'outs' was far less a feature of Scottish political life than it was under wealthier and more centralized monarchies. What did produce the three crises that are the only examples of such struggles was not exclusion from office, but exclusion from the king. The crisis of 1482 was another example of Stewart infighting; the ruling clique, Avandale, Argyll, and William Schevez, archbishop of St Andrews, were attacked by the king's half-uncles, the earls of Atholl and Buchan and the bishop-elect of Moray, not because of their offices but because they were the men close to James. The 1488 rebellion did produce one rebel motivated by loss of office, the sacked

chancellor Argyll; it was an exceptional case because this earl, heavil
involved in central government for a decade, was himself such a
exception. And the minor rebellion of 1489, ostensibly to avenge
James III's murder, was actually an attack on the families of Hume
and Hepburn, those former rebels who were now all-powerful with the
new king. The fragmentary contemporary chronicle which says that ir
1482 the rebel lords 'slew ane part of the kingis housald and other par
thai banysyt' makes the crucial point that those who might block direct
access to the king were the real threat. The later legend of James III,
which put the emphasis wrongly on low-born favourites, still reflects a
basic reality about the nature of Scottish government: for the great
laymen, formal position mattered very little, but personal familiarity
with the king mattered much. In any case, two rebellions against the
most remote of the Stewart kings, and one in the unique circumstances
of the accession of his son, hardly disturbed the general pattern of
Scottish politics.

They do, however, underline the supreme importance of personal
contact within a political structure that was institutionally under-
developed, and therefore help to explain the particular ways in which
the monarchy fostered its own image. It never indulged in the quasi-
religious propaganda used by the English and French kings. No Scottish king touched for the King's Evil; James VI was further to offend his
English subjects by showing extreme distaste for the practice. Like so
much else, its methods were more prosaic, and highly effective. This
was an age when, following the example of the fifteenth-century
Burgundian court, the monarchs of Europe were building up their
courts as places of formality and elegance, centres of culture and
political life. Those European monarchs James III, IV, and V did likewise. The buildings, the clothes, the pageants, the lifestyle of their
courts, were all sufficiently lavish to display to their subjects at home
and visitors from abroad the impressiveness of the Scottish crown; the
careful lay-out of the rooms through which ambassadors were led to
the king's presence in one wing of Linlithgow palace, built by James V,
and James I's magnificent Great Hall in the opposite wing, used for the
court performance in 1540 of David Lindsay's brilliant *Satyre of the
Thrie Estaitis*, stand as testimony to their cultivation of royal
splendour.

These things enhanced their personal prestige. Politically, the
heightened importance of the court brought advantages rather different from those sought by, for example, the English monarchy. The
Scottish kings were not seeking greater control over their nobility, not

trying to reduce the level of local autonomy, for that would have weakened the crown along with the aristocracy. Rather, they were trying to strengthen their personal links with the men who were crucially important to them in the localities. It has been perceptively pointed out that 'an earl at court may often have achieved more in five minutes than Alex Inglis (the clerk-register) at umpteen meetings of the council'.[2] Equally, the king might achieve a great deal in these five minutes. For a personal monarchy ruling over a disparate kingdom, the court was particularly appropriate as the political centre. It offered the ideal meeting-place for the king and his 'natural counsellors'. They did indeed want to be asked for counsel, but not in the context of a council dealing with detailed and sometimes trivial business. Parliament suited them better, but it was, above all, the court that could attract them. The desire to attract, not to overawe, explains why no Scottish king of the late fifteenth or sixteenth century ever tried to insist on the personal cult which produced the adulation encouraged by Henry VIII and Elizabeth. Good relations were what mattered. Because they depended so much on personality, they were achieved with supreme success by the most attractive of these kings, James IV, as they were to be again — as descriptions of his court make clear — by the easy-going James VI.

Absence of a personality cult did not mean absence of the cult of kingship. Outwith the court, the vast expenditure on artillery, the supremely expensive status-symbol, and, in the case of James IV, the navy, show the same pre-occupation with regal display; it is ironic, but somehow not inappropriate, that the one unpopular king, James III, should have had the bad luck to lose a gift of artillery from Sigismund, archduke of Austria, which sank in a storm *en route* to Scotland in 1481. Yet it was James's exalted ideas of kingship that set the scene for the future. The concept of empire first occurs in the records of his reign. It also occurs on his coinage, for the silver groat issued in the last years of his reign has a three-quarter face portrait of the king, the first of its kind north of the Alps, and James wears not the open crown of kings, but the closed crown of the emperor.

At the same time, the idea of personal kingship was carefully maintained. The strength of kinship and lordship throughout the localities of Scotland was subsumed and unified by the concept of the king as

[2]A.L. Brown, 'The Scottish "Establishment" in the later Fifteenth Century', *Juridical Review*, new ser., 23 (1978), p. 105

the supreme embodiment of both; again, it was left to James VI to arti-culate it, when he likened the king to the father of his children. In contrast to other European royal styles, the monarchs described them-selves not as kings of Scotland but as kings of the Scots. This concen-tration on the familial nature of kingship reinforced succession by primogeniture, that theoretic but not always practical source of strength. Yet the monarchy never laid claim to a long and glorious ancestry, showing no interest in the ancient and legendary king-list used by historians and chroniclers. Instead, they took the prosaic and made it royal. They emphasized their origins as stewards, first to the counts of Dol in Brittany and then, in the twelfth century, to the kings of Scotland. Those who had once looked after the king's household now looked after the kingdom. The Latin version of their name was 'seneschallus', the word for steward; and they gave themselves the vernacular title Steward of Scotland.

The remarkable ability with which the crown portrayed itself as the supreme expression of both the attitudes of an outward-looking society and the attitudes of a localized one, was a major source of its consider-able authority. Its power brings out sharply the sometimes blurred dividing-line between politics and government. It is an important dis-tinction. Despite the almost unique degree of centralization and bureaucracy that existed in England, the localities were by no means entirely amenable to the dictates of the king's government in London. Conversely, there was a degree of control within Scottish society which was maintained without a highly sophisticated government machine. The monarchy did, of course, have a civil service; indeed, the prolif-eration of financial officials reflects one of its strongest interests. More generally, because red-tape is one of the most prolific organisms known to man, even Scottish bureaucracy was steadily increasing, so that, for example, a royal grant now went through six stages of authentication. But the major institutions of government, parlia-ment, convention (general council), and council, were still ill-defined, and remained so; when the great lawyers of the late sixteenth century, Sir John Skene of Curriehill and Sir Thomas Craig of Riccarton, attempted to distinguish the authority of parliamentary act and council ordinance – defined in fourteenth-century England – they had to confess themselves at a loss.

The Scottish parliament has suffered by comparison with that unusual phenomenon the English one, in particular because it remained a small body, which did not attract the shire gentry. In fact, the more important local landowners were coming in a new guise, as lords of parliament,[3] but there was nothing like the vocal English house of Commons. Specifically, absence of taxation and war was a major reason for the difference. Generally, comparison with the English parliament is less instructive than comparison with the Estates of Europe; in France, the empire, Aragon and Castile, Poland, Sweden, as in Scotland, the national assembly was an assembly of higher nobility and clergy, and of townsmen.

That means that the Scottish parliament was composed of the leaders of rural, ecclesiastical, and urban society. The thesis that it was a weak body must therefore depend on the unlikely idea that the most powerful people in the kingdom changed from eagles to doves when they entered parliament. As the one formal link between centre and locality, it actually mattered far more to have men prepared to speak with an independent voice on behalf of the localities than to have large numbers of people. Equally from the king's point of view, a weak parliament would have been of little use. This was the highest court in the land. King-in-parliament was the law-giver; and from the time of James I there had poured out, from its almost annual meetings, an immense amount of law, on matters ranging from issues of national importance to the ban on the destruction of birds' nests and the obligation on the lieges to deal with that persistent threat to crops, the 'guld' or corn-marigold. Royal policy transmitted to the localities, regional interests brought before parliament, both required the same thing: that as the intermediary parliament should have an authoritative voice.

The price that the monarchy had to pay was that the voice could also be critical. Inevitably, James III suffered most; the early criticism of his foreign policy was followed by a string of complaints from parliaments throughout his reign, up to 1487, about his failure to take an interest in justice other than personal profit through the sale of remissions (pardons). These issues affected both the country and the localities; and they raised questions about the exercise of royal power. On these, parliament would speak. On the other hand, parliament could be an essential ally, as it was for James V. The rising threat of religious dissent probably encouraged a closing of ranks; James's determination to maintain the old church was underwritten by repeated legislation in support of the church against heretics and heretical literature. Because

[3]The emergence of this group is discussed in the important article by A. Grant, 'The development of the Scottish peerage', *Scottish Historical Review* LVII (1978), pp. 1–27.

it was reinforcing the *status quo* and not, like the Reformation parliament in England, overturning it, James V's parliament looks more neutral. In fact, king-in-parliament in the 1530s in both countries claimed to determine the religious position of the people. It was a dramatic claim. In Scotland, where there was no effective king after James's death in 1542, this use of parliament's authority was the forerunner to the sensational parliament of 1560 which did exactly the same thing, this time dictating Scotland's Protestantism, and doing so without licence from the monarchy, indeed in open defiance of it.

The combination of religious upheaval and the need to summon parliaments during minorities, ensured that the Scottish parliament did not share the decline of the Estates in France, Spain, and Germany. But kings and regents continued to use two other bodies which were on the whole more easily controlled, conventions, and a privy council with astonishingly wide competence. The attraction of both was obvious enough. Conventions could meet quickly, not being subject to the 40-day rule; and not everyone who had the right to come to parliament need be summoned. For political crises, particularly during minorities, they were invaluable. So useful were they to regents, indeed, particularly in the minorities of Mary and James VI, that by the end of the century the principle that at least a convention that taxed must be fully attended by the three estates had been forced on both regent Morton in the 1570s and the king in the 1580s. Before that, the rules were conveniently flexible.

The privy council, because it retained legislative and judicial powers, and was never reduced to an advisory capacity, was even more invaluable. It was small — quorums were normally under 10 — and it was the body closest to the king. For that reason, parliament tried to have a say in its membership; up until 1598, councils were sometimes chosen in parliament. But it was the minorities, as much as royal policy, that kept the council strong; parliament's nomination of councillors to remain with the young king in rotation was designed to restrict the power of either regent or any one faction. This could rebound disastrously, as it did in 1525, when the earl of Angus simply refused to hand the king over to the next group of councillors, and thus seized political control. But normally the council did provide a check. And as the most regular and by far the most hard-worked of the government institutions, it had a crucial rôle; even the partial survival of council records, which describe only its judicial work in the late fifteenth century, show that at least for some periods of the year being a councillor was a full-time occupation.

It was dominated by a distinctive group within the king's government, the professional administrators and lawyers. As yet, they were almost exclusively churchmen, university graduates who sought a career in the king's service, and hoped, through royal preferment, to gain benefices. The highest ambition was a bishopric; people like William Elphinstone, successively bishop of Ross and Aberdeen, and Thomas Spens, bishop of Galloway and then Aberdeen, are both examples of civil servants who sat regularly on the council, went on embassies, and made it to the top. Less fortunate was Archibald Whitelaw, secretary from 1462 until 1493, a distinguished scholar and collector of books, a man who had a moment of diplomatic fame when he delivered an oration in Ciceronian Latin to Richard III at Nottingham in 1484; for all that, he died as archdeacon of Lothian. These people were the mainstay of government; the clergy were still the literate élite, almost the only people with legal training. Their rôle was not primarily political, although the dividing-line is not absolute, for on the king's council they were involved in political decisions; hence the sad scene in 1513 when the aged Elphinstone, after a lifetime of royal service going back to the reign of James III, tried despairingly and unsuccessfully to halt the rush of enthusiasm for war against England. In general, however, the fact that such men survived political crises ensured a degree of continuity and administrative expertise, less dramatic but more stable than the shifts within the political world.

Professor Brown's analysis of the sederunts of James III's council shows how important these people were compared to the laity. The earls hardly ever turned up; apart from Argyll and the earl of Crawford, a close associate of the king who was regularly in the royal household, other magnates like Atholl, Angus, and Erroll attended less than five out of a total of 198, and the most powerful northern earl, Huntly, never attended at all. Lords of parliament came rather more frequently, but the 58 attendances of John Lord Carlisle were still unusually high. This reflects traditional attitudes. Yet for reasons that were not the result of royal policy, and that cannot indeed be satisfactorily explained, this is the period when a profound change in government circles is first detectable. Literate laymen were challenging the professional monopoly of the clergy, emulating clerics by making a career in royal service and getting rewards; John Lord Carlisle seems to have owed his lordship of parliament and grants of lands in the south-west to service in the king's administration. More striking examples were Richard Lawson, graduate of St Andrews, lawyer, and provost of Edinburgh, and John Ross of Montgrenan, also a lawyer, and, like Lawson, king's advocate. Of James III's five chancellors, two were laymen who between them held office for 27 out of the 28 years of the reign; of the five who served James IV, three were laymen, and a fourth, the king's brother, difficult to classify, for he was both duke of Ross and archbishop of St Andrews. That is in marked contrast to the run of clerical chancellors until the reign of James II, broken only once in the 1340s. The change was as yet in infancy, and it was to take another century before its effects were fully felt. But these were the men of the future.

More rapid was the development of the law. Justice in Scotland was an extraordinary mixture of royal justice, where there was a degree of professional expertise, and local justice which was largely amateur. But even royal justice was haphazard to a degree; before the reign of James IV the king's council, consisting of clerical lawyers and whichever amateur laymen happened to be present, simply turned to judicial business when a backlog had piled up, and then spent a fortnight or so getting through as much as they could. James IV rationalized this system; his Session met daily in Edinburgh, clearly as a response to pressure of business. Then in 1532 came the establishment of the College of Justice, which was not the great new beginning after the 'Dark Age' traditionally believed in by legal historians, but was certainly a landmark.

The inspiration for these developments did not come primarily from the crown. With the exception of James III, the monarchy rightly saw that their responsibility to maintain law and order could be more effectively fulfilled in the localities. Moreover, they were not idealists. They wanted their councils to be free to deal with their business, and not to be endlessly clogged up with the complaints of their subjects; thus they consistently tried to force justice back into the local courts, leaving the council as an appeal court. James V used the idea of the College of Justice as a device to persuade the pope to allow him to tax the church. The paid bench which he claimed was essential for the improvement of justice remained unpaid, while the money went into the king's pockets. It is the palaces of Falkland and Stirling, not the College of Justice, that are the real monuments to the ambitions of James V.

The impact was made by the lawyers themselves, who seized the chances offered by pressure on the crown, and by the sharp practice of James V. The growing demand for 'professional' justice increasingly strengthened their hand in defining their rights, and so establishing a monopoly, as lawyers will. The judges of the new Court of Session reacted strongly to infringements of their competence; in 1533 they removed a case over a disputed tenement in Montrose from the commissary court of St Andrews. They also extended that competence, claiming the right to hear a case of land-ownership in 1543 on the grounds that the court had had such competence 'thir divers yeiris'. It had not; the old Session had dealt with cases of possession, but cases involving ownership had been sent back to the local judges.

They also took on the king. They were circumspect enough not to threaten strike-action if they were not paid until after James V's death. But they were quick to invoke their statutes of 1532, one of which forbade the king to interfere in the administration of justice; in 1533 defendants who produced a letter from the king supporting their case had the letter dismissed, while the king was told to keep out. The 'ordinary' lords of session — the president and 14 judges, 7 lay, 7 clerical — fought a long battle with the crown over its excessive use of its right to appoint 'extraordinary' lords. They failed to persuade the crown to keep the numbers down to the three or four allowed by the 1532 statutes, or even the six agreed with Mary of Guise, regent in the 1550s. But they gradually imposed their own standards of entry into their exclusive ranks, and they became a distinct and powerful institution. 'Royal' justice was no longer the 'king's' justice. Nor was it the justice offered by the professional clerics of the past. The original composition of the court in 1532 already indicates that the laity were pushing their way into the law, as they were into government, and after the Reformation they took over entirely from the clergy. It was still in the field of civil justice that the lawyers had their real success; criminal justice did not yet have a central court. But in 1514 the office of justice-general was created for the earl of Argyll, whose family held it until 1628. The existence of a single and supreme criminal official was the first step towards the creation of the High Court of Justiciary in the late sixteenth century. The disappearance of the amateur, the gradual exclusion of royal influence, and the emergence of a lay legal profession were part of a process that began before 1500 and was to have a profound effect on the attitudes of society to justice and the law.

In any government a system of checks and balances will naturally operate as the various institutions, including the crown, seek to develop their vested interests at the expense of the others. The effect of this will vary from country to country, depending on the relative strengths of monarchy, landowners, clergy, and lawyers. The Scottish lawyers, emerging as a strong professional caste, were able to dictate their terms with increasing success. Politically, a strong monarchy maintained a strong council with extensive powers, but also had to accept an active parliament, regularly summoned; the balance was therefore closer to the situation in England, though by no means identical, than to that of the continental countries where the Estates lost out to king and council. But a long tradition of greater indifference by the Scottish localities to the centre lessened the demand for exact definition of powers. That is a constitutional matter; and constitutional sophistication is not necessarily the same as political power. The development of Scottish government was the product of vitality, not the product of weakness. The circumstances of the late fifteenth and early sixteenth centuries were such that the king's full personal power was employed only occasionally, and only against individuals; his government was rarely called on to cope with more than the general maintenance of an acceptable degree of order. That government, which collectively stood between the power of individuals in the localities and the power of the individual on the throne, restrained and moderated both.

2

The Local Community

In his article on 'The county community and the making of public opinion in fourteenth century England', J.R. Maddicott analyses the politically-conscious English counties, their ability to articulate reactions to the demands of government, and the need of that government to sell its policies.[1] A less demanding government will inevitably have a different relationship with the localities; it impinges less because it asks for less. The local communities of Scotland, for many the sum total of their experience, were largely left to run their own affairs; the guiding hand, to an even greater extent than in England, was that of the local landowners. The relatively quiescent nature of Scottish political life was to a considerable degree the result of the fact that the crown did not seek to alter the relationship between the localities and the centre. The king was expected to show concern, by sending down his justices from time to time and, on occasion, appearing in person. Links with the capital were maintained through parliament, where sectional and regional interests could be represented and particular problems aired; not every part of Scotland was over-run by marigolds and wolves, but those that were, like the abbey of Cupar Angus whose estates were apparently infested with the marigold, could petition parliament and have their complaints formulated into a general act which could then be invoked. The court also provided a meeting-place, not only for kings and local lords, but also for local lords with one another. Between them, peripatetic kings, their courts, and their annual parliaments transformed the natural insularity of the local community into an awareness of itself as part of a greater whole. That was all that was required, in the political and social circumstances of early-modern Scotland.

It is, of course, in terms of local society that Scotland is so often

[1]*Transactions of the Royal Historical Society*, 5th ser., 28 (1978), pp. 27–43.

portrayed as lawless and turbulent. The dramatic 'national' events are extremely limited in number. When the early-sixteenth-century scholar John Major complained about economic instability which resulted from short-term leases and the wanton destruction of crops by people at feud, or when James VI succinctly advised his son, in *Basilikon Doron*, to 'roote out these barbarous feides', they were referring to local conditions. But when scholars produced their academic analyses, or parliament or council issued legislation about the need to improve law and order, even when a king wrote a manual of kingship, they were not describing an eternal norm; they were talking about the exceptions, the cases of breakdown of the norm, as much as parliament and journalists do today. There was feuding. There were also strong forces for stability in local society.

One method of assessment is the degree of stability among the landed members of society. Various factors appear to militate against stability; the gradual move from a territorial to an honorific peerage, virtually complete by the reign of James III, and the fact that land was now extensively a commodity for buying and selling, meant that the concept of loyalty was increasingly divorced from landed − feudal − relationships. Moreover, the fragmentation of estates meant that the wealthiest landowners, earls, lords, and greater barons, had holdings scattered sometimes through several shires; in the late fifteenth century the earls of Huntly held eleven baronies, nine in the northern shires of Aberdeen, Banff, Moray, and Inverness, one in Perthshire, and one in Berwick. The strain thus put on inheritance encouraged the increasing use of entails to heirs male, and this − a subject that awaits detailed study − must have exacerbated the position of younger sons, although in pre-Reformation Scotland the church and military service abroad still provided the traditional outlets, while trade, law, and administration were beginning to offer others. It also encouraged the legal consolidation of estates; thus Alexander Ogilvy of Deskford had his various lands and baronies erected into the single barony of Ogilvy in 1517.

The real disaster to any landowning family was inability to keep its lands, either because of failure of male heirs or forfeiture. K.B. McFarlane has shown that in fifteenth-century England the failure-rate was, on average, every third generation. In Scotland, among the higher nobility at least, the record was considerably better. The earldoms of Buchan and Bothwell changed hands, because of failure of male heirs in the Stewart and Hepburn families. Much more typical was the steady succession of Gordons to the earldom of Huntly,

Campbells to Argyll, Keiths to Marischal, Kennedies to Cassillis, and so on; these were all families who, when they got their earldoms in the two great periods of creation, the reigns of James II and IV, had already demonstrated genetic stability over several generations, as had the Lindsays, who had held the earldom of Crawford since 1398 with only a minor hiccough in the succession in 1542 when the son of the eighth earl was 'excluded from the succession for wickedness'. Nor were there many forfeitures, in a country free from dynastic disputes at the top, and with a monarchy as inclined to conciliate as to punish. The first forfeiture in the Huntly family came in 1562; no earl of Argyll was forfeited until 1619. Occasional groups did suffer temporary forfeiture: the supporters of the would-be usurper Albany, brother of James III, once the king had regained his authority after the Lauder crisis, and the Red Douglases and their associates in James V's reign. But the only permanent forfeiture in the five reigns from James III to James VI was that of the Lord of the Isles in 1493.

The detailed analysis of the 150 years before 1460 made by Dr Grant shows considerably more fluctuation, indeed 'radical changes both in personnel and institutionally'. By the mid fifteenth century the upheavals were virtually over. Eight new earls were added to the rump of the older comital families left after the crown's attack on the Stewarts and Black Douglases, and a further seven families were ennobled by James IV. The nobility had been transformed. There now existed a high level of personal stability among the leading families of the localities. This was crucially important. The fundamental bonds of society were forged not through land but through kinship and personal lordship. So strong were they that at least one late-sixteenth-century commentator assessed the power of the nobility not just on their landed wealth but also on the number of men in their followings, which could be even more important. Thus Lord Ogilvy was 'a man of no greate lyvinge, but of a good number of landed men of his surname (kindred), which makes his power in Angus the greater', while the earl of Glencairn, though crippled by 'morgages wher with some of his auncestors have entangled a good parte thereof', nevertheless had 'reasonable great' power because of his 'surname and frendes'. Given an attitude like this, continuity among the people at the top of local society mattered even more than geographic cohesion of their estates, for loyalty to a family or lord was personal loyalty, whereas land had become the basis of a legal and fiscal relationship between landlord and tenant.

Kinship survived as the basic form of obligation in local society partly because the crown never challenged it, and partly because of the nature of the Scottish kingroup. It was agnatic, that is, dependant on an ancestor, whether real or mythical, in the male line, and recognized as a bond between male relatives. Females — mothers, sisters, daughters — were not part of this bond; they were added to, or removed from, the kingroup by marriage. Women retained their own family name when they married, which reflected the fact that a marriage alliance might create or reinforce a bond of friendship between two kindreds, but it did not create ties of kinship. The strength of agnatic kinship was that it avoided the problems of conflicting loyalties, which weakened the alternative form, cognatic kinship, in which both paternal and maternal relatives were included in the kindred, and brothers-in-law, for example, had equal claims with full brothers. Moreover, the kingroup was readily identifiable, at least in the lowlands, because of the use of the surname, which provided a simple method of distinguishing those who were one's kin from those who were not; indeed, the word 'surname' or 'name' became synonymous with 'kindred'. The other factor which dictated ties of kin was geographic unity. The Gordons, despite their outlying estates in Perthshire and Berwickshire, were a northern kingroup. Distance made fulfilment of the obligations of kinship difficult to the point where they could be disregarded.

Identification of one's kin in a society where kinship is fundamental, but where inevitably kindreds overlap, is never a simple business. The nature of the Scottish kingroup reduced the complexities as far as possible; so it remained strong. This was true also of lordship. There is extensive evidence about late-medieval and early-modern lordship because of the remarkable survival of some 800 contracts, made between *c*. 1450 and 1603 either by lords promising mutual support or, in the great majority of cases, by lords and their men binding themselves to protect and serve one another: contracts of friendship and bonds of maintenance and manrent. They show that lordship was seen in terms of kinship, and involved the same obligations; men who were not kinsmen of a great lord undertook and wrote down the obligations that were natural to, and therefore unwritten by, the kin. They used the language of kinship. The word 'friend' still carried something of its original connotation of kinsman, referring to someone who would act as kin; 'kindnes' — kinship — turns up repeatedly.

Perhaps the most impressive aspect of these bonds is that they were almost all made for life or in perpetuity. It was extremely rare for men to make bonds with more than one lord, and the exceptions sometimes had a particular reason. Dependants of the Campbells of Cawdor and Glenorchy recognized that their immediate allegiance was to the cadet branches of the Campbells of Inveraray, earls of Argyll, and therefore referred to their higher allegiance; and it was regular practice to reserve allegiance to regents during royal minorities, which was virtually equivalent to the automatic exception, in all bonds, of allegiance to the crown. Those who did give more than one bond of manrent included a clause stating their previous obligation, and on occasion added a promise of neutrality in case of conflict between their lords, as Neil Stewart of Fothergill did in his bond to John earl of Atholl in 1478. But when, in 1602, Andrew Hering of Littleblair promised his lord, Francis earl of Erroll, 'my onelie dependance', he was speaking, in effect, for almost all grantors of bonds of manrent. The heads of smaller kindreds, the Cheynes of Essilmont, the Munros of Foulis, the Irvines of Drum, the Stewarts of Duror, and countless others, bound themselves and their kinsmen and followers to the heads of greater kindreds, the earls of Erroll, Huntly, Argyll, and to them only. Thus again the problem of divided loyalties was averted. This can hardly have been accidental; the ethos of loyalty was fundamental in theory, and of immense importance in practice, in a society where men depended so heavily on personal relationships, personal support. The great advantage of the bond of the fifteenth and sixteenth centuries was that it was easier to demand single-minded loyalty in return for protection of a man's position and possessions when the personal nature of lordship was once again pre-eminent than it had been when service was associated with land, for no lord could prevent his vassals acquiring fiefs from others.

Nevertheless, the relatively clear-cut structure of magnate followings in Scotland did not mean that tensions were taken out of the localities. The very fact that these bonds were written down in their hundreds is not just a reflection of an increasingly document-conscious age, although in a century when for the first time men began to record their I.O.U.s for trifling debts, that was certainly part of it. It was also a direct consequence of the strains that the reconstruction of the nobility imposed on the communities. The essential feature of a bond of manrent was that it was an obligation by a lesser man to a greater. But it may be that these bonds did not so much reflect established order as provide a means of bolstering it up. The Gordons, Campbells, Montgomeries, singled out by the crown and given earldoms, were not immediately distinguishable from their former social equals, the barons and lairds, in terms of their wealth and local standing. Some families did build up vast estates, but that took time; some, like the earls of Erroll, never seem to have held significantly more land than a great local family like the Cheynes of Essilmont. One piece of evidence that suggests the extent of the problem for these new comital families is the list of hostages for James I in 1424, which gives their money values. Campbell of Argyll was already among the wealthiest. But at the lowest level was Alexander, lord of Gordon, valued at 400 merks, worth only half as much as Hay of Erroll, whose descendants as earls of Erroll were always junior partners of the Gordon earls of Huntly, and worth less also than Dunbar of Cumnok, whose family would later, as lairds, give bonds of manrent to the earls of Huntly. In these circumstances, the written bond was an ideal way for these new families to assert superiority.

The obsession with status which characterized this period also suggests the extent to which social and economic distinctions between the greater and lesser were perhaps becoming blurred and challenged; men are not likely to be obsessed with status if they do not feel their position threatened. The first sumptuary act defining status and its rights was passed in 1430; it specified the dress people could wear according to their rank. It had an economic as well as a social purpose; it was designed to restrain spending. But the rules that successive parliaments laid down about the dress one could wear, the food one could eat, the arms one could bear, the size of retinues, and the fact that wives were allowed to dress according to their husbands' position in society and not above it, reflect a considerable degree of status-consciousness. The whole emphasis was on the position of the lord; 'sentinal yeomen' in lords' retinues could dress rather better than yeomen on the land, for example. Those below the highest rank were equally conscious of status; Gilbert Menzies of Pitfodells assured George earl of Huntly in 1588 that he would serve him like 'utheris gentilmen. . .of our rank and estait'. 'Sharpening self-consciousness about their social status', as F.R.H. du Boulay describes it, is a feature of both English and European society of this period; it is clearly evident in Scotland also, probably because of redistribution of wealth, and almost certainly because of redistribution of titles.

Thus the theoretic strength of kinship and lordship, although often translated into practice, also concealed weaknesses which from time to time flared into open violence. The majority of lairds who gave their bonds to the new aristocracy did so willingly enough, and the relationship worked to the mutual advantage of both. But there was never any question of a dominant group of lords and a subservient group of lairds. Most of the lairds whose allegiance was sought were themselves powerful men; that was their attraction to their lords. They were heavily involved in the affairs of their localities. Some were barons, with baronial courts; some acted as sheriffs-depute, which in practice meant that they did the work; they sat on local assizes; they were called in as private arbitrators. They were the backbone of local society. Indeed, they were more than that; even more than the aristocracy they were the crucial determinant factor in Scottish society as a whole. In the course of the sixteenth century they were to play a major role in the Reformation movement, more significant in the long run than that of the magnates. And it was when they began to move out of the localities and claim a place in central government that the long-established pattern of society was radically and irrevocably altered. It is difficult to overestimate the importance of the shire gentry. Certainly the aristocracy were fully aware of that importance.

Just as the magnates regarded themselves as the king's 'natural counsellors', so the lairds were the 'natural counsellors' of the earls; giving counsel was one of the most important clauses in their bonds, because it gave them a voice in the affairs of their lord for which their assistance might be sought. How much it mattered is seen in the bitter complaint in 1586 by two northern members of the Campbell kin, remote from the centre of power in Inveraray, during the minority of the seventh earl, when they felt excluded from the inner ring of councillors; 'my lordis speciall freindis', they said, 'can nocht haif excesse [access] to his Lordship to do thair luissum affairis, nor yitt to giff thair oppinioun as thai war wont to giff to his lordships predicessouris of befoir'. Co-operation, not autocratic authority, was an essential part of good lordship.

In a minority of cases even co-operation was barely possible. Some families were brought reluctantly into the orbit of a lord's affinity, and when occasion offered itself, moved into opposition. In the 1530s various Argyllshire families, led by the Macdonalds and the Macleans, made considerable hay while the sun of the king's favour shone on them and was withdrawn from the earl of Argyll. Alexander Macdonald of Islay, summoned before the council in 1531 by Argyll, found himself with a clear field when Argyll, with remarkable stupidity, failed to turn up; he refuted Argyll's charges, and made a moving statement about his loyalty to the crown and his desire to maintain order in the Isles, where, he claimed, the house of Argyll was the greatest troublemaker. The king chose to believe him, and Argyll was in turn summoned to answer for his dealings, and imprisoned.

James's refusal earlier in the year to grant him the lieutenancy over the Isles had opened the way for those who looked with a jealous eye on the steady increase of Campbell power, and the personal ineptitude of this earl did the rest.

This episode illustrates three factors that could affect local stability. The Gordons and the Campbells are the supreme examples of the 'new' families of the fifteenth century whose power and wealth were consistently built up, to the advantage of their kin but to the visible disadvantage of at least some of the prominent lesser landowners of their localities. The state of cold war, for example, that existed between the Gordons and the Forbes, punctuated by attempts to strengthen the relationship by making bonds, and by outbreaks of feud, can be immediately understood by looking at a map of the north-east; the Forbes's principal seat of Druminor was close to Huntly, and hemmed in by Gordon strongholds. The Campbell success story was even more remarkable than that of the Gordons, partly because they were the one family who significantly departed from the norm and maintained their influence well outside the immediate area of their own lands; they kept close links with remote cadet branches of the kindred who would normally have functioned independently, the Campbells of Glenorchy in Perthshire, and the Campbells of Cawdor on the Moray Firth. The fact that they made written bonds with these kinsmen — an exception to the rule — demonstrates the strains that geographic distance put on the tie of kinship; but they managed to cope with these strains, at the inevitable expense of arousing considerable hostility.

The second factor was personality. The earl who was humiliated by James V was the one weak member of an otherwise exceptionally able and tough line of earls. Personality was of crucial importance, counting for far more than institutional position. The dealings of the other earls of Argyll with the families who resented their power — notably the Macdonalds, whom they were steadily undermining in Kintyre — resembles nothing so much as a keeper controlling a pack of snarling dogs. They paid detailed attention not only to their own control over the major local families, but also to the relations of these families with one another. They insisted that men who wanted to enjoy Campbell protection must support their friends and adherents; and the sweeteners offered in the form of assistance in both general and specific circumstances were balanced by the threat to withdraw protection. It was no empty threat. A graphic picture of what loss of Campbell friendship meant is provided by Lauchlan Maclean of Duart in 1578, complaining to the council that when he tried, like a loyal subject, to come to the lowlands and pay the king's mails, he and his servants were beaten up and imprisoned by Argyll's adherents; after this one-sided savagery it is not surprising that within a year Lauchlan had made his peace. Campbell policy was a judicious and effective mixture of negotiation where possible, formalized by the making of bonds, and force where diplomacy failed. Its success depended ultimately on the strength of personality of the men who pursued this policy.

The third element is the part played by the king. It was not the only occasion when a hostile laird invoked James V's support against Argyll. John Lamont of Inveryne, summoned before Argyll as sheriff in 1540, as the defendant in a case of disputed possession which he was almost certainly going to lose, thoughtfully provided himself with a signet-letter forbidding Argyll to hear the case because of his feud with Lamont: a feud that Lamont asserted and Argyll, his lord, more justifiably denied. Remote and intermittent though its exercise might be, royal authority was undoubtedly acknowledged as ultimate. It could be invoked, or brought to bear by the kings themselves, when they drove the ayres in person or descended on the borders and Isles, as James IV and V did. It was not necessarily resented; when it imposed order it was welcomed. When sacrilege was added to a case of particular brutality in 1490, when the master of Drummond and his followers burned 120 Murrays in the kirk of Monzievaird, the king immediately stepped in, and, despite appeals for remission, the master was executed. The family remained loyal; indeed, it did more, for the master's sister Margaret became the king's most favoured mistress. But in terms of local stability, royal authority was a double-edged weapon. It could be exploited, as Macdonald and Lamont exploited it; and the personal likes and dislikes of a powerful king could be as harmful to order in the localities as royal severity could be beneficial.

The tensions and rivalries within the affinity of any lord inevitably weakened the lord's own authority. Moreover, even if the majority of his followers were loyal, as seems to have been the normal pattern, that might simply mean that two lords at feud had solid and readily identifiable blocks of support. The greatest potential cause of disorder in the localities was not the petty thieving or brawls or even murders by the tenants and peasants; it was the quarrels over land or honour or status by the men of power. Yet even in a society with a strong military ethos, men still desired to die in their beds, to know that their heirs would succeed peacefully and that their possessions and lands would remain intact; James VI was correct when he told his son that 'the most part of your people will ever favour justice'. There is no more impressive feature of Scottish local society — a society lacking any of the institutional controls to which modern society is accustomed — than the sanctions which it put on outbreaks of violence and feud, and the means of control it used. There survived in Scotland, up until the seventeenth century, a highly developed form of the bloodfeud, not just in its bloody form, but as a force for peace.

It depended on two things: the widespread acceptances of the principle of compensation rather than retribution as the best way to settle crimes and disputes, and the acceptance of the authority of lord or head of kin, or of chosen arbiters, to decide on and impose a compensation settlement. It offered the advantages of a quick settlement, in contrast to the endless delays of actions before the courts, and also a heightened chance of permanence precisely because it was imposed locally, and by local lords. It survived as an alternative to the courts, not in opposition to them; when in 1500 William Lord Graham and John Lord Oliphant drew up a contract of friendship which included their mutual obligation to deal with the disputes of their followers — a frequent clause in such contracts — they agreed that if they failed to settle such disputes, the plaintiff should take the case to court. The point was to achieve a result, not to quibble about the means, or maintain one kind of justice — the justice of the feud, in which the lord played the prominent part — at the expense of another, the increasingly professionalized justice of the lawyers and the courts. The monarchy itself, as part of its general acceptance of the efficacy of local justice, supported the justice of the feud. Royal remissions were to be given only after the aggrieved party was satisfied by the offender. There is no doubt of their acceptance of this kind of justice.

As in so much else, the personal authority of the lord was the crucial factor in ensuring that this justice was effective. Lamont of Inveryne had already outmatched Argyll long before 1540. In 1532 he had refused to accept the judgement of arbiters chosen by himself and his opponent in a land dispute, despite their backing by the earl; the arbiters rather weakly recommended that his opponent should go to law, and that Lamont should accept a decision by the courts without 'ony grwnchying or rancour of mynd'. By contrast, David Lord Drummond was completely in control of the settlement for the kin of the murdered George Drummond of Leidcreif in 1554. He successfully rejected the initial offers made by the murderers, the lairds of Drumlochy, Ardblair, and Gormack as insultingly paltry, and forced new terms, which brought Drumlochy into his service, and which provided husbands — Drumlochy's son and cousin — for the daughter and sister of his dead kinsman. Compensation was based on the attempt to undo the effects of a crime. Money might achieve that; equally, the fact that the murderer, by making provision for the unmarried female relatives of his victim, took over the rôle of their protector was a simple and yet strikingly effective method of emendation.

There were many such successful settlements which brought feud to an end. As a final sanction the giving and accepting of compensation was itself a matter of formality and ceremony, performed as publicly as possible. In 1563 Lord Boyd sought forgiveness of Niel Montgomery of Langshaw at Irvine, the scene of his father's murder of Neil's father, falling on his knees and offering a naked sword by the point, that classic symbol of submission. Then he gave compensation of 1800 merks, and received from Neil the 'letter of slanis', the written acknowledgement that the feud was over and friendship would exist between the two from now on. Reconciliation as well as compensation was a vital element; hence the publicity attached to it, and also the frequent attempts to give the losing party to a dispute, particularly a dispute over land, his own compensation in the form of cancellation of outstanding debts, or a lease of land. The whole emphasis was put on restoring peace and trying to ensure that the peace would be lasting. Thus it was important not to leave the loser in a state of outraged grievance, and to demonstrate openly that the feud was ended and both sides were satisfied.

It did not always work. Yet the fact that its principles depended on satisfying people who had been wronged, and doing so not with the majesty of the law but with the authority of the men who stood at the head of the local community as the embodiment of the accepted concepts of kinship and lordship, made it a natural and effective means of containing crime and civil dispute. Contemporary understanding of 'feud' went far beyond, and far below, the full-scale blood feud, with two kindreds or affinities fighting it out; the word covered civil dispute, with no bloodshed, and also a single murder. The feud in Scotland was therefore both more extensive and less violent than has sometimes been suggested. That, and the way in which local societies dealt with local feuds, suggest grounds for re-thinking the question of the lawlessness of local society.

The men who were involved in feud and the settlement of feud were also those who maintained order through the local sheriff, baronial or regality courts, or, more informally, through their power to withhold the tacks (leases) held by their tenants. The latter element is demonstrated in the records of a great ecclesiastical landlord, the abbey of Coupar Angus. In 1466 part of their land of Syokis was leased to Dic Scot for five years, under threat of loss 'if he shall not be sober and temperate, preserving more strictly a kindly intercourse with his neighbours and relatives', while in 1494 the tenement of Dunfallandy was let to Alexander Gow, son of the previous tenant, with the instruction that he should 'carefully keep the wood and be obedient to his mother'. Tensions created by men living in close proximity — where a neighbour was persistently drunk, or pastured too many beasts on the common ground, or refused to observe his boundaries — are seen again in the records of the local courts, which are full of cases where a tenant provoked beyond endurance was brought before the court for 'fylin of the grund with violent blud'. Violence at the level of a brawl and a punch-up which often resulted in blood-letting was common. But Scottish soil was not endlessly defiled and awash with blood. Landlords and local judges, reinforced by the occasional injection of royal justice for the rarer major crimes, seem to have been able to maintain an acceptable degree of order; in general, the register of Coupar shows a high level of stability among its tenants, with frequent renewals of leases to families who proved satisfactory enough. As a further safeguard, there were the 'birlaw courts' — a Scandinavian word which suggests an institution of some antiquity — which were courts composed of local worthies who had no legal expertise; they were themselves tenants, sometimes acting as part of the baron's court and sometimes as a separate institution, backed up by the baron's court. Their function was to ensure 'good neighbourhood'; they dealt with controversies between tenants, being responsible for keeping or restoring the peace rather than imposing penalties, and they held their position purely by virtue of their local standing and good reputation in the locality. These 'community' courts lingered on into the very different world of the eighteenth century. In the fifteenth and sixteenth, they are a remarkable illustration of the wider social point suggested by T.C. Smout: the relationship between landlord and tenant was as yet more than that of landlord and rent-payer, partly because tenants were not easy to replace and partly because they were still essential not only as providers of food for the lord's kitchen but also as men for his following, in his peaceful and military pursuits. While the lord's status was reflected by the size of his retinue and his security by the ability to summon men who would fight for him, so the tenant's co-operation, rather than his passive and perhaps surly obedience, was at a premium. This did not mean that all tenants were well treated, as we shall see. It did mean that, as in the upper reaches of society, there was still a degree of personal contact between lord and tenant which reflected the lord's personal needs and which encouraged a high level of social concern, as contemporary legislation shows; this was to change only later, as the population grew, and as the lord's needs changed.

The structure of local society and the controls within it were still common to every part of Scotland, including the highlands and borders. The awareness of some sort of distinction between highland and lowland was first expressed by John of Fordun in the late fourteenth century, in his famous passage about the two peoples of Scotland, the wild Scots − *ferina gens* − rough, thieving, and lazy, and the domesticated Scots − *domestica gens* − cultured, law-abiding, and devout. The continuing existence of the last of the old provinces of Scotland, the Lordship of the Isles, where each lord was inaugurated in a ceremony that contained all the main elements of the inauguration of Celtic kings, and where a considerable degree of political independence was maintained, produced in the Scottish monarchy the same frustrations and aggression that fifteenth-century French kings felt for the semi-independent Celtic province of Brittany and its dukes, and the same result: political annihilation, by James IV and his contemporary Louis XII. The geographic and political expansion of Middle Scots, the language of poets and government as well as great numbers of the population, reinforced the idea of highland isolation and even backwardness. The borders, which stretched from southern Scotland down into northern England, with a political boundary running through them that owed little to geography and nothing to social custom, were also seen by the government as increasingly troublesome. They were indeed a part of the country with a lot of raiding and cattle-rustling, minor feuding, and sometimes rather more; the Scottish side tended to be the area of greater trouble, simply because of the number of settlements and the existence of the great border abbeys, grown wealthy on sheep-farming, as compared to the relative lack of habitation on the English side. Nevertheless, both highlands and borders were not the distinctive units they later became. The increasing lowland interest in documentation, records of land-grants, rentals, and so on, spilled over into the highlands; kin and bloodfeud, a lasting feature of highland society, were as familiar in the lowlands, where, indeed, some of the words associated with feud were borrowed from the Gaelic west. When James IV finished off the work begun by James I and destroyed the Lordship of the Isles in the 1490s, it was a political move; this king, who spoke Gaelic himself, never showed the utter contempt for Gaelic society and Gaelic culture that was so marked an attitude of James VI. His attempt to replace Macdonald domination by that of the Campbells probably did create greater social tensions within highland society, and therefore heightened the government's impression of a particularly turbulent part of the kingdom in the course of the sixteenth century. The later history of the highlands, the popular images of Glencoe – in oversimplified form, another Campbell–Macdonald fight – and the Forty-Five, and Walter Scott's romantic domestication of the noble savage and invention of modern tartan, all combine to create the idea of a gulf which had always existed. In the early sixteenth century the gulf was beginning to open; but there were still many bridges across it.

In the course of the sixteenth century, despite the years of minority and lack of direction from the crown, two forces in society were beginning to break down the structure of the local community, at least in the lowlands. One was the new interest of the lairds in law and government; the other was the astonishingly effective organization of the Reformed kirk, which created a link between its national and local assemblies stronger and more immediate than anything Scotland had hitherto experienced. The comparative autonomy of the regions, the amateur and private methods of providing justice, even kinship itself, were all weaker by 1600 than they had been in 1500. But the difference is not an adverse comment on the older system, and does not mean that local society necessarily became more stable.

3

Town and Country

To speak of Scotland as a poor country is a truism. To talk about the Scottish economy is much more difficult. There were several 'economies', all interrelated up to a point, but also functioning independently, in a way that would be impossible today. The difficulty of communications, bad transport, and the *laissez-faire* approach of the government meant that long-term and comprehensive planning would have been virtually impossible, even if it had been thought of; and on the whole, it does not seem to have been thought of. The mainly pastoral farming of the highland and border areas contrasted with the mainly agricultural farming of the lowlands and east-coast strip, and interaction between the two was severely limited; at the end of the sixteenth century Sir Thomas Craig claimed that cheese was sent to the lowlands in time of shortage, and occasionally the council issued directives about the movement of food, but in practice both areas depended much more on what they themselves produced than on exchange of foodstuffs with the other. There was also a clear distinction between east and west. It was the east coast that maintained trading links with the continent and the Baltic, and there burghs grew up. By contrast, there was little urban life in the west. Ayr was reasonably flourishing, with its established trade with Ireland and to an extent with the continent, and occasionally wine from France and even iron from Spain were landed at Kirkcudbright, but with the exception of Glasgow, which was beginning to develop, other west coast burghs remained small in number and size, operating within a local context. The other major contrast was between the royal burghs with their money economy, and the countryside. Obviously the distinction was not complete. The burghs depended for food and trading goods on the produce of their rural hinterlands; Edinburgh's position as the largest of the Scottish burghs, even before it became finally established as the capital, has been attributed to the wealth of Lothian, 'the maist plentuus ground of Scotland', according to Hector Boece. But the major burghs were strongly conscious of their autonomy, complaining continuously about attempts by lords on the land to interfere with their affairs. Moreover, the burghs were themselves divided. From the fifteenth century we hear of royal burghs as opposed to burghs of barony; only the royal burghs could engage in foreign trade, a privilege which they hung on to with desperate tenacity until the late seventeenth century, leaving the burghs of barony as small local communities, dealing largely in barter in kind.

The first impression of economic life is of stagnation and sometimes worse than stagnation. Four-fifths of the population made their living from the land, using traditional agricultural methods. Land was divided into infield and outfield; bere, oats, peas, beans, wheat, flax, and hemp were sown on the better land, the infield, oats on the outfield, all of them at the mercy of a difficult climate. Farming was group farming, based on the lowland farmtoun or kirktoun, or the highland baile, as the centre of an area that was notionally two or three ploughgangs, that is, the area that two or three ploughteams could keep under cultivation; the land was allocated in rigs, which could be reallocated from time to time, or let permanently, and farmed by husbandmen and subtenants. Where possible, the rigs ran downhill, thus sharing out the wet and dry land. This was the only way of coping with the problem of drainage, and far from adequate; yet the nineteenth-century historian W.F. Skene pointed out, from personal observation, that the runrig tenants fared better, in particularly wet or dry years, than those with their own crofts. In some areas, such as Kintyre, a light horse plough was used; otherwise, the plough was the heavy wooden plough with an iron coulter, normally drawn by oxen, which were cheaper to feed and better at the job than horses. Along with the bitterly resented obligation to grind corn in the lord's mill, which produced violent hatred of the miller and numerous cases in the baronial courts, tenants had an annual obligation to provide oxen for the lord's plough. That obligation is the subject of one of the few popular songs to survive, the 'Plough Song' dating from the end of the fifteenth century, which begins 'My heartly service to you, my Lord', and goes on to describe the ancient and toothless ox produced for the lord's plough which 'goeth backward' in verse one; by verse two, 'the old ox Tripfree he be dead', whereupon the tenants harness themselves to the plough. Ploughing was the subject of legislation restricting powers of distraint; in 1503, and again in 1581, it was laid down that horses, oxen, and anything pertaining to the plough were to be exempt from distraint in time of ploughing.

The first signs of agricultural improvement were not seen until the seventeenth century. Equally, there was very little initiative in developing Scottish crafts in the late fifteenth and early sixteenth centuries. The Scots did begin to cast their own artillery in the mid 1470s, under foreign instruction it would seem, in view of the payment of five guineas to 'Rannald Franche man that maid the gwn' in 1474. The siting of the work was extraordinary; the Black Friars of Edinburgh were given eight pounds by James III for repairing their house 'riven at the zetting of the gwn'. Metal-working was beginning to develop; four Scots turned up in Moscow in 1507 as specialists in artillery. In the long run this was to become the one part of Scottish craftsmanship that claimed serious foreign attention, not in the making of guns, but in the much less militaristic gold- and silver-work for which Edinburgh goldsmiths became renowned in the late sixteenth century. James IV's ship-building and the palaces of James IV and V also provided high, if temporary, employment. But there was little else. Scotland had long depended on her wool trade, and continued to do so, despite the general decline of this trade, which can be traced back to the early fifteenth century, if not earlier; indeed, the quality of Scottish wool had deteriorated much earlier, as a result of sheep-scab, first recorded in the late thirteenth century. Certainly exports had dropped by the mid fifteenth century, and although they then levelled off, there seems to have been a further drop in the early sixteenth century. Yet traditional attitudes died hard. The decline did not have the effect, as it did in England, of encouraging cloth-making; the Scots contented themselves with the production of poor-quality rough cloth. They continued to think in terms of trade rather than technology. The increased trade in fish, of which Scotland had plenty, did not produce better equipment; Scottish ships and gear remained inferior to those of her main competitors from Holland and Bremen.

Lack of native craftsmanship seriously imbalanced Scottish trade. Exports were almost entirely unprocessed raw materials, wool, hides, salt, fish, animals on the hoof, coal. But there was a shortage even of some basic raw materials, iron, good-quality salt, increasingly timber and, in bad years, grain. And Scotland was almost wholly dependant on imports for manufactured and luxury goods, which were both necessary to and much demanded by the wealthier sections of society, king, aristocrats, the greater churchmen, and the rich among the burgesses. Insistence on a lofty lifestyle, and the need to import basic goods, combined to create the problem of chronic shortage of bullion.

A further scourge was the repeated visitations of the plague. Inevitably it was the towns that suffered most from these random and terrifying outbreaks, sometimes widespread, sometimes hitting individual areas; Aberdeen does not seem to have shared the great outbreak in Edinburgh in the early 1530s, but was afflicted in 1546. The fear and horror it created is seen in the savage penalties imposed by the town councils for concealing plague. In August 1530 David Duly was sentenced by the Edinburgh council to be hanged before his front door for failing to report his wife's sickness before she died; the rope broke, and the council decided that, because he was 'ane pure man with small barnis', they would 'for pete of him' commute the sentence to banishment. It is a graphic and hideous little incident, and the prospects for the banished Duly and his small bairns make 'pity' a not altogether appropriate word.

The government did little or nothing to encourage economic development, partly because it could not, and partly because it had no positive ideas to offer. In time of dearth, parliament and council pushed out well-intentioned legislation, designed to prevent regrating (buying up surpluses for sale at a profit), to ration the amount of victuals that could be stored during lean years, to ban exports, mainly of food and tallow. These acts were never effective. The machinery to enforce them did not exist, and the localism of society militated against general action, even in times of crisis.

The crown's main obsession was financial, and parliament and council joined with it in worrying; most parliaments agonized about 'the mone'. Depreciation was one easy answer; the 352 pennies minted from a pound of silver in 1393 had become 1,680 in 1483. Indeed, the political crisis of 1482 must be set in the context of an economic crisis, of which we know all too little, but is reflected in the violent hostility to the king's introduction of the heavily debased coinage known as the 'black money' in 1480, which was 'cried down and demonetised' in 1482, and lingered on in memory to become part of the later legend of James III. Parliament's own approach was very limited; there is little sign that it ever took a less simplistic view of economic problems than it had in 1455 when it announced that 'the poverte of the crowne is oftymis the caus of the poverte of the Realme'. Crown and parliament together showed a passionate desire to have the country 'stuffit of Bulyeon', as parliament said in 1478, and having got the bullion, to keep it; it was the classic 'money under the bed' mentality. The act of 1473, for example, forbidding the import of English cloth, was not a protectionist measure designed to help Scottish weavers, although that may have been a side-effect; its real purpose was to insist that bullion, not cloth, must be imported in exchange for Scottish exports. The same mentality lay behind James I's invention of the crime of barratry – going to Rome in search of benefices without royal licence – because it involved taking money out of the country. Yet the repeated legislation on bullion was already meaningless before it was even issued by parliament. Kings, landowners, merchants – the most conspicuous spenders – were not going to give up their wines, silks, leather goods, spices, artillery, the luxury goods from abroad, for the sake of their economic theory.

But poverty has two faces, the absolute and the comparative. In comparative terms, Scotland was an impoverished European country, with a pitifully small volume of trade. At home, most of the population lived according to what each individual year brought them; there was no cushioning against a bad year, when climate and disease destroyed crops and life. But that does not mean absolute poverty. There are some signs that, compared with the second half of the sixteenth century, and compared with the state of both urban and rural communities in many parts of Europe in the first half, the situation in Scotland was relatively stable and reasonably good. In the catalogue of economic problems of late-fifteenth-and early-sixteenth-century Scotland, there are two significant omissions, war and the price-rise. When the great powers France and Spain were pushed by bankruptcy of their governments into making the peace of Cateau-Cambrésis in 1559, they were joined by their two satellites, England and Scotland. England was also in severe economic straits, from which that parsimonious genius Elizabeth was to rescue it. Scotland, having consistently kept her contacts with Europe within the peaceful fields of academic and economic life since 1513, was not. And although the price-rise that afflicted Europe from the late fifteenth century would make itself felt when goods were imported, Scotland was not badly affected until after 1560. In Europe, the central 40 years of the sixteenth century seem to have been generally the worst. In Scotland, the most severe impact came rather later. The Edinburgh records show that, with the exception of a brief period from late 1547 until early 1553 when, mainly because of war, the price of bread doubled, the cost of a loaf of wheaten bread, weighing between 16 and 18 ounces, remained static at 2d.; and prices of wine and ale, for example, were also fairly static. Wages are difficult to estimate, being often paid in kind or recorded only for short-term work; but the *Accounts of the Master of Works* and *Treasurer's Accounts* provide the figures of

15s.–18s. for masons per week, and 5s.–10s. for barrowmen, and again these levels held until the middle of the century. Only after 1560 was there a sharp increase.

Although there was depreciation of the coinage, which was one of the principal causes of the price rise, the other strains on the European economy, war and population growth, were not significant factors in early-sixteenth-century Scottish economic life; there is little evidence that the population was becoming too great for the resources of the country before the late sixteenth century. One notable consequence was that urban life in Scotland, and certainly relations between towns and government, were peaceful to a degree rare in Europe. Figures such as the 50 per cent of the inhabitants of Coventry who in 1524 could not pay the minimum rate of the lay subsidy, 4d., or the estimate that half the population of most European towns lived on the poverty line, suggest a picture much more grim than that which emerges from the admittedly incomplete Scottish records. There was certainly no conflict in Scotland like that between Charles V and the towns of the Netherlands, where the emperor's policy of encroachment into town privileges and demands for money significantly weakened the towns, let alone the revolt of the *comuneros* of Castile against the emperor in 1520–1. The Scottish merchants were in the extraordinarily favourable position of being the main producers of money for the crown at a time when the crown had no particular reason to demand it; they had a bargaining lever which was operating in the realms of the potential, and they made full use of it to gain privileges for themselves in an age when their European contemporaries in France, Spain, and the empire were losing them. Moreover, such records as we have do not indicate a high level of urban unrest. There were no bread riots; moreover the belated impact of the price-rise meant that it was not co-terminous with the beginnings of religious dissent.

The merchants of the royal burghs, therefore, had a free hand to pursue their own interests; it was of immense advantage to them that the government could talk but not act. They also benefited from the long periods when Scotland was not at war, although this was not a complete protection, for wars involving Scotland's trading partners hit Scottish trade. In 1524 they were complaining bitterly about the Auld Alliance because it hampered trade with England, Flanders, and Spain. The crown was generally more enthusiastic about links with France than the merchants; in 1467, for example, it added to the legislation that moved the Low Countries staple from Bruges to Middelburg an act telling the merchants that La Rochelle and Bordeaux were lawful ports. But the Scots got little out of the French until Louis XII, in desperate straits in 1510, gave an exemption of customs with Normandy, and further privileges in Norman trade were negotiated by regent Albany in 1518. Much later, in 1602, James VI's suggestion of a Scottish conservator in France, on the lines of the arrangements with the Low Countries, was blocked by the merchants of the royal burghs.

Until the end of the fifteenth century the merchants' own interests lay primarily in the Low Countries. Indeed, this link may help to explain the failure of the Scots to develop their cloth industry, because it seems that there was no real pressure on them to do so. There was still a ready market for wool in Flanders; and the Scots made enough cloth for sale to the urban poor in Flanders, while importing the much finer Flemish cloth. Interest in this trading link was not one-sided. The history of the staple, established in Bruges by the end of the fourteenth century, moved to Middelburgh in 1467, and finally settled at Veere in 1541, is in part the result of competition by these towns; as part of his negotiations with James V in 1527, Charles V offered renewal of the 100-year-old commercial treaty with the Low Countries, backing the claims of Middelburgh against those of Veere, which had entered into negotiations on its own behalf with James.

Trade was only one feature of the strong Scottish links with Flanders, a comparatively neglected area which scholars of Scottish art and cultural life are beginning to open up; the wealthy and thriving Burgundian territories, centre of religious revival and with the most impressive court in northern Europe, offered even more than France to a country as consciously European as Scotland. The economic decline of Flanders in the 1490s, however, the closer ties which James IV and V made with France, and a growing thirst for wine — for wine imports increased steadily during the sixteenth century, despite rising prices — began to swing the balance of Scottish trade to France. The evidence is patchy, but the Edinburgh customs book of 1537–8 shows that, of the 49 ships listed, only 8 went to the Netherlands, while 25 went to France; political relations, recently reinforced by James V's two French marriages, may suggest that this volume of trade was unusually high, but it seems likely that it reflects a general trend. Scottish merchants did not only turn to France. Scottish shipping to the Baltic increased rapidly, from 8 in the mid 1470s to 21 in 1497 and 43 in 1503, and Scottish merchants in 1483 made a killing on salt, undercutting Baltic prices. Useful commercial links were undoubtedly helped by Scotland's rôle as the stronger partner in political and diplomatic relations. They were also strengthened by the Scots who made careers in Denmark, of whom the Shetlander David Sinclair, the king's administrator — *foud* — in Shetland after 1488, and governor of Bergen castle in 1496–7, is an outstanding and early example. The merchants themselves had established communities in Copenhagen and the towns of the Sound by the end of the fifteenth century; and in the first half of the sixteenth century the crown's demand for timber for its ambitious ship and building programmes, as well as the need for iron, produced a rapid development of trade with Sweden, to the point when, in 1546, Scottish merchants were second only to the Dutch in trade with Nylöse (later Gothenburg). There were even glimmerings of revival of trade with England, reflected in the act of 1473, and again in 1482, when Berwick and Carlisle were made legal ports of entry for Scottish goods.

The confidence of the merchants of this period also comes out in their activities within the burghs. Scotland has nothing to offer like the great parish churches of the Cotswolds which a wealthy English merchant class could put up. But this was a period of building, or at least restoring and embellishing the burgh churches, founding new altars, pressing for collegiate status; St Michael's, Linlithgow, its tower overshadowing the neighbouring royal palace, is a supreme example, and there are many others. It is also from this time that the leading burgesses began to take over from the church as the providers of hospitals and schools, a trend that, however involuntarily, was to weaken the church's grip on society. And they were buying their way into landed society, even if as yet on a small scale; Professor Nicholson's analysis of sales of land in James IV's reign shows that the aristocracy and gentry sold more than they bought, whereas the 11 merchants from Edinburgh and 14 others sold little and bought much. It is therefore difficult to reconcile the merchants with the traditional idea of Scottish poverty. 'Your proffeit daylie dois incres', wrote the court poet William Dunbar in his scathing attack on the Edinburgh merchants. That describes them better. They were the real success-story of early-modern Scotland, as status-conscious as those on the land, and in a much stronger position to enforce their superiority.

In 1469, and again in 1474, parliament underwrote that superiority over the craftsmen, giving legal backing to a position virtually assured by the mid fourteenth century, and now made impregnable. They became the unchallenged ruling oligarchy; the first act allowed the old council to choose the new, giving representatives of the crafts a say only in the election of the provost and bailies, and the second stated that four members of the retiring council should sit on the new. Although the craftsmen began to get corporate recognition for themselves, beginning with the skinners of Edinburgh who were given their seal of cause in 1474, they continued to lose out; in 1493 their control of price-setting and standards of workmanship was transferred to the bailies. They were never entirely silenced; their rôle in the burgh, even though Scottish technology was so undeveloped, made it impossible to reduce them to complete subservience, and their formal and unchallenged part in burgh pageantry is a visible sign of that. But they did not have the merchants' voice in government nor their bargaining power.

The same confidence is seen in the relationship of the major burghs with the surrounding countryside. Not only the king, but also the lords looked on the concentration of money and goods within the burghs with an envious eye. Edinburgh was particularly vulnerable; in the 1510s and 1520s there was a constant struggle between Hamiltons and Douglases for control of the burgh, through the office of provost which alternated between them, and a dramatic street fight known as 'Cleanse the Causeway' in 1520, when the Hamiltons were temporarily driven out. But the position of the capital was unusual. The wealthy and important burgh of Aberdeen was more successful in controlling its affairs, by accepting realistically that alliance with one powerful lord would give it the best chance of keeping others out. In 1463 it gave a bond of manrent to Alexander earl of Huntly in return for his maintenance, thus formally initiating a relationship that was to last for 130 years. In practice, Huntly controlled the provostship, which was held for generations by his dependants, the family of Menzies of Pitfodells. The burgh successfully resisted Lord Forbes' demand in 1530 for the tun of wine claimed because he protected their salmon fishings on the Dee and the Don; it retorted that those who should have protected in fact destroyed. It also resisted infiltration from within. In 1525 John Collison tried to get voting rights in the election of provost for four Aberdeenshire lairds. This was turned down; and a marginal note was added to the council's decision, tartly pointing out that Collison was related by marriage to these lairds: 'ane ambesowus proud man was this John Colesoun'. That was a little hard; there were many such 'ambesowus proud men' among the merchants of Scotland.

They also succeeded in keeping the merchants of the non-royal burghs out of foreign trade, despite the dramatic increase in the number of these burghs; indeed, that must have heightened their determination. It has been suggested that, because of the importance of kin or lord as the focal point of rural society, there was less need for rural capitals such as Norwich and York; English county towns did not have a Scottish equivalent until the eighteenth century. The burghs of barony undoubtedly remained small, and were less administrative centres than little service communities; the nearest one can get to them is the little nineteenth-century village of Moscow in Ayrshire, where round the centre provided by a pub − or, it might be, the lord's castle − there grew up a hamlet, with the local carpenter, the shoemaker, and so on bartering their services in return for local produce. It was very different from the money economy and international operations of the royal burghs. But the 178 founded between 1450 and 1625 were too many to be ignored, and eventually the royal burghs were forced to give up their monopoly.

Wealth was not only to be found in the burghs. The depreciation of the coinage did not have wholly adverse effects; it brought more money into circulation. Kind, not money, was still the main source of the wealth of the landowners, enabling them to live well and maintain large households; provisions for the Christmas visit of Andrew Durie, abbot of Melrose, to Mauchline in 1527 included a puncheon of wine, two cows, six sheep, three swans, salmon, and much else. A lavish table in a comparatively unadorned castle was still the lifestyle of the gentry. But from the late fourteenth century there are signs that money was being more widely used. Masons require cash; and the rapid proliferation of the little tower houses throughout Scotland, built as much for reasons of prestige − for stone was the prestigious building material − as for defence, suggests that some lairds did have money to spend. Foreign luxuries and elaborate buildings were no longer reserved for the greatest in society. The use of money seems to have been extending down the social scale, further reducing the gulf between aristocracy and gentry. It must have extended even below the gentry. The mid sixteenth century witnessed an immense upheaval in the pattern of landtenure, with the widespread introduction of feuing. The feu was a matter of higher rents, often monetary rents. It was by no means only the top men in society who managed to find the money.

As in the towns, so in the countryside there is little sign of unrest before the impact of feuing. Lack of agricultural innovation at least meant lack of uprisings in rural society, such as Kett's rebellion in Norfolk and the outbreak in the south-west in 1549, which were reactions primarily against enclosure. There is indeed a general absence of social unrest in Scotland; peasant risings on the scale of the Peasants' Revolt or the Jacquerie are not a feature of Scottish life, for reasons which are hard to explain, but must presumably be related to the close personal structure of society, as John Major argued when he wrote about the immense, even blind, loyalty of tenants and peasants to their lords. The leaders of peasant society, took positive pride, according to Major, in involvement in their lords' affairs, including their aggressive affairs; that in itself could provide an outlet for local aggressions, and where they led, lesser men were likely to follow, for the poorest members of society were not in a position to take an independent line. There was in any case little to take an independent line about in the early sixteenth century. We do not know enough about diet, although Major was fairly positive on the subject; he wrote a cookery lesson on the making of oatcakes, pointing out that this 'bread of the peasants' fed those who made up the mass of English and Scottish armies, 'a proof that oatcake is not a thing to be sneered at'. For most people diet was grain-based, with some vegetables, milk products, and possibly fish; meat was a luxury. There is no clear evidence of shortage; the period when dearth became a real horror was the late sixteenth century. Even the complexities of landtenure did not produce in practice the degree of instability that in theory could have been expected.

Major claimed that the short-term lease, the common form of tenure, militated against improvement to land because of the built-in insecurity. Dr Margaret Sanderson's study of kirk lands, however, shows that his strictures must be modified. There was a trend towards longer leases. Between 1464 and 1516 the abbey of Coupar, a highly effective estate manager, leased 418 holdings: 87 were for life, 289 for five years, and the others from 19 to 1 year. Of the 257 leases from 1539 to 1560, 150 were for life, and of the other 107, 47 were converted to life. Even the preponderance of short-term leases in the earlier period did not mean uncertain livelihood. Leases were often renewed. Coupar's grange of Airlie, for example, was held by the Spalding family for over 100 years, and on the estates of Paisley abbey between 1526 and 1555, 64 per cent of new tenants were related to the previous ones, while the fact that the majority of holdings changed hands only once shows a high level of stability. In practice, therefore, there was similarity between the lease, even the short-term lease, and the other usual form of tenure, the rental, which was normally given for life. Even failure to keep up with the rent did not necessarily involve loss of land; in 1476 Coupar gave a one-year lease of Dunfallandy to Donald and Andrew Macgow, despite three years arrears of rent, which were 'superseded without any remission. . .in hope of good and better management'. Not every landlord was an extortionist on the make. The ethos of protection included charity to small tenants from whom lords got small fiscal returns as well as maintenance of those more powerful people from whom they got service. It is seen again in what was probably a tragic case on the Coupar estates; leprosy has been suggested as the reason for the five-year lease of Kethyk in 1466, which John Barbour had held, to Anne Porter his wife, with the condition that after the first year's sowing Barbour should 'depart from his wife and healthy children to a place which he shall choose suitable to his infirmity'.

The personal ethos of society was the basis for a third kind of tenure, kindly tenancy, which gave a right to land on the grounds of kindness – kinship – to the last holder. Kindness was a reality, not a concept; it could be given away, sold, bequeathed, used as a dowry, divided between sons. Kindly tenants were not necessarily small tenants; some were lairds. And there could be a distinction between the right to the tenure and the form of it; George Campbell of Cessnock, kindly tenant of the abbey of Melrose, held his land by rental. But very often kindly tenants did not have written evidence of their tenure, relying rather on the claim to have held the land 'past memory of man'. This was to make their position particularly precarious when the feuing movement radically altered Scottish land-tenure.

Nevertheless, a tenant who could produce a written title was protected by the law; and even the rights of those who could not were not necessarily abandoned, although the fact that much of the farming population depended on unwritten agreements suggests that Major's account of the effects of insecurity cannot be ignored. Yet many people did have security of tenure. What they did not have was security against regular increases of rents when their leases were renewed. And what they could not do was to guarantee that their heirs would inherit. It was these two things which gave the feu its immense advantage.

Instances of grants in feu-ferme can be found since the twelfth century. But even the Stewart monarchy took some time to realize the short-term advantages, despite the 1458 act which advised the king to feu his lands. James IV was the first king who did to any extent. In the sixteenth century feuing became common on church lands; the church was panicked into feuing, as many of its feu-charters said, by James V's massive taxation in the 1530s, by general uncertainty about its future, and in southern Scotland, by the devastation of church buildings by the English in the 1540s. Given the amount of good land held by the church, thanks to the generosity of the twelfth- and thirteenth-century kings, feuing created a new class in rural society, when former tenants became in effect landowners, and prospered. Feuing looked very similar to leasing or renting; it involved a grassum (down-payment on entry) and annual feu-duty, and double duty in the year when the feuar died and his heir succeeded. But in this lay the crucial difference. The feu was hereditary.

In the first generation of a feu, the advantages were all to the superior. When James IV feued the lands of Ettrick Forest, his former rents, £525 in 1501, rose 522 per cent to £2,672 in gross terms, and even in real terms, 400 per cent to £1,639. Grassums and annual feu-duties were raised when a tack was transformed to a feu, and some-times the new feuars were required to pay an extra sum every three, five, or seven years in compensation to the landlord for the loss of his grassum on the renewal of a lease. For the king, for any other secular landlord, and for a church that believed itself to be in desperate straits, it was a very quick way of raising money. But in the long term feuing worked in the interests of the feuar. The value of money fell steadily; the silver value of coins was halved between 1513 and 1570, and halved again by 1600. But the feus were fixed from the beginning, and, as the acts of 1503 and 1540 said, they were perpetual. It was therefore almost impossible to raise feu-duties to keep pace with inflation, and in real terms feuars paid increasingly less, superiors got less.

The social distribution of the feuars differs on the crown and the kirk lands. Dr Madden's study of Ettrick Forest shows that 4 per cent of the new feuars were nobles, 45 per cent lairds, 15 per cent smaller tenants — people designated 'in' a holding, which signified that they did not possess it — and 36 per cent who are names without designation. Dr Sanderson's figures for the church lands show a decrease in the number of nobles and lairds — 3 per cent and 29 per cent respec-tively — compared to 44 per cent of people 'in' holdings, and 13 per cent of undesignated names; in addition, 8 per cent were burgesses, and 6 per cent clerics and lawyers. These figures may reflect a differ-ent social distribution on the lands before feuing began. More impor-tant is the fact that, even on the crown lands, the number of people who possessed land heritably for the first time marginally outweighed the established landowners who took on feus, and on the church lands notably outweighed them. When David Lindsay, in the *Satyre of the Thrie Estaitis*, castigated the new breed of 'gearking gentill men that neither will he work or can' he was exaggerating the problem, as Major had done the problem of leasing. But the sudden infusion into local society of a new group of landed proprietors, many of whom were to succeed in increasing their wealth, was one of the most dramatic changes in Scottish society, although until work comparable to Dr Sanderson's study of the early feuars is done for those who inherited the feus in the late sixteenth and seventeenth centuries, it is impossible to understand the full implications of that change.

Writing in 1930, I.F. Grant claimed that feuing 'undoubtedly made for the unhappiness of large numbers of people, and it increased the gloom of the period of greatest mental stress that Scotland had been called on to endure'. Dr Sanderson questions the 'unneccessarily sinister reputation' of the feuing movement, and justifies this by demonstrating that on the kirk lands an impressive 63 per cent of the sitting tenants were able to take on the financial burden of converting their holdings to feus. There was evident feeling that sitting tenants should not be arbitrarily dispossessed. In 1510 Adam Scott of Tushielaw would get the feu of Gilsmancleuch only if the sitting tenant, George Hume, refused it; and when in 1578 the kindly tenants of the bishopric of Dunblane petitioned parliament against the bishop's proposed feu of his lands to the earl of Montrose, whose influence had got him the bishopric, parliament upheld the tenants and, despite an appeal from the earl, maintained their decision that the feu should not be confirmed until the tenants were satisfied for their kindness.

There were, inevitably, those who suffered. Thirty-seven per cent did not become feuars, and might end up like the former tenant in the barony of Kilwinning, forced to become his neighbour's servant when his inability to raise the money meant dispossession. Even the wealthy could be caught. The earl of Huntly became feuar of the lordships of Strathdee and Cromar in 1530 for a grassum of 2,000 merks and a feu-duty of £238; the grant was caught in James V's act of revocation, and the new composition demanded by the king was too much for the earl. Moreover, feuing offered wonderful opportunities for speculation in land; the lord justice clerk who held a feu on the Scone estates made far more from the four tenants he put into the lands than he paid. The gloom of contemporary writers like Lindsay and Robert Wedderburn, probable author of the *Complaynte of Scotlande*, whose Labour complained to Dame Scotia that 'I am exilit fra my takkis and fra my steddyngis, the malis and fermis of the grond that I laubyr is hychtit to sic ane price that it is fors to me & vyf and barnys to drynk vattir', was not wholly misplaced.

Almost all the great literary figures of the period, Major, Boece, Henryson, Dunbar, Lindsay, and others, turned their attention to economic life. They were not uncritical; they can be absolved from the suggestion of propaganda for foreign consumption, such as underlay the glowing account by d'Ayala to be read in the Spanish court. So their praises as well as their strictures may be taken to reflect, not wholly inaccurately, a reasonably stable society. The feuing movement changed that, and did so at precisely the time when religious uncertainty had begun.

4

Poets, Scholars, and Gentlemen

The question has been asked whether it is possible that the attempt by James IV's protegé, John Damien de Falcusis, abbot of Tongland, to fly from the battlements of Stirling castle is an echo of the world of Leonardo da Vinci. Such was the interest in what was happening in Europe that the answer may well be yes, although it then has to be admitted that nothing more typifies the prosaic nature of Scottish society; Damien neither flew nor died a dramatic death, but dropped gracelessly down into a midden, from which he picked himself up and complained that he had been cheated, for the feathers of hens which 'covet the mydding and not the skyis' had been infiltrated into the wings of eagles' feathers which should have borne him aloft.

Yet Damien's farcical leap into the limelight hardly does justice to the sheer exuberance of Scottish cultural and intellectual life in the late fifteenth and early sixteenth centuries. Whether its sum total justifies the term 'Renaissance Scotland' is neither an answerable nor even a necessary question. Nor is it in the end profitable to debate whether the relative peace in the reign of James IV, and again in the reign of James VI, provided the necessary context for that exuberance; Italy itself was hardly a haven of peace. Much more important is the question of sufficient surplus of wealth to encourage patronage; and if that was there in abundance in the Italian towns, so did it exist, on a much more limited scale, for the crown, the church, the greater towns, and the aristocracy in Scotland. We have in any case a distorted picture because of accident of survival; only in the relentless rhythm of William Dunbar's great poem, popularly known as the *Lament for the Makaris*, do we get an impression of the number of Scottish poets of the fifteenth century, for none of the work of 'Maister John Clerk' or 'gentill Roull of Corstorphine' and many others named in the poem survives. Moreover the talent, sometimes spilling over into genius, which made James IV's desire for a cultured and impressive court so easy of fulfilment, was ultimately the result of individual chance. What is important is that in this age, when kings sought a place in Renaissance politics, and merchants showed a keen eye for the centres of commercial wealth in northern Renaissance Europe, Scottish poets at home and Scottish scholars abroad were strongly conscious of also being part of a wider world.

We know hardly anything about native artists. As in England, the monarchy may have had 'model' portraits, which formed the basis for later reproductions and variations; if so, Daniel Myten's somewhat dreary portrait of James IV does not inspire confidence in the original. Names that survive are those of painters rather than artists, men like Alexander Chalmer, employed to embellish the king's ships, and make canvas beasts with wooden wings for a tournament in 1507. But if Scotland did not produce much itself, it had the taste to go for the best; and the best in the late fifteenth century for northern Europe was the Netherlands. The lovely and delicate hanging lamp in St John's kirk, Perth, survives as an example of Scottish contact with the Low Countries, and the Book of Hours of James IV and Margaret Tudor as a fine example of Flemish illumination. Tabernacles and images of St Catherine and St John were brought from Flanders to Dunkeld by Bishop Brown, and vestments and hangings by the abbot of Holyrood when he visited Bruges in 1494. Even Flemish tombstones enjoyed a vogue; Schevez, James duke of Ross, and others imported tombstones from Bruges, and for this life Schevez had a portrait medal done of himself, probably by Quinten Massys. Some contact in the other direction may have existed; it has been reasonably conjectured that Alexander Bening, one of the great Flemish miniaturists and father-in-law of the Scots merchant Andrew Halyburton, conservator of the staple at Middelburg, may have come from the Edinburgh family of Benings, who produced a number of artists in the sixteenth century. Certainly, Flemish contact brought to Scotland one of the great works of art of the age, the Trinity panels. These are among the larger of the nine surviving paintings by Hugo van der Goes; they depict James III and Margaret of Denmark, and Edward Bonkil, provost of Trinity College, Edinburgh, who commissioned them in the 1470s. The style follows Van Eyck's *Virgin in the Church*. The painting itself is a marvellously evocative rendering of the vision of the Trinity during the Saturday vespers, when to the earthly liturgy of the provost, praying to the Virgin, was added the heavenly liturgy of the unseen angels, singing and playing the organ. The power of music is compellingly portrayed in the Trinity altarpiece.

The Scots also went to the Netherlands as the country which led the world in music; Guillaume Dufay and his successors made the Netherlands the Vienna or Berlin of the fifteenth and early sixteenth centuries. John Broune, lutanist, was sent there in 1473, and was followed in 1498 by Thomas Inglis and John Fethy. Fethy came back to Scotland as master of the song-school in Aberdeen and then Edinburgh; he introduced the new skill of five-fingered organ-playing; and the elaborate part-writing of the one piece of his music that survives indicates the presence in Scotland of a musician of high talent. His impact can be seen in the work of a pupil of his Aberdeen song-school, Robert Black, who wrote organ music that has all the liveliness suitable for the small organ, and is amazingly attractive, if unfamiliar to generations nurtured on Bach and the music of the massive and sonorous modern pipe-organ. Otherwise, two folk-songs, court part-songs, and the church music of Robert Carver, who wrote five masses for the Chapel Royal at Stirling, including a hauntingly lovely mass for six voices in 1520, are the main survivals of Scottish music: just enough to reflect the quality and style of what once existed. There is no doubt about the importance of music in secular and ecclesiastical society. One of his court musicians, Thomas Wode, has left us the thumbnail sketch of James V insisting in joining in the singing in a harsh and raucous voice. The existence of the song-schools in the burghs, where basic literary skills were taught, but where the teaching of music to supply choristers for the church was more important, shows that Scotland took the desire for good music seriously. There is also a hint that it followed one development in the Netherlands: the emergence of the professional musician, the salaried singer or organist; the cathedral of Antwerp employed a professional organist in the 1470s. In 1531 the 'hale toun' of Aberdeen sacked all its singers 'for their demerits. . . done to God and tham', except for the aged Andrew Coupar, who should continue to be paid his fee. This interest in music makes it difficult to discount the tradition, preserved by the Piedmontese scholar Giovanni Ferrerio who taught at Kinloss in the 1530s, that the musician William Rogers — in legend, a 'favourite' of James III — did found a school of music.

As in art and music, so in architecture contacts with the Netherlands were strong. Holyrood, St Mary's Tower in Dundee, and St Mary's, Haddington, all owe something to Flemish influence; indeed, a Fleming worked at Holyrood, and trading contacts make that influence on the burgh churches readily understandable. On the other hand, the French master-mason John Morrow was employed at Melrose abbey and Glasgow cathedral; and Stirling and Falkland, the great palaces of James V, were not surprisingly the work of masons imported from France. Like so much else, architecture shows a mixture of foreign and native features, with perhaps increasing emphasis on the native in this case, notably in the lairds' tower-houses, basically simple constructions, but capable of considerable and ingenious variation in design and decoration. Architecture reflects the double-vision of early-modern Scotland, the desire to combine things Scottish with things European.

The basis of interest abroad was, once again, confidence at home; and in two areas of its cultural life, the linguistic and the literary, Scotland could be very confident indeed. Middle Scots was emerging as the language of literature, government, and the educated section of the population. The French-speaking aristocracy of earlier centuries had become, by the late fourteenth century, a Scots-speaking aristocracy, lapping up the first great vernacular work, Barbour's epic poem *The Brus*. There were two major vernacular works in the early fifteenth century, James I's remarkable poem *The Kingis Quair*, and the verse chronicle of Andrew of Wyntoun, a work interesting for literary and historical reasons, but less appealing with its monotonous and jingling verse. In the late fifteenth and early sixteenth centuries there was a proliferation of translations of French works into Scots, like the *Book of Alexander*, *Lancelot of the Laik*, and the *Porteous of Noblenes*. Under the patronage of the Sinclairs, Gilbert Hay produced translations of chivalric works, *The Buke of the Law of Armys* and the *Order of Knychthode*, and of that most famous and influential treatise on kingship, the *Secreta Secretorum*, an Arabic work believed to be Aristotle's advice to Alexander the Great. And the 1470s saw the writing of the second great vernacular epic, *The Wallace*, which, to a greater extent than Barbour's *Brus*, derived from oral tradition which had been developed and embellished for almost two centuries, producing a central character raised to a level of spiritual heroism far above the human figure of Barbour's King Robert.

This corpus of prose and poetry for a knightly and aristocratic audience used the same language that its audience employed in government. Much earlier than in England, vernacular became the language of government in Scotland. From the reign of James I almost all parliamentary legislation was in Scots, and the council records and treasurer's accounts are in Scots as far back as they survive, to the 1470s; only the register of the great seal and the exchequer rolls continued to use Latin. The adoption of Scots by the ruling élite had considerable social and literary impact. It undoubtedly enhanced the prestige of the language. In 1400 it had been a subject of apology by the earl of March in his famous letter to Henry IV, when he explained that 'Inglysche' was 'mare clere to myn understandyng than Latyne or Fraunche'. In 1500 it was the accepted language of the great as well as the majority of the ordinary people. March called it English, and that was the word used by fifteenth-century writers. In a sense they were correct. Middle Scots is very close to the language spoken in northern England; it derives substantially from Old English, although there are both Gaelic and French influences. But from the late fourteenth century it became increasingly a separate dialect, with distinctive forms; the English ending 'red', for example, became 'rent' in Scots, in words like 'hatrent' (hatred), 'kinrent' (kindred) and so on. And it had a distinctive life of its own, with sometimes astonishingly literal and attractive forms of expression; 'the rysand of the son and the gangand to rest of that ilk' is a wordy but appealing version of 'sunrise and sunset'. It was not a language of measured dignity. It is not, perhaps, the language that would be regarded as ideal for the earliest translation of Virgil's *Aeneid* in Britain, written by Gavin Douglas in the early sixteenth century; Douglas himself modestly deprecated his 'lewit barbour tong', but negated the apology when he stated with pride:

> This buke I dedicait
> Written in the language of the Scottis natioun.

Yet if it cannot be imagined as a medium for Shakespeare, its lasting qualities and vitality did produce the medium for the genius of Burns, while in the twentieth century the *Drunk Man looks at the Thistle* is a supreme example of what could be achieved at the hand of a master, Hugh McDiarmid, when he changed his mind about the impossibility of Scots as a language for the poet. The flowering of Scots cannot simply be attributed to the fact that the aristocracy turned from French to Scots. But it did have an effect. It became the language of the court, and therefore of the court poets.

Its wider social effect is a matter for speculation. It is only possible to guess that in Scotland the idea of a common language, shared by the Scottish and English aristocracies − even if the southern English would in fact have had difficulty in understanding Scots − may have had a gradual effect on the hostility that all good Scots should feel to the English. The change from a society where the upper ranks spoke

French to one another and Scots, or sometimes Gaelic, to their servants and estate-officials, to a society where the same language was used for all, was considerable, and may well have reinforced the bonds of kinship and personal lordship, as well as the relationship between landlord and tenant. More generally, it is difficult to imagine that in this age of the developing nation-state it did not have a unifying force, and add to men's awareness of their nationality.

In one crucial area, however, it certainly increased disunity between Scottish lowland and Gaelic highland. Geographically, Gaelic had been declining since the twelfth century. Nevertheless, Major's claim that Gaelic was still the language of half of the population was not outrageously inaccurate; in 1400 all but the borders, lowland belt, and east-coast strip was apparently Gaelic-speaking, which suggests a high survival-rate, for half of the population lived north of the Tay. It was not until the end of the fifteenth century that Gaelic clearly became a 'second-class' language. There is no more illuminating spectacle to illustrate the effect of this than the way in which the sixteenth-century Campbell lairds of Glenorchy got bonds of manrent from their dependants; the makers of the bonds came along and gave verbal promises, in Gaelic, and then watched the Campbell notaries − one of whom wrote a glorious Italic script − writing these promises down in what, to the grantors, was a wholly foreign language, Scots, and struggling hopelessly with their outlandish names.

By the mid fifteenth century the sport of Gaelic-bashing had begun. The Elgin priest Richard Holland, in his *Buke of the Howlat*, used the Gaelic phrase 'beannachd Dhe' − God's blessing − to poke fun at 'a bard out of Ireland with Bannachadee' who spoke pidgin Gaelic, 'Glunton, guk dynynd dach hal mischy doch'. Dunbar, in his *Flyting of Dunbar and Kennedy* − 'flyting' being a quarrel in verse − attacked the poet from Gaelic-speaking Carrick in Ayrshire:

> I tak on me a pair of Lothian hippis
> Sall fairer Inglis mak and mair parfyte
> Than thow can blabber with thy Carrick lippis. . . .
> Thou art but gluntoch

'gluntoch', like Holland's 'glunton', being a derisory lowland word from Gaelic 'glundubh', black knee. But Kennedy was at least allowed to reply:

> Irische . . . sud be all trew Scottis mennis lede

It was the gud langage of this land . . .
Quhill Corspatrick, that we of tresoun rede . . .
Throu his tresoun broght Inglis rumplis in.

This suggests that contempt was still leavened with humour in 1500, as it was not 1600. Yet d'Ayala's way of describing James IV's knowledge of Gaelic, that he spoke 'the language of the savages', must reflect court opinion to some extent. There was nothing to counter the advance of Middle Scots, the language of the aristocracy, the fashionable poets, Fordun's 'domestic Scots'. The very word 'Scots' had been taken over. In 1400 'lingua Scotica' meant Gaelic. In 1500 'Scottis' was used, at least by Douglas, to refer to the language of the lowlander. And in 1600 James VI fondly imagined that he could civilize the Isles by teaching the people to speak an increasingly Anglicized form of that language.

By now the esoteric tradition of the bards was foreign to the lowlands; there is a world of difference between the history and poetry of the bards and that of the lowland writers. One difference is that in the highlands the two were not distinct. There was developing, in the increasingly literate and record-conscious lowlands, an awareness of the sense of the past, a distinction between past and present, which was absent from Gaelic writing. The six-day drinking-spree described by the seventeenth-century poet Niall Mor, one of the long line of MacMhuirich bards who can be traced back to the thirteenth century, was actually an account of a contemporary orgy at Dunvegan in 1613; but it can have been no more and no less immediate to its audience than accounts of the feasting and banqueting of long-dead Macdonalds. This quality of timelessness is very much part of the attitude of a non-literary society, dependant on a closed literary élite, whose work is designed to remind those in the present of the glories not so much of the past as of their families, their society; the prestige of the present lord is enhanced by the deeds of his ancestors, and it is in a real sense in praise of him that these deeds are recounted. A non-literate society is not a society without culture, although more literate societies have a distressing tendency to regard it as such, as the lowlanders did the highlanders. The immense prestige of the MacMhuirich bards and the Macbeth physicians, the long and highly technical training in the bardic schools to learn the skills necessary for poetry written according to strict and complex rules, make nonsense of their attitude. Moreover, while Gaelic society tenaciously preserved its own traditions, it was by no means isolated. Some of the bardic poetry was love-poetry, inspired by continental influence; Gaelic medical manuscripts are translations of Latin treatises from the great medical schools of Europe, Padua, Salerno, and Montpellier. And there is nothing insular about a society that could produce, in the mid sixteenth century, a notary called Socrates MacEwan.

The distinction between literate lowland and non-literate highland was by no means complete. The great compilation of Gaelic poetry, the *Book of the Dean of Lismore*, produced in the early sixteenth century by James MacGregor and his poet brother Duncan, mainly for the courts of the greater chiefs, is the major example of poetry of oral tradition finding its way onto the written page. Moreover, contact with the lowlands was maintained by scholars who came to the lowland universities. John Carswell, superintendant of Argyll, and translator of the Book of Common Order – the first book to be printed in Scottish or Irish Gaelic – may have been trained in a bardic school, and was certainly a student at St Andrews in the early 1540s; Roderick Maclean, bishop of the Isles in the mid sixteenth century, combined education at home with the path to higher education so familiar to lowland scholars when he went to the university of Wittenberg in 1534. The most renowned of all sixteenth-century Scots scholars, George Buchanan, was a Gaelic-speaker, and although his career was to lie in the field of European learning and Scottish lowland politics, his most remarkable achievement was his recognition of the common origin of all the Celtic languages, Breton, Welsh, Irish, Scots. But on the whole, contact between highland and lowland was a one-way process. The early-sixteenth-century *Chronicle of Fortingall*, written by a MacGregor of Glenstrae partly in Latin and partly in Scots, symbolizes the problem for Gaelic culture, and the need felt to compromise and adapt, which was not matched by corresponding interest in the more complacent lowlands.

The three great names of lowland poetry in the late fifteenth and early sixteenth centuries are Robert Henryson, William Dunbar, and Gavin Douglas. Of these, only Dunbar was, strictly speaking, a 'court' poet, wholly dependant on court patronage, and thoroughly sour about how niggardly it was, and how little he was regarded at court, compared with the:

> kirkmen, courtmen and craftismen fyne,
> divinouris, rethoris and philosophouris,
> astrologis, artistis and oratouris . . .
> musicianis, minstrelis and mirrie singaris,

> pryntouris, payntouris and potingaris . . .
> schulderaris and schoveris that hes no schame.

It is a lovely description of the court of James IV, not least because of the brilliant description in the last line of the archetypal courtier, of all courts in all ages. But Dunbar, in his own eyes the greatest ornament of all, remained 'amang the laif, unworthy be ane place to have'. He was unnecessarily bitter; his annual pension of £80 was not, by the standards of the day, ungenerous. In any case, he had the last word; it is the work of this great 'maker' which has survived as the testimony to the vitality of the court of James IV. His poetry ranged from lively and scurrilous 'flyting' and sharp-edged satire from which none was exempt, whether the 'fenzeit freir of Tungland', the merchants of Edinburgh, those at court, even the king, to the deeply moving and powerful allegories and religious verse such as the *Dance of the Sevin Deidly Sinnis* and the *Tabill of Confession*. The influences detectable in Dunbar's work are many and varied: the follower of Chaucer, Lydgate, and Gower, the Scottish Francois Villon, with his bitter wit and self-awareness, the north-European, with his dance of death in the *Lament for the Makaris*, echoing the eschatological art of the Netherlands. These are evidence not of lack of originality in Dunbar but of his European stature as a poet of great range and inspiration, and sour and endearing humanity.

Robert Henryson, writing mainly in the reign of James III, was not attached to the court. He was a Dunfermline schoolmaster, working close to the abbey whose collection of manuscripts show it to have been one of the major cultural centres of late-fifteenth-century Scotland; it may have been the abbot, Richard Bothwell, who persuaded Henryson to move from the university of Glasgow to the grammar school of Dunfermline. His pupils were privileged; this is the man generally regarded as the greatest of the poets. His themes, the vanity of the world, the need for moral reform, derive from medieval rhetoric; his language reflects humanist influence. In the *Testament of Cresseid* he took up Chaucer's theme, and took it much further; the divine punishment of Cresseid's leprosy leads to the terrible moment when Troilus sees her again, so disfigured that he does not recognize her, but is somehow reminded of his lost love; and the poem ends on a note of profound human pity for the tragic woman who

> under this stane, late lipper, lyis deid.

He was a scholarly poet who made use of a wide variety of sources, Boethius, 'Aesop', Chaucer. He was familiar with the writings of Boccaccio; there are parallels with the *De Genealogia Deorum*, for example, but not slavish following; the cold wintery hostility of his Saturn in *Cresseid* is not Boccaccio's Saturn, while in the *Morall Fabillis* the classical imagery of Boccaccio is replaced with concentration on the recreative power of literature. To describe him as a 'renaissance' poet would be a misleading attempt to classify a man who, like many in the early stages of the humanist movement, does not fit black and white categories. It is, in any event, always different to classify towering talent, in this age or any other.

Gavin Douglas was a member of one of the great aristocratic families, third son of Archibald earl of Angus, provost of St Giles in Edinburgh from 1503, and bishop of Dunkeld from 1515. His *Palice of Honour* reflects his aristocratic background; the men of faith, philosophy, and poetry surround the palace where Honour sits with princes and heroes of just wars. His masterpiece was the *Eneados* (Aeneid), the astonishing achievement of the translation into Scots, with a deliberate attempt at verbal accuracy, of a work composed in a language whose construction, rhythm, and sonority were very difficult. He wrote for his own circle, royal and aristocratic. But he sought a wider audience, including those to whom the poem would have to be read aloud; and he had a concept of the educational value of his enterprise: 'Thank me tharfor, masteris of grammar sculys'.

His background gives him something in common with the greatest poet of the next reign, Sir David Lindsay, diplomat and courtier. At least one of the poems of this widely travelled man, the *Dreme*, suggests, as Dr R.D.S. Jack has argued, a knowledge of the Italian vernacular as well·as Italian humanism, for its model was *The Divine Comedy*. He wrote a considerable amount of poetry, the *Papyngo*, the *Monarche*, and much else, as well as the dazzling play for which he is best known, the *Satyre of the Thrie Estaitis*, performed at the court in 1540, and in a much longer form in public at Edinburgh and Cupar in the 1550s. It is extremely good theatre; the language problem is no barrier to its enjoyment by audiences who have seen its revival in Edinburgh and Glasgow in the twentieth century. But it is more than that. Like Lindsay's other writings, it offers a wealth of comment on sixteenth-century Scotland, as well as advice to the king. After the court performance, James V is said to have turned to the bishops present and threatened to pack them off to his uncle, Henry VIII, if they would not listen and reform themselves; and indeed their embarrassment, as they watched the relentless pillorying of the wealth and lack of spirituality and even human concern of the leaders of the church, can readily be imagined. It is unlikely that Lindsay was a crypto-protestant, as has been suggested. It is certain that he was a man thoroughly aware of the great religious issues of his day, and the great social problems, at home and abroad; and he wrote about them with biting wit.

Apart from poetry, the other great interest of the period was historical writing, a carefully constructed account of Scotland's past, pressed into the service of present ambitions and national awareness, and thus to an extent similar to Gaelic poetry, but with a wider purpose, a chronological framework and a consciously scholarly approach. On the surface it looks like 'nationalist' history in the restricted context of relations with England, following the tradition first committed to writing in Barbour's *Brus*. That was, of course, part of it. The origin myths, which asserted that the Scots were the descendants of the Greek prince Gathelos and his Egyptian wife Scota, gave grounds for scoring off the English with their Trojan descent, for everyone knew that the Greeks beat the Trojans. Even the great hero Arthur became a monster of moral iniquity and treachery because of his double-dealing with the Scots and the Picts, and with the noble Mordred, son of the king of the Picts. But national awareness was much more positive than that, in a country whose council could refer, in 1552, to the existence of the Auld Alliance 'sen the tyme of Achaus king of Scotland and Charlis the Maine king of France'. Already in the early fifteenth century Wyntoun had set out to depict Scotland's place in world history, and it was that approach which was the key to Scottish historical writing. As, by the end of the century, churchmen were engaged in establishing a history of Scottish sanctity, so they were producing a secular history, both of which gave Scotland a past such as other nations had. Thus the collection of legends and tall tales strung together by the renowned scholar and principal of Aberdeen, Hector Boece — tales that at least had the merit of providing Shakespeare with his witches in *Macbeth* — were immensely popular, patronized by James V, and translated into Scots at his expense by John Bellenden in the 1530s. Boece's 'history' was much more to the taste of his audience than the cool scholarly analysis by his contemporary John Mair or Major, whose *History of Greater Britain*, published in 1520, made the mistake of arguing strongly for union with England; in the aftermath of Flodden, war with England was something to be avoided at all costs, but closer ties were as yet too strong meat.

That unfashionable scholastic Major did something never matched by the humanist Boece. He questioned the legitimacy of the origin myths, the earliest scholar to do so in Scotland, barely a generation after another pioneer in the field, the French scholar Robert Gaguin. Moreover, he produced the most extensive analysis of kingship of the period, the first reasoned statement of something that was to become a crucial issue in the late sixteenth century, in the hands of George Buchanan. History was beginning to be used as political didactic. Already there was a long-established genre of *specula principum*, going back to Isocrates and Xenophon, and proliferating in the early sixteenth century, most notably in the *Institutio Principis Christiani* of Erasmus. In Scotland, Gilbert Hay's translation of the *Secreta Secretorum* had contributed to this genre. But most advice to princes was given in verse, such as Henryson's *Lyoun and the Mous*, the anonymous *Thre Prestis of Peblis*, and the poem attached to the chronicle *Liber Pluscardensis*, and in the sixteenth century, Lindsay's *Monarche*, William Lauder's *Office and Dewtie of Kyngis*, and others. Much of it was limited to the basic theme of the king's responsibility to do justice, which was conceived in far more than strictly legal terms, for it comprised good government which would produce order and stability; from that followed comment on the king's moral character, and his need of counsel, though only the *Liber Pluscardensis* poem advanced the astonishing theory that councillors should be chosen for ability, not rank. Historical writing was beginning to take on this flavour. Boece's 40 mythical kings could be deprived of office if they lived immoral lives — as most of the 40 did. Much closer to home, it is in the early sixteenth century that the legend of James III began to develop; the earliest hint is in the remarkable 'world' history, the *Roit and Quheill of Time*, written by the Jedburgh friar Adam Abell in 1533. This was to grow into a systematic historical and even moral explanation which stood events on their head and brought into prominence the evil counsellors, James's low-born favourites. It was a valuable weapon at the end of the century, when the past was used to justify the crisis of Mary's reign. In the early sixteenth century history was not yet employed in this way. But the trend was already visible.

In 1507–8 one of the most dramatic developments of fifteenth-century Europe was introduced to Scotland; the Edinburgh burgesses Walter Chepman and Andrew Millar set up the first Scottish printing-press. In general, the revolutionary change from the laborious and expensive business of producing manuscripts to the easy production of vast numbers of printed books can hardly be overestimated. Dunbar certainly benefited from Chepman and Millar, and so did his public. But Scottish scholars still preferred to send their work to the great European centres, especially Antwerp and Paris, thus keeping themselves firmly within the wider world of scholarship. The real interest of the Scottish printing press is the fact that it was welcomed by the king as a means of promoting government business; it was to print 'bukis of our lawis, actis of parliament, chroniclis, mess bukis'. It is one indication of the deliberate attempt to put cultural developments, and education itself, to the service of the state. The same motive encouraged Bishop Elphinstone to establish a new university at Aberdeen, where law would be taught; he intended to provide a new centre for the training of professional lawyers, exactly as the 'Education act' of 1496 demanded. That act directed the eldest sons of the greater landowners to go to school to learn 'perfyte Latyne'; when this hurdle was over, they were then to go to the schools of law — that is, the universities — so that for the first time the country would have judges in the local courts who had professional expertise. The laity were to become literate.

Almost certainly, this legislation was not a cause, however, but a consequence of what Dr G.G. Simpson has called a 'silent revolution' in lay literacy in the previous half-century. He has estimated that at least 60 per cent of the nobility were by now able to sign their names. One source that demonstrates the change is the corpus of bonds of manrent; with almost unbelievable mathematical precision, in a body of documents that comes mainly from the period 1450–1600, the signature began to accompany the seal from 1500, and took over entirely after 1550. Evidence of the ability to sign one's name is not in itself evidence of more than the most elementary literacy. But the fact that the signature became acceptable as legal authentication is undoubtedly evidence of something very dramatic indeed.

Modern society regards literacy as something good and necessary in itself, and makes life difficult to the point of impossibility for those who do not acquire the skills to cope with the ever-increasing amount of documentation now somehow equated with civilization. It is therefore hard for people today to conceive of a society such as that of early-modern Scotland where literacy was only a means to an end, one path, but not a necessary path, to a career. We tend to listen sympathetically to the strictures of contemporary scholars such as John Major and, later in the sixteenth century, James Melville, who castigated the nobility and gentry for their lack of enthusiasm for book-learning;

they were demanding what we now take for granted: lay literacy. But their criticism was unduly harsh. The fact that laymen were beginning to acquire literary skills for themselves was not just a natural development from a state of non-culture to a state of culture. It was a massive and even revolutionary change in the value-judgements of a whole society.

As late as the mid fifteenth century the literate were still a recognizable élite, and still almost entirely a clerical élite. They were necessary for the business of government and the law. They were also necessary for the purpose of entertainment. They wrote the poems and histories for a non-literate aristocratic and gentry audience, and they read them to that audience. Inevitably, this clerical and literate closed-shop had something of a mystique. But that mystique was tarnished by a degree of contempt, even hostility, from the laity. Many of the literate were, after all, in the position of servants, as government officials, chaplains in the lord's household doing double-duty as his clerks, and so on. Their very existence meant that there was literally no occasion when a great layman had to read anything for himself; if there was a dispute over his lands a clerical servant could find the relevant charter in his charter-chest and read the details of the grant; if he wanted tales of military exploits after dinner a servant could read romances or suitable extracts from chronicles to him.

Why, then, should the laity want to learn the skills of the subordinate? For them, getting on in life was achieved by living in conspicuous splendour, being admired for their military skills, adding to their lands by marriage alliances and royal favour. For good social reasons the need to impress their fellow-men was all-important; the need to read and write was irrelevant. Even in the changed world of the sixteenth century that value was still held dear; the highly-educated English knight Sir Thomas Eliot could say in 1531, in his *Boke named the Governour*, that 'continuous study without manner of exercise shortly exhausteth the spirits vital.. . .The most honourable exercise. . .that beseemeth the estate of every noble person is to ride surely and clean on a great horse and a rough, which undoubtedly. . . importeth a majesty and a dread to inferior persons'. Moreover, the idea that their inability to read meant that they were 'uneducated' would have made no sense to the non-literate layman. This was an age when the verb 'to read' normally meant 'to read aloud', and also 'to be read to'. Gilbert Hay said that it was good for kings and princes to have legends and romances read to them, and kings and princes would have agreed. They were highly cultured creatures, thoroughly conversant with the literature of their age; they commissioned it, and had it read to them.

For all that, it is nevertheless the case that by the end of the fifteenth century attitudes were beginning to change and the literate layman was no longer a social oddity. A strong argument has been advanced by Roderick Lyall that two of Dunbar's 'makers', James Affleck and Sir John the Ross, were the laymen James Auchinlek, son of Sir John Auchinlek of that ilk, and his father-in-law John Ross of Hawkhead. In the early sixteenth century the earl of Argyll was not only the patron of bards but may have gone to a bardic school himself. There is no doubt about the trained lawyers of the 1480s and 1490s, John Ross of Montgrenan and Richard Lawson, provost of Edinburgh, or about Lord Sinclair, patron of Gavin Douglas and 'fader of bukis'; this family, noted for its education and patronage of literature, could read the books on the shelves of its library, established, apparently, by William Sinclair of Roslin in the mid fifteenth century, and containing, by the sixteenth century, Einhard's *Life of Charlemagne*, a Latin *Odyssey*, and the *Iliad* and the *Odyssey* in Greek.

This change is as inexplicable in Scottish society as it is in any other. One possible explanation is economic; the Linear B tablets, after all, dealt mainly with trade, and mass literacy tends to be a feature of industrialized societies. But there is no evidence that the thriving merchants of late-fifteenth-century Scotland gave a lead in the growth of lay literacy. It is more probable that the lead came from the crown, not from its legislation, such as the 1496 act, but from personal example. James I was certainly literate, as were his successors; what the king approved was likely to gain favour among his greatest lay subjects. It is also possible that fear of being regarded as backward compared to the English, with their Inns of Court and professional lay lawyers, and to the literate laymen of Europe, acted as a spur to the Scottish aristocracy. And it may be that the self-generating proliferation of government documentation did for the first time make them feel conscious of a gulf between the amateur and the professional which put them at a disadvantage. All these are possibilities, even probabilities; no more. The only certainty is that a change of great magnitude with profound implications for society was taking place. By 1600 it was necessary, as it had not been in 1500, for any layman who wanted a prominent place in Scottish government and society to know how to read and write.

In the late fifteenth and early sixteenth century those laymen who were literate were probably educated by private tutors, for the schools and universities were still almost exclusively clerical, although there are some signs that after 1496 a few laymen did begin to attend university, and one, Patrick Hume of Fastcastle, obtained licence for himself and his wife to go to Paris to study. Hume was following in clerical footsteps. Elphinstone's dream of a law school at Aberdeen foundered, like Bishop Turnbull's before him at Glasgow, because scholars who came to Scottish universities to take their first degrees then went abroad to become part of the world of the cosmopolitan scholar. In particular, they shared the belief of Guillaume Budé that Paris was the new Athens, and to Paris they flocked as students and teachers. But it was not only to Paris. Dr John Durkan, whose work has opened up a new dimension in Scottish intellectual history, has produced a series of studies that show where academic life flourished in northern Europe, there were the Scots. They went to the universities of Orleans, Cologne, Wittenberg, Louvain, Vienna, and others, and they went in considerable numbers; one of them, Sir John Rutherford — 'rhetor fortis' — became a member of Montaigne's household; another, Henry Scrimgeour from Dundee, was a noted collector of books and manuscripts, and librarian of the great Fugger collection at Augsburg. They had contacts with the great neo-platonists of the academy of Florence, Marsilio Ficino and Giovanni Pico della Mirandola, and with the famous humanist Johannes Reuchlin, who learned Hebrew in order to search out the mysteries of the Cabala; the cabalistic alphabet on a book owned by John Greenlaw of Haddington, and the copy of Guillaume Postel's *Cosmographicae Disciplinae Compendium* owned by the lawyer James Balfour of Pittendreich, show Scotsmen entering 'that strange third world between dogmatic Catholicism and dogmatic Protestantism' in which men sought certainty.

Scottish scholars did not go abroad as self-conscious products of a backward society; they went as members of an academic community, and they believed — and others agreed with them — that they had something to contribute. In an age dominated by Luther and Erasmus, their contribution was more than merely academic. The rivalry between Major and Boece when they returned to Scotland from Paris and wrote their histories extended into the critical area of religious debate. Major was involved in the examination of Erasmus's works when the Sorbonne attacked him. Boece, long a friend of Erasmus, and responsible for the introduction of Erasmian learning into his university of Aberdeen, promptly went to his defence. This time, Major was on the right side. Erasmus's letter to James V, reminding him that he had tutored James's uncles in an attempt to seek his support, elicited a gracious reply, but no more; Erasmus's writings, as well known in Scotland as elsewhere, were becoming suspect to the uneasy churchmen of Scotland in the 1530s, and the enthusiasm for Erasmian humanism, marked in earlier decades, collapsed to the point where, at the trial of John Borthwick in 1540, his *Paraphrases* were declared heretical. It was not Major's only part in religious issues. Professor J.K. Cameron has pointed out that it was Major who, by attacking Luther, first brought him to the attention of one of his pupils who was to have a profound effect on sixteenth-century Europe: John Calvin. Major and Boece were the leading members of the group of scholars who, perhaps more than any other group within Scottish society, so fully exemplified the combination of interest at home and interest abroad; intellectually, this was an age of immense receptiveness and involvement. It was involvement in both the Europe of the Renaissance and the Europe of the Reformation; in the persons of Scottish scholars the searchings of the mind and the searchings of the spirit came together.

II

The Reformation

5

The Pre-Reformation Church

As in other European countries the Reformation in Scotland dominates sixteenth-century history. More than in most European countries it has left both a church and a historiographical legacy which still haunt the minds of Scots at home and determine their image abroad. Even in this secular age there is the occasional religious historian who writes with passion of the sinister dominance of Rome in the four centuries preceding the Reformation, these centuries of the 'black terrors of the soul' which Calvinism dispelled, as J.S. McEwen wrote in his book *The Faith of John Knox*, which marked the fourth centenary of the Reformation. And there lingers on the romantic idea of the 'Celtic church' of the dark ages, that church locked in the spiritual purity of its own isolation, with its uncorrupted faith lost to Scotland in the twelfth century and not to be rediscovered until Calvinism triumphed over papalism in 1560.

The fourth centenary of the Reformation, however, produced two remarkable works, one by an episcopalian, the other by a group of mainly Catholic writers: Gordon Donaldson's classic study *The Scottish Reformation*, and the Scottish Catholic Historical Association's *Essays on the Scottish Reformation*, edited by David McRoberts. These books destroyed the excesses of the old view. Yet the opening up of interpretations that put welcome emphasis on 'social', 'political', or 'economic' factors may reduce those men of undoubted burning religious conviction who lived through and guided the troubled years of the Reformation to an isolated, even rather freakish group. This is only to say that Reformation studies are now in a healthy state of flux, as scholars turn to other aspects of the period. As in the Reformation period itself, old certainties have disappeared for good, and a new search for understanding is under way.

The difficulties begin when looking at the last century of the medieval church, which suffers from the particular problem of any

period leading up to a cataclysm. It is virtually impossible not to allow
its end to overshadow its existence, and assume the inevitability not
just of reform — something acknowledged by many loyal Catholics
throughout Europe at the time — but of Protestant Reformation.
Such a view is encouraged by the strong and sometimes violent reactions of the Protestant reformers themselves. But the Reformation is
not in itself reliable evidence of the corrupt state of the old church. It
was not simply a clean-up job, a smoother path to salvation; it offered
a quite different path, a clear alternative. And insofar as it was a
clean-up, the zeal of the reformers, while natural, could be excessive.
Moreover, for all their criticisms, the reformers inherited and retained
attitudes and beliefs from their predecessors. In education and social
concern they took over and built on the work of the old church. Calvin
'sought to realise at least some ideals of the great medieval Popes', and
he was followed in this by John Knox and Andrew Melville, with their
vision of a universal church. And the struggle between church and
state in post-Reformation Scotland was in microcosm only an extension of the great medieval struggle between the spiritual and temporal
powers, with Melville and James VI playing out the rôles of pope and
emperor. Wholesale collapse and corruption is not the context in
which the Reformation came about. Much of what the reformers
attacked was not new, so that the fundamental question about the
church is not why it had become immeasureably worse, but why it
ceased to satisfy.

The old church was certainly not dying in the late fifteenth century,
when two long-term problems about its place as part of the church
universal were resolved. The crown achieved formal control of
appointments to major benefices within the kingdom; and Scotland's
unique position as a province of the church without an archbishop
was ended with the establishment of the archbishopric of St Andrews
in 1472. The first came about because, with the collapse of papal
prestige as a result of the Great Schism, the Scottish monarchy, like
other secular powers in Europe, seized its chance to improve upon its
own control of appointments by making substantial inroads into even
the theoretic rights of the papacy. By the end of the reign of James II it
was clear that the king had the backing of the greater clergy, who were
making agreements about the extension of the crown's rights without
reference to the pope. Formal recognition of where the realities of
power lay came with the Indult of 1487, by which Innocent VIII
acknowledged that the crown had eight months in which to nominate
a successor when a vacancy occurred in any major benefice or abbey

valued at more than 200 florins. This was one of a series of such concessions by the papacy, to Ferdinand and Isabella of Spain, and to
François I of France in 1516. But these concessions only underwrote an
existing situation; they did not create a new one.

Ironically enough, the creation of St Andrews as a metropolitan see
was a last-ditch attempt by the papacy to retrieve a position visibly
slipping from its grasp. Archbishops were undersirable creatures
because their personal power stood between the pope and the local
province; and Scotland's position, defined in 1192 as 'special daughter
of the see of Rome', which meant that Scottish bishops were immediately subject to the pope and not to a Scottish archbishop, was
uniquely ideal, even if it offered less in practice than the same position
with regard to the church in France, Germany, or England would have
done. Now, in a short-sighted effort to retain control, Sixtus IV gave
away that position and elevated Patrick Graham, bishop of St
Andrews and a strong supporter of the papal position against that of
the crown, in the hope that Graham would use his new authority over
the Scottish episcopate in papal interests. It was a bad bet. Graham's
appointment even to the bishopric had been unpopular. The new
archbishop thought it prudent, in the face of hostility from king and
church, to skulk abroad for a year after he was given metropolitan
status. Whether he was in fact mad, as was said, or driven to nervous
breakdown by the pressures on him, which included excommunication in 1475 and deposition in 1477, both from within Scotland, his
record as archbishop was so dismal that the pope did not lift a finger to
save him. His successor was a man very close to James III, William
Schevez.

The papacy had gambled with its source of power and lost, for the
church in Scotland was now organized under a metropolitan who
would speak not with the voice of the pope, but with the voice of the
king. Nor does the long-awaited archbishopric, which at last put
Scotland on a par with other provinces of the church, seem to have
interested the Scots in terms of their international standing, enthusiastic though they were about that standing in other ways. Instead,
the whole business degenerated into a squalid internal power struggle.
By the end of James III's reign the bishops of Moray, Aberdeen, and
Glasgow had successfully lobbied the Curia and obtained exemptions
from the jurisdiction of St Andrews; and pressure from Glasgow,
encouraged by James IV, was to wring a second archbishopric out of
the papacy, for Robert Blacader in 1492.

The attitudes of crown and church in Scotland do not reflect at this stage — any more than Gallican ones — a desire to detach themselves from the church universal, much less incipient protestantism. The origins of the struggle lie far back in the eleventh and twelfth centuries, and the astonishing achievement of the papacy in expanding its spiritual headship of the church into an institutional control of a European-wide organization. From the twelfth century, Rome, a small and half-ruinous city with hundreds of churches standing in its midst, became the legal and bureaucratic centre of Europe; and the Scots joined their contemporaries in the long trek to Rome or, in the fourteenth century, to Avignon, not only the faithful on pilgrimage, but clerics seeking benefices, laymen and women seeking marital annulments, and both seeking forgiveness for sins. The new papal position inevitably brought the papacy into conflict with secular rulers; for in their kingdoms were a crucially important group, the educated clergy on whom they depended heavily in government, but who as clerics owed allegiance to, and sought favours from, an outsider who was not only the great spiritual authority in the West but also a great temporal lord, involved — as James IV found to his cost — in politics, diplomacy, and war. Naturally the papacy regarded the business of choosing the major clergy as its concern, for these were the men who would uphold its power, put its directives into effect, co-operate with papal collectors in gathering its revenues, maintain the true faith against heretics. Equally naturally, the king fought for control of men who were prominent in his government, and indeed for the right to reward them in the way they wanted, by providing them with benefices within the church — literally in lieu of salary, which no medieval or early-modern government could afford to pay. These were practical considerations which produced an uneasy balance of power throughout the Middle Ages. When the late-fifteenth-century monarchy took its chance and tipped the balance decisively in its favour, it was simply demonstrating that it knew the rules of the power-game as well as its European contemporaries, and as well as the papacy.

The ultimate legal authority of the papacy was never denied; even after 1560 men still went to Rome, as they had always done, in order to leave no doubt about their position as clerics or even as feuars of church lands, and it was a real problem for the government to stop them. The numerous petitions of the lesser clergy show how unchallenged the principle was; for while the bishoprics might be familiar to the Curia, it could hardly know of the small benefices, the vicarages to which, among the welter of miscellaneous business, it might provide three or four candidates at once, all clamouring to fill the same vacancy. The state of sheer muddle which could attend papal provisions is seen in the case of the parish church of Dunlop (Ayrshire), to which Robert Blacader, clerk of St Andrews, was provided in June 1493, and Constantine Murray, priest of Glasgow in July 1493, while in fact the benefice went to a third claimant, John Stewart. This casts a new and puzzling light on the way the church worked at local level, but puzzling only to modern eyes, for this kind of jockeying for place seems to have worried no-one; it was not a matter for criticism, whereas the fact that John Stewart had now added a third benefice to the two he already held would be. Likewise, the creation of the archbishopric did not interrupt contact with Rome. It may even have encouraged it. The eyes of the bishops — sometimes envious and resentful eyes — were now focused on the man sitting in St Andrews rather than on the man sitting in the chair of Peter. And when the archbishop was a member of the mighty family of Hamilton, as was the last Catholic holder of the position, political opponents might also find him a more threatening figure than a mere bishop would have been. There was one safety-valve; they, and many others, appealed from his court to the court of Rome.

The position of the papacy in pre-Reformation Scotland seems to have been seen almost entirely in this legalistic light. Mainly out of habit, and sometimes for more positive reasons, men continued to invoke its legal authority. There may have been rather more; in a vague and remote way the notion of the papacy, not altogether unlike the notion of the king for many people, may have given a comforting sense of unity. There was virtually no challenge to the papacy until in 1547 John Knox burst forth with his dramatic demand to destroy not individual members of the papacy but the roots of the whole. For Scotland there had been very little to challenge, for the papacy did not threaten, as it did in France and Germany; there was nothing like the relentless attack on its powers by German scholars as well as political leaders. But its position was weak, nevertheless. The great reforming popes of the earlier period had led the reform of the church; now, a series of worldly and politically-motivated men held back the reform sought from within the church, and opened the way to Luther. In Scotland the response to a papacy whose spiritual authority was very low was the dangerous one of indifference.

The papal concession to the crown in 1487 has been regarded as a fatal blow to the church, on the grounds that James IV and V took advantage of it to make scandalous appointments to the major benefices. Royal bastards, even children, became prominent members of the clerical estate, flooding into the benefice-market; and the hitherto occasional practice of appointing a churchman to hold an abbey 'in commendam' during a vacancy became a permanent feature, with the sinister addition that the commendator of the sixteenth century was normally a layman, or at best a layman who took minor orders, as a mere technicality. Certainly this produced some remarkable holders of benefices. Twice, for example, James IV managed to get papal sanction for the appointment to St Andrews of two close relatives: his brother James, whose other titles, duke of Ormond and earl of Ross, cast doubt on his interest in a career in the church, for the prince-bishop was not a feature of Scottish society; and then his illegitimate son Alexander, aged 11 at the time of his nomination in 1504. But these appointments do not simply demonstrate that the effect of the Indult was to plunge the church down to a new level of corrupt practice. 'Only nineteen years old, already dissolute and not yet literate' is not a reference to a sixteenth-century Scottish nominee; it is Sir Richard Southern's description of Henry of Gueldre, Innocent IV's choice for the bishopric of Liege in 1247. No Scottish bishop of the last years of the old church ever matched Bishop Henry. Nor does the youth of Alexander Stewart appear quite so unique, or so clearly evidence of Catholic corruption, when set in the context of a number of late-sixteenth-century German appointments of children and adolescents, at Naumburg and Bremen, for example; with one exception, these were Protestant elections, made for the purpose of intruding a well-connected Protestant into a formerly Catholic diocese.

Whatever the merits or otherwise of James's first appointment, his second was not unscrupulously irresponsible. He had his son Alexander highly educated, both in Scotland and in foreign universities. At Padua and Siena he was a pupil of Erasmus, such a pupil as to inspire a moving and glowing tribute from Erasmus when he was killed at Flodden: 'something of mine was lost there too' was his sad comment on the death of a brilliant and gentle scholar. Alexander's active part in the foundation of a new college in the university of St Andrews, St Leonard's, established for the education of 20 poor clerks in 1512 — the best-known but not the only example of his interest in his diocese in the brief three years when he administered it — suggest that the king's own interest in education and piety must be taken into the reckoning when discussing the motives of James IV.

These are the most notable examples of the king's insistence on his own nominees; in European terms they amount to very little. Nepotism was undoubtedly a matter for criticism throughout the church, but it was hardly the rock on which the church foundered. The same applies to non-royal nepotism. In this society where ties of kin were so fundamental the famous example of the three Chisholms who were successively bishops of Dunblane may have looked less sinister than it does to modern eyes. The church is rooted in society, and is bound to reflect the values of that society, whether Catholic or Protestant. Such public examples in high places before 1560 were not very different in essence from the reformed ministers who sent their sons to school and university to follow them into the ministry, thus establishing small-scale dynasties; 'the church-race', as the seventeenth-century writer Drummond of Hawthornden caustically commented, 'marry only among themselves'.

More generally, the late-fifteenth- and sixteenth-century episcopate may have contained some lurid members, like Patrick Hepburn, bishop of Moray from 1538 to 1573, whose exercise of his office was based on spiritual indifference and worldly consideration. But it contained also a greater number of remarkable men, highly educated, much concerned with their dioceses, and caught up with the general feeling that was sweeping Europe from the beginning of the sixteenth century that reform — some kind of reform — was needed, men like William Elphinstone, bishop of Aberdeen, Robert Reid, bishop of Orkney, and even John Hamilton, archbishop of St Andrews, whose reputation for learning and religious fervour even Knox recorded, although he promptly put it down to hypocrisy. That episcopate was not more corrupt, less committed, than earlier generations of bishops; it was the same sort of hotch-potch, with the same range of men. It may be that none of them was great enough to produce the kind of inspired leadership that could have restored confidence in the collapsing world of the 1550s, but some at least saw the need for such leadership, and tried to provide it, in the impressive series of reforming councils held in the decade before the Reformation, exactly the period of the Council of Trent.

Four centuries of Protestant thought have made it almost impossible to understand the mentality of the medieval bishop. From 1560 the kirk forbade its ministers to hold secular office, thus ending the possibility of the clergy playing a leading rôle in affairs of state. But no bishop ever questioned that dual rôle; most of them were bishops because of it. William Elphinstone was a notable beneficiary of royal service. He was also a great bishop. He was heavily involved in affairs of the world. But he also took a strong interest in his diocese, and gave that interest tangible expression. Earlier bishops had built cathedrals. That option was no longer open, though many bishops rebuilt and embellished, as Elphinstone did at St Machar's, and his contemporary Blacader at Glasgow, adding the aisle that bears his name. But they could and did found universities, at St Andrews, Glasgow, and Aberdeen. Elphinstone himself did more. He replaced the Sarum Use, derived from England — believed, inevitably though wrongly, to have been foisted on Scotland by the arch-destroyer of things Scottish, Edward I — with a new Scottish liturgy. In a series of liturgical works, including the *Martyrology of Aberdeen* (*c*. 1490) and the *Aberdeen Breviary* (1509–10), he rediscovered or introduced the cult of Scottish saints; where a mere handful had hitherto had a place in the liturgical observance of the Scottish church, Elphinstone now produced over 70 drawn from all parts of Scotland. This ecclesiastical activity was part of the general and self-conscious interest in Scotland's distinctive place as a European nation, not an increasing Scottishness for its own sake; the province of the church in Scotland was now provided with its own holy men, as other provinces of the church universal had long had. More personally, it puts Elphinstone in a unique category among the Scottish bishops, for this episcopal enterprise had much more relevance than most to the lives and religious observances of the ordinary parishioner. A good bishop — he who left his diocese enriched, more noteworthy than he found it — would have his name remembered for all time, by the dignitaries of his cathedral, the members of his university, the tourists of later centuries. How far his parishioners felt themselves enriched by the new university or additional aisle is a very different question.

That question provides the one real point of identification with the medieval bishop, for lack of contact between the bishop and the majority of the members of his church is a common feature of any episcopal church, at any time. This in itself is a reminder that, as in so many aspects of the Reformation, when we hear criticism we are hearing the voice of the articulate minority, not the voice of the unhappy masses, who were presumably indifferent rather than unhappy until told otherwise. Such criticisms, though often savagely directed against individuals — witness John Knox's repeated and vitriolic attacks on that 'bloody wolf, the Cardinal', David Beaton — tell us not that bishops were worse than their predecessors but that expectations were changing. When the archbishop of York or the archbishop of St Andrews emulated the warrior-pope Julius II and went into battle, they were offending against an ideal even more than bishop Odo of Bayeux had done in 1066. When they appeared in their traditional rôle, as princes of the world and princes of the church, the attack on them was not new, but it had a wider scholarly base and a new level of support which made it altogether more deadly. But the problem of the pre-Reformation episcopate – on balance, active, even reforming – is much more complex than simply the corruption suggested by the reformers. Expectations were indeed changing, but at least part of the Reformed church saw the answer in modifying the rôle of the bishop, not abolishing it.

Bishops were headline-hitters. So also were the monasteries, another apparent sign of visible weakness in the church. Like the bishops, abbots and prioresses, monks and nuns suffered from the savage wit of Lindsay. The picture of religious institutions in which spiritual vitality had been replaced by unashamed enjoyment of the things of the world, and, even worse, financial and sexual corruption, was the basis for wonderful propaganda which grew to proportions far beyond the comments of the Visitors of the English monasteries in the 1530s, or of Lindsay himself. Lindsay's most scandalous attacks were directed not against the monks, who on the whole were criticized simply for indulging in a life of ease, but against that group who had never been prominent in the Scottish church, the nuns. When we do read the occasional reference to something more than the enjoyment of 'helsum aill', in a passage in which the abbot claims that:

> My paramours is baith als fat and fair
> As ony wench into the toun of Ayr'

it can be assumed that concern with rhyme rather than the particular corruption of south-west Scotland dictated the example. Moreover, although Lindsay's language and examples were Scots, his canvas was much wider. One of his most brilliant creations, Sir Robert Rome-raker, the pardoner with his fraudulent relics, was not drawn from an abuse common in Scotland, where few references to pardoners exist. It is a reminder that Lindsay was writing in an age that had seen the spark of Lutheran reform ignited by that most famous of pardoners, John Tetzel.

Apart from the small and unimportant abbey of Saddell in Kintyre, suppressed by 1508, it is difficult to find cases of really substantial decline in the monasteries. At Paisley, for example, where one of the monks took part in the first recorded curling match in Scottish history, in 1541, the maximum number of monks was 25, so that the 19 who made up the community in 1543, and who included 4 novices, do not suggest a dying monastery. The great and lovely border abbey of Melrose was harder hit by English destruction in 1545 than by the coming of the Reformation; the community of 32 monks in 1536 had declined to the 17 known in the 1550s. Extensive rebuilding was a feature of the fifteenth rather than the sixteenth century. But evidence of intellectual and cultural vitality, seen in fifteenth-century Dunfermline and Culross, is paralleled by the quite astonishing flowering at the northern abbey of Kinloss, where two successive abbots, Thomas Chrystall and Robert Reid, built up a library, established close contacts with the university of Aberdeen, and attracted a scholar of European standing, Giovanni Ferrerio, as a teacher in the abbey in the 1530s and 1540s.

Criticism was not confined to those outside. Reid's activity at Kinloss was designed to give reality to his vision of the church reformed, which exactly agreed with that of the great European reformers like Ximenes and Vives. And the Augustinian canon Robert Richardson, who had first introduced Ferrerio to Reid, wrote in 1530 his *Commentary on the Rule of St Augustine*, dedicated to abbot Alexander Myln of Cambuskenneth. Myln, like Reid, was a reforming abbot. Richardson, drawing on the example of the reformed monastery of St Victor in Paris, and behind that, Windesheim and the inspiration of Thomas à Kempis, produced at Myln's request his own account of what must be done to renew and reform the monastic life. By one of the extraordinary coincidences of history, Richardson the reforming Augustinian was studying in Paris at the same time as Ignatius Loyola, in 1530. In 1543 Paul III confirmed Loyola's new order, the Society of Jesus; in the same year Henry VIII sent Richardson to Scotland as a Protestant preacher. One man who had done something to urge reform within the church had given up the struggle.

The efforts of men like Reid and Myln failed. They have been wholly overshadowed by the great scandal of the lay commendators, imposed on the monasteries to an extent unparalleled in Europe. The effect of the Indult was certainly more damaging to the monasteries than to the episcopate, and the villain of the piece was James V. It is impossible to understand James's own religious position. His preference for churchmen was a matter of comment in the 1530s; his Wolsey, Cardinal Beaton, enjoyed a secular and ecclesiastical position unique in Scotland. He consistently opposed Protestant reform and put pressure on his episcopate to initiate reform from within; he was far too aware of the intellectual and religious currents of the day to be blind to the need. Yet the price he exacted for his support of the leaders of the church was heavy taxation. For the papacy, the price of his resistance to the blandishments of Henry VIII was the agreement that such taxes should be levied; in addition, he bullied Paul III into underwriting his nominations of his illegitimate children to lay commendatorships. With cheerful candour he confessed that his youth had led him to succumb to the temptations of the flesh; nevertheless, His Holiness would commend his desire to fulfil his duty as a father to provide for his children, and as these children, despite their tender years, showed such precocious piety that they would be an ornament to the church, so he sought benefices for them. Such blatancy has its attractive side. Less entertaining is the fact that the monasteries of Kelso, Melrose, Coldingham, St Andrews, and Holyrood were all held by James's sons; and within three months of his death in 1542 parliament agreed that the new regent, Arran, should pocket all the revenues surplus to the children's needs, to help him finance his 'greit hous', then running him to 'mair sumpteous expense' than even the late king had incurred. These things do not suggest that, however much effort was made by the abbots and monks to halt the rot within the monasteries, the attitude of the king, and the leading laymen, was other than cynical.

Yet it is possible to question whether this cynicism was either destructive or an outward sign of religious indifference. The monasteries were a very special case. Luther, from without the church, Erasmus from within, both attacked the idea that Christian vocation could be lived in the relative isolation − even the selfish isolation − of the monastery. Abbot Reid himself was not trying to renew the old ideal so much as reform it, putting his community to the service of the world, and making it respond to the demand for intellectual and spiritual leadership; Kinloss became, in effect, a college attached to the university of Aberdeen, which is not the traditional rôle of the monastery. James, the patron of Erasmus's friend Boece, principal of that university, and an enthusiast for Erasmian humanism until he took fright in the 1530s, might well have felt it possible to write off the monasteries without writing off the church. It was the logical development of the fact that the monastic ideal had lost its powers of inspiration some two centuries earlier; the last monastery to be founded in Scotland was the strict order of Carthusians at Perth, by James I, following Henry V's example at Sion. Ultimately, poverty is an impossible ideal. The history of monasticism is the history of the never-ending cycle of the efforts and failures of men to achieve it, and in so doing, to draw others to awareness and love of God. It is also the history of the fundamental question of how the Christian can best serve God. In the twelfth century, one of the great ages of European monasticism, that 'sair sanct for the croun', David I, had responded to the spiritual mood of the time by endowing monasteries with a lavish hand. In the sixteenth century, the age that saw the monastic ideal of poverty in complete decline, and itself no longer believed in the ideal of Christian isolation, James V tried to take it all back, and went a long way towards doing so.

Indifference to one form of religious expression, monasticism, is very far from indifference to the church. For motives which no doubt ranged from 'fire-insurance' to genuine devotion, wealthy laymen still turned to the clergy for prayers for their souls and the souls of their families, with perhaps even more conscious concern than twelfth-century kings had done, for the idea of purgatory had developed markedly in the thirteenth century. And they believed as much in the need to seek God's favour — as well, no doubt, as impressing their neighbours — by giving part of their worldly goods to the church. They gave these instincts new expression by founding and endowing collegiate churches; 42 were in existence by the time of the Reformation, and of these, a quarter were sixteenth-century foundations. They range from the very simple, like that founded by William Lord Crichton in 1449, to the neighbouring glorious freak at Roslin, established in the same year as Crichton, but a world away in its riotous and fantastic decoration: the simple and the ornate, to the glory of God and the founder, and for the salvation of souls. On a smaller scale, the simple and lovely sacrament-house in the little parish church of Cullen in Banffshire, built by Alexander Ogilvy of that ilk in the 1540s, is one of a number of examples of a fashion found in north-eastern Scotland in the mid sixteenth century. These endowments and gifts to the church, made on a wider scale than ever before by the laity, stand as a reminder that the last century before the Reformation, for all the evident abuse, was a religious age. Scotland undoubtedly fits into Chadwick's general argument that 'the Reformation came not so much because Europe was irreligious as because it was religious'.

That argument is further supported by another group of religious, who were surviving, in contrast to the monasteries, with remarkable success: the friars. They had a new lease of life in the late fifteenth century; the order of Observant Friars was organized as a Scottish province from 1467, while the older Franciscans and the Dominicans were recognized as forming separate Scottish provinces in the early 1480s. Unlike the monasteries, they continued to attract endowments until the eve of the Reformation, and this may be because they did come closer to meeting the new demands; even Lindsay suggests that they still fulfilled their function of preaching. Certainly there were among the friars a number of notable counterparts to Reid and Myln, who seem to have had more of an impact than those in the monasteries. The leading figure was John Adamson, Provincial of the Black Friars, who won general approval from the General Chapter in Rome in 1518 for his work in Scotland. Under Adamson's guidance libraries were built up in the various houses, in Aberdeen, Edinburgh, Glasgow, St Andrews, Perth, and Elgin; an impressive number of friars from Scotland had degrees approved; and several of them were prominent teachers in the three universities. Moreover, as the storm-clouds of Reformation increasingly menaced the church, there came to Scotland in 1535 one of the most remarkable spirits of his time, John Royaerts, Commissary in Scotland. Royaerts' influence extended far beyond his own preaching, for which he was renowned; his books of sermons provided a model for his disciples. John Watson, for example, appointed in 1547 as canon and special preacher in Aberdeen owned and relied heavily on Royaerts' works. His notes on Royaerts' Pentecostal sermon on the subject of those who would do anything to avoid hearing sermons, or who paid little heed to them, were extensive; but these sermons, and presumably Watson's own, were well worth the hearing, with their emphasis on God and Christ, their offer of hope for mankind, their reliance on the Bible.

When the Reformation came the fate of the friars was very different from that of the monks. There was no suppression of the monasteries, which were allowed to decline and dwindle away in relative peace. The friars came under savage attack. Most of their houses were destroyed in 1559 and 1560. Because they were in the towns, they were more immediately subject to criticism, and accessible to Protestant looters. But the attack on them may also demonstrate their strength. What they were already doing was perhaps too close for comfort to what the Protestants wanted to do. The vision of those within the church who sought reform was often very close to the vision of those outside the church. Unlike the monks, the friars did produce early Protestant reformers, including one of the great leaders of the future, John Willock. Theologically divided, Willock and Watson had still much in common.

A world away from men like these stands the maligned and pathetic figure of the parish priest, desperately poor, ill-educated, sexually immoral, covetous of his parishioners' goods while indifferent to their spiritual well-being. As such, he was massively criticized in the six-teenth century, again notably in the *Thrie Estaitis*, with its devastating portrayal of the Poor Man ruined by the savage exactions of the 'cors-present', the funeral-payment; successive deaths in the family had meant successive additions to the worldly goods and livestock of the priest. And the early-sixteenth-century stone cross at Campbeltown leaves no doubt that in some areas concubinage was not only public but a positive means of adornment, for the cross was put up by a parish priest and the son who succeeded him as priest.

Criticism of the parish clergy was not new; it is a recurrent theme in medieval Europe. Indeed, the Scottish clergy in earlier centuries were remarkably free from the abuse and vilification from which con-temporaries suffered, and which was heaped on them in the decades before the Reformation. This is the more surprising because of the system of appropriations in Scotland, whereby the bulk of the revenues of the parishes were appropriated by the religious institutions, cathe-drals, monasteries, collegiate churches, and universities. This practice had begun in the twelfth century, and had been going with a swing ever since. By the sixteenth century 86 per cent of all parish churches were appropriated, and in some cases the proportion was higher, reaching 95 per cent in the diocese of Aberdeen. With the exception of Switzerland, there was nothing like this in any other province of the church. It is, understandably, regarded as one of the great abuses of the church in Scotland, for the inevitable result of drawing off parish revenues, leaving the church in the hands of an extremely badly-paid vicar, was to ensure that the parish clergy in Scotland were the impoverished dregs of the clerical profession. Small wonder, then, that they were the target of insistent criticism about their greed and their lack of education.

But the problem is more complex than that. The Aberdeen figure comes from a part of the country where, perhaps partly because of that figure, there was a strong reforming tradition within the old church, and a strong survival of Catholicism after 1560. Moreover, it was not only the high level of appropriations that kept the parish clergy a depressed group. The real problem was that a clerical career before the Reformation encompassed a range of job opportunities extend-ing far beyond the ministry. The fact that the modern word 'clerk' then referred to a cleric is a reminder of the time when the clergy had a monopoly of positions in government and the law that demanded literary skills. The ambitious and bright young man of pre-Reformation Scotland, and indeed pre-Reformation Europe, might come from humble origins, for provision was made for poor scholars, but he would certainly not end there; government and diplomatic service, along with preferment in the church, or an academic career in the schools and universities, or as a private tutor, were open to him, and he would not turn to the parish ministry. The vicar to whom the religious institutions entrusted the parishes within their gift was likely to be the man who failed to make it to better things. Not all were uneducated; William Tunno, vicar of Manor in the 1550s, supplemented his miserable stipend of 24 merks allotted to him by the parson, the archdeacon of Glasgow, with a temporary appointment as schoolmaster of Peebles. But men could serve with very little education indeed. Archibald Hay's complaint to Cardinal Beaton about the ordination of men who 'hardly know the order of the alphabet' may be the exaggeration of a notable scholar, impatient of the limitations of lesser men; but in the rural areas especially, the clergy were characterized more by their mumbling of Latin than by their education and ability to preach.

That situation existed everywhere, however, and to that extent the high level of appropriations in Scotland only compounded an existing problem. Moreover, there is no reason to suppose that the parish clergy of the sixteenth century were worse than their predecessors. It is therefore once again a matter of changing expectations, as a greater premium than ever before was put on the need for an educated clergy, not only by churchmen, but by the growing number of literate laymen; for increasing literacy among the laity inevitably cast a new and damaging light on the clergy. But it is important to remember who the critics were. The adverse comments that have come down to us are, by definition, the comments of the articulate minority, the men of learning like Hay, whose major ambition was to found a new college at St Andrews and introduce the study of Greek; or David Lindsay. Even the 'popular literature', the mid-sixteenth-century collection of ballads hostile to the old church, was the product of educated men. Their expectations have so much in common with modern expectations of the clergy that it becomes all too easy to forget that a good sermon does not necessarily mean a good pastor. Perhaps in listening sympathetically to the voice of the educated minority, we exaggerate the shortcomings of the parish clergy. What we never hear is the authentic voice of the ordinary parishioner; we do not know whether he reacted with horror or boredom — as well as curiosity — when he had his first experience of a Reformed service, with its inordinately long sermon, but we may suspect that perhaps he did. Chaucer's parson in the fourteenth century, and in the nineteenth the curé d'Ars, whose spectacular failure to pass the simplest examinations did not prevent him from becoming a priest of rare and inspiring spirituality, both suggest that a clergy lacking higher education may not have rendered only bad service.

The other strand of criticism levelled against the parish clergy, their rapacious exactions of mortuary dues and other offerings from people unable to afford them, probably has more substance as a genuine source of tension between the priest and his parishioners. 'Na penny, na paternoster' is an extreme but succinct and compelling statement of the problem; and while few may have suffered quite as much as Lindsay's Poor Man, it was undoubtedly a matter of concern, even to James V, who demanded reform of the abuse. The criticism of the educated élite may have arisen from their desire for a better educated clergy; the present low standards made the demand for money peculiarly offensive. Just possibly, new strains imposed by the feuing movement, both on those who had to find more money for their feus, and those who lost out, may have made clerical demands more strident as lay ability, or willingness, to pay became less.

But many of the clergy were themselves in desperate straits. After the initial decade of the Reformed church, when there were cases of hardship, it is hard to find any examples of Reformed ministers living on stipends that came anywhere near the pittances paid to pre-Reformation vicars, like Tunno's 24 merks, or the 15 merks paid to the vicar of Alva in Banffshire, out of a total revenue from the parish of £80. Their only additional sources of revenue came from their glebes, which they could farm and whose surplus produce they could sell, and from payment for particular services, baptisms, marriages, and funerals, which is still in fact a normal feature of the church in modern times, although not always so explicitly demanded. They were then caught by the reforming councils, which demanded that priests must not have a lifestyle too close to that of their parishioners, but must wear distinctive clerical dress, and not engage in trading; they found themselves the subject of sermons, such as that of the Aberdeen theologian William Hay, who criticized the laity for their reluctance to pay reasonable dues, but joined in the condemnation of the clergy's abuse of these dues; they saw the great churchmen, with their conspicuous wealth, deliberating in the reforming councils about the possibility of raising the minimum stipend of 10 merks, fixed in the thirteenth century, to 20 or 24 merks, at a time when a professional man would be paid £80–£100 per annum, and, as Professor Donaldson has pointed out, the wealth of the church was sufficient to provide each parish with about £300 each year. They were left with the triple burdens of poverty, abuse, and no solution; even the abuse was not always justified, for the rectors of the parish were entitled to claim the 'corspresent', and, in the case of Melrose abbey, for example, sometimes did.

That was one of the most glaring weaknesses of the pre-Reformation church. But there is also evidence of remarkable vitality. Receptiveness to European trends is seen not only in reforming ideas, but also in popular devotion, again inspired mainly by the Netherlands. The Haliblude Play at Aberdeen, for example, seems to have been based on the annual procession at Bruges, where the devotion originated, and the one surviving example in Britain of a medieval banner, the so-called Fetternear Banner, was almost certainly embroidered in the early sixteenth century for the confraternity of the Holy Blood of St Giles, Edinburgh. In 1533 Thomas Douchtie turned up in Scotland with an image of the Virgin, apparently after fighting the Turks, and established a hermitage at Loretto, near Edinburgh, thus introducing the devotion made popular in Europe some 30 years earlier when Julius II gave his approval to the shrine at Loretto in Italy, where the 'house of the Virgin' had miraculously established itself. Loretto had sufficient appeal as a pilgrimage centre to attract James V – on foot, from Stirling – and the caustic wit of Lindsay, while Douchtie's name was used in a satire on the Franciscans, written by one of the leading Protestant nobles, Alexander earl of Glencairn.

A more sinister form of contact with Europe, from the church's point of view, was the Lutheran literature which began to circulate in the east-coast burghs, prompting a panicky act banning it in 1525. Yet there is surprisingly little evidence of heresy. There was an act on the statute book, *De heretico comburendo*, passed by James I in 1425, apparently in imitation of Henry IV's act rather than to meet a real need; even the enthusiasm of that grim churchman Laurence of Lindores for extirpating heresy foundered on his inability to find more than three or four heretics to burn. Wycliffe's influence does seem to have spread briefly into south-west Scotland, although we know little more than the fact that in the 1490s there apparently existed a group described years later by Knox as the Lollards of Kyle. And there is one hint of the existence of vernacular heretical literature, presumably of the type that had such an impact in England, in the work of 'popular' theology *The Merroure of Wisdome*, written by John Ireland in the late fifteenth century with the same purpose as the earlier orthodox vernacular works such as the fourteenth-century *Catechism* of Archbishop Thursby of York; Ireland claimed that 'many errouris agane the faith and haly doctrine of jhesu and the kyrk ar writtin in this tounge and in Inglis, at a part of the pepil of the realme are infekit with'. But even the half-century before the Reformation produced comparatively little heresy. Knox did what he could with the sensational burnings of Patrick Hamilton in 1528 and George Wishart in 1545, but these and the few other cases gave him very little to go on, and certainly no opportunity to produce a Book of Martyrs.

This may explain why those who sought reform of the church from within were confident of success for so long. The initiative certainly lay with them. Indeed, Scotland presents the extraordinary spectacle of what was almost a 'Counter-reformation' taking place before the Reformation itself, in the series of reforming councils held by Archbishop Hamilton between 1549 and 1559. Four years earlier, the General Council of the church, long sought by the leading Catholic churchmen, opened at Trent. Its first session ended in 1547. Its decrees were published in 1548 and used by the Scottish council of 1549. No Scottish bishop went to Trent. But a prominent member of the council, a man close to the pope and leader of the commission that drew up the Tridentine decree on justification, was one of the most remarkable churchmen of the sixteenth century, Robert Wauchope. Blind, or almost so, he was yet a scholar of distinction, a close and admired friend of Loyola, Salmeron, and Cardinal Contarini, and sufficiently renowned to be attacked by Melancthon as a 'Parisian sophist, a blind Scot, who at Paris raged with utmost ferocity against the Christians'. Through Wauchope the Scottish church had the authenticated copy of the early Tridentine decrees in time for its first provincial council.

That council was summoned 'for the reformation of morals in the Church of Scotland and for the extirpation of heresy'. It attacked concubinage, clerics engaging in trade, clerics dressing as laymen. But its major concern was provision for teaching. Every cathedral chapter was to have its theologians and canonist, every monastery its teacher of doctrine; bishops and rectors were to preach four times each year, and vicars every Sunday and on major feast-days. This was followed up at the second council in 1552 with the publication of Hamilton's *Catechism*, a long vernacular work, in clear and forceful language, setting out to explain the Ten Commandments, the Creed, the seven sacraments, the Pater Noster and Ave Maria, and answering the questions to whom and for whom men should pray. That council recorded with pride and confidence 'how many frightful heresies have, within the last few years, run riot in many divers parts of this realm, but have now at last been checked by the providence of the all-good and Almighty God, the singular goodwill of princes, and the vigilance and zeal of the prelates for the Catholick faith, and seem almost extinguished'. They had some reason for pride, for in at least some dioceses, in Orkney, Aberdeen, Glasgow, and St Andrews, the programme of reform was being implemented. Even as late as 1559 the church was still confident. The council of that year took the opening up of the church's services to the laity a stage further when it introduced common prayers, litanies, and evening prayers in the vernacular, and produced a simple exhortation to be given before communion, the so-called 'Two-penny faith', which may be the one surviving example of such exhortations on all the sacraments. It declared its intention to hold another council. That council never met.

Yet the confidence of the reforming Catholics, although misplaced, was not simply blind. Maintaining the *status quo*, in a conservative society, has its own strength; and if their confidence compares with some of the leading Protestants, John Knox and Erskine of Dun, who were equally certain that they knew the will of God, it contrasts with others who were not: men like John Davidson, principal of Glasgow University, whose conversion in 1559 came as a complete shock to his close friends Archbishop Beaton of Glasgow and Giovanni Ferrerio; or John Winram, one of the authors of the *First Book of Discipline* in 1560, but in 1558, as sub-prior of St Andrews, prominent at the trial and execution of the protestant Walter Myln. Their complexity of spirit is wholly understandable. To Catholics, on the other hand, the document of 1558 issued by the dean and chapter of Aberdeen setting out the need for reform − and rather embarrassingly suggesting that the bishop should set an example by ridding himself of 'the gentill woman be quhom he is gretlie sclanderit' − was a reminder of the fact that all was not yet achieved, not the sounding of a death-knell.

The reasons why they failed are many and varied. But even in their own terms their vision was too limited and restricted, impressive though it was, and impressive though the men who tried to make it a reality were. It was not enough to think in terms of a more spiritual life within the monasteries and cathedral chapters, or in terms of a more inspiring lead from the top, provided by a better-educated minority of churchmen. For that cut out too many people, and put too much emphasis on the traditional rôle of the higher clergy as the literate educated élite. It cut out the parish clergy, with their grievous problem for which no solution was even attempted. Even more fatal, it cut out the aspirations of the laity.

6

The Growth of Protestantism

'There are three things of which one should be infinitely afraid in every principality – huge debts, a royal minority, and a disturbance in religion. For there is not one of these three which is not sufficient in itself to bring mutation to a state', said the political writer Estienne Pasquier in the late sixteenth century.[1] Two of these evils, minority and religious disturbance, hit Scotland in the 1540s, and 1550s. Instability is evident at every level of society, as traditional beliefs and ways of doing things, and established order, gave way to uncertainty and fear. From the politicians at the top, caught between the pressures from the 'auld inemeis', England, and the 'auld ally', France, to the small peasant at the bottom, threatened by the rapidly changing pattern of landholding, the same reaction can be seen. Mid-sixteenth-century Scotland was caught up in the political, social, and religious turmoil that swept every part of Europe.

Yet although it did cause 'mutation', that turmoil was, paradoxically, less violent than most, precisely because minority and religious disturbance came together. The structure of Scottish society, and long experience of minorities, made the absence of a king much easier to bear than it was in those other European countries, France, Portugal, England, the Netherlands, afflicted by a plague of female and infant rulers in the 1550s and 1560s. Indeed, the death of that unusually autocratic ruler James V immediately reduced the tension building up because of the new level of authority within the state. Thus the problem of religious dissension during the minority was to an extent minimized by the absence of a strong political lead. The Protestants, as yet numerically small, but with a significance and influence out of all proportion to their numbers, did not have an easy road to Reformation,

[1] Quoted in the indispensable article by J.H. Elliott, 'Revolution and Continuity in Early Modern Europe', *Past and Present* 42 (February 1969), p. 45.

but were never faced with sustained and really effective challenge; one factor that undermined the efforts of the reformers within the old church was that they were not given clear support by the regency government of Mary of Guise until the crisis years of 1559–60, when it was too late. It was a dangerous weakness for those who were trying to restore confidence in the church.

One problem was the increasingly visible inability of the pre-Reformation church to maintain its traditional and clear-cut rôle, not only as the repository and sole interpreter of Christian doctrine in the West, where it was directly under attack by the Protestants, but more insidiously and perhaps more fatally, in its social and economic rôle, as the provider of teachers, lawyers, and doctors, and as the wealthiest landowner in Scotland. This decline goes back at least to the fifteenth century, as Dr. I.B.Cowan has shown, when in some of the burghs, such as Edinburgh, Peebles, and Aberdeen, the laity had taken the initiative from the clergy in establishing and running schools and hospitals. It was accelerated in the sixteenth, with the emergence of literate laymen, beginning to push their way into the preserves of the church, in law, education, and government. As that happened the church's pervasive rôle in society shrank further, and men's eyes became more sharply focused on its fulfilment of its spiritual functions. And that made its position as the wealthiest institution in Scotland a matter for resentment, vilification, and plunder. The great individual churchmen like Cardinal Beaton, of whom an English observer wrote in 1543 that 'he kepethe a great hous of substantial men and gevethe greate ffees and such a house as was never holden in Scotlande undre a king', or the general ostentation of stone-built churches and monasteries, dominating burgh, village, and countryside, brought the church under fire. By comparison with other European countries, the attack on the wealth of the church came late in Scotland. It came when a new educated lay élite, for the first time violently critical of an uneducated clergy, was also for the first time demanding a place for itself which made the ecclesiastical politicians, lawyers, and eventually even teachers redundant.

This was, however, a gradual process. More immediate was the debilitating spectacle of an institution with an income 10 times that of the crown rushing into panic reaction when the crown attacked that wealth and trying to meet the threat by the rapid and extensive feuing of its lands. Statistical analysis has shown that the feuing movement did not cause as much hardship as used to be thought. Nevertheless, one-third of the church's tenants did not manage to convert their holdings into feu-ferme. Contemporary comments which suggest bleakness and misery, such as those of Lindsay or the *Complaynte of Scotland*, have little value as an accurate statistical picture, but great value in indicating the doubts and tensions, even the sense of shock and alienation, which inevitably accompanied a dramatic change in land-tenure:

> Our tennentis cryis alace alace
> That reuth and pity is away

wrote the mid-sixteenth-century poet Richard Maitland of Lethington. Opportunities for speculators and middle-men, for landlords to replace a manageable rent with an unmanageable feu, fear of what was going to happen, probably even among those who did succeed in retaining their lands under the new form of tenure: these things encouraged a new level of distrust between tenants and their ecclesiastical landlords. Moreover, friction between new lay commendator and established hereditary bailie, and the practice by some commendators of intruding their kinsmen, as David Beaton did at Arbroath in the 1520s, and John Hamilton at Paisley, added fuel to the feeling that this was a period of insecurity and upheaval. Parliament's frantic legislation of 1546 demanding order in 'putting and laying men furth of thair takkis and stedingis' and forbidding 'convocations' of landlords and tenants is in marked contrast to the fifteenth-century legislation which offered protection to tenants against oppressive landlords, and creates a compelling image of very troubled times. None of this stopped with the Reformation. But it was too closely associated with the pre-Reformation church to leave that church unscathed.

Nor did the church benefit from those who made it, and became feuars. The relationship between new feuar and clerical landlord was different from that of old tenant and landlord. The old relationship had a personal immediacy which could, from the tenant's point of view, be good, as it was on the Coupar estates. As that went, so the church's position was weakened. 'There is something about proprietorship, however small', as Dr Sanderson says, 'which breeds a certain self-awareness of the kind which could be constructively absorbed into the participatory rôle of a congregation in the Reformed Church'. The old church, aware of the need for action, was too absorbed in the attempt to make the old ways work better, and too caught up in its own financial problem, to offer any outlet for such self-assertiveness among the laity.

The feuing of kirk lands may well, therefore, have undermined the church's image in the eyes of both those who gained and those who lost. They did not all flock to join the Protestants, but they swelled the ranks of those laymen critical of and frustrated by the church. The effects of this remain a matter for speculation. Yet it is a profound irony that the church itself created uncertainties in a society economically and socially still relatively stable. The absence of rural and urban unrest in Scotland compared to other European countries has already been commented on. The feuing movement in which the church played so large a part was clearly seen at the time as the major cause of social disturbance. That disturbance did not show up in localized rebellions, as in England; it remained a more passive dissatisfaction. Nevertheless, it minimized support for the church when the final crisis came.

The level of unrest, which was not simply a matter of Protestant influence, can be detected in the legislation of the same decades as witnessed the feuing of kirk lands, when the government tried to shore up respect for the church, which was now visibly collapsing. There were repeated acts against those who defied excommunication, beginning in 1535. A spiritual sanction widely used for secular and economic reasons against those who failed to pay their teinds, for example, was badly debased. The state's efforts hardly restored the moral authority of the church when it concentrated on the threat to distrain the goods of the excommunicate so that the cleric who had cursed him might obtain the money for which sentence had been given.

More generally, the string of acts issued by James V in 1541 demanding that honour should be given to all the sacraments, to the Virgin and saints, and to statues and images tell the same story. Indeed, they show how wide was the spectrum of breakdown, ranging from fundamental attack on doctrine to popular piety turned to mockery. The early-seventeenth-century historian and minister David Calderwood, drawing on Knox's *History*, Fox's *Book of Martyrs*, and the register of the Justice Courts, described in moving and hideous detail the execution of a group of inhabitants of Perth in 1544, with the final horror of the one woman involved handing over the baby at her breast to a nurse immediately before being drowned. Some of these people certainly ranked as heretics, accused of meeting to hear and expound Scripture. But one of the accusations was concerned with 'hanging up the image of Sanct Francis on a cord, nailing of ramme's hornes to his head, and a kowe's rump to his taile'; and one of the accused was James Hunter who, 'being a simple man, and without learning, and a fleschour by occupation, could be charged with no great knowledge in doctrine'. There were, presumably, many James Hunters. This man, and those anonymous rebels who demanded to attend Mass and receive the sacrament while under sentence of cursing, were not primarily committed to reform from without, though their restlessness and lack of reverence for the old church made them an obvious source from which the leading Protestants could seek support. Their dissatisfaction was already finding expression in isolated attacks on individuals within the church long before the period of orchestrated destruction in 1559–60. For such people, the well-intentioned efforts of the clerical reformers, and the more ambivalent efforts of the state, solved nothing.

The problem was that the state, while prepared to give the church its backing, did not wholly see eye-to-eye with the ecclesiastical reformers. Indeed, for all his refusal to follow the example of his uncle, Henry VIII, James V came very close in practice to doing the same thing, and replacing a Catholic church with the pope at its head with a Catholic church under the king. Even before James himself was in control of events, an act of 1526 had suggested something of this trend. It legislated against 'evil disposit personis' who seized bishops' palaces during vacancies, and kept abbeys 'in secular menis handis'. This would have been admirable had it not been that the real offence was doing these things without royal licence, the crime treason, and the effect, very carefully distinguished, 'in hie displesour of god almichty, our haly fader the pope, and in contempcioun of oure soverane lordis auctorite'. This distinction, and the extent to which James V gave a lead in keeping abbeys 'in secular menis handis', give his act in his 'reformation' parliament of 1541 against impugning the pope's authority, under pain of death and forfeiture, all the appearance of a damp squib. Little better was his open prayer that the kirkmen, now 'lychtlyit and contempnit' because of their 'unhonestie and misreule. . .in witt, knawlege and maneris', should reform themselves, when the only sanction he proposed was the invoking of remedy from the pope.

Neither this parliament, nor the parliament of 1552 which once again issued a series of acts demanding an increase in moral behaviour and respect for the church, have anything like the power and driving-force of the Reformation parliament in 1560 nor its follow-up in 1563, when the state put its weight behind the spiritual authority of the new church. 'Incorrigibill adulteraris', for example, in 1552 would be put to the horn (outlawed), a punishment as over-used by the state as cursing was by the church, and as little regarded. In 1563 the 'abominabill and fylthy vice and cryme of adulterie' was punishable by death. By the early seventeenth century the secular powers were less willing to maintain this extreme position; the zeal of the early days had cooled, and the state was more concerned with the problems of property associated with marital breakdown and adultery. But the immediate contrast of the two pre-Reformation parliaments and those that first underwrote the existence of the new church show all the difference between the groping confusion of one church and the confident deter-mination of the other. The political backing of the state reflects both these conditions.

Confusion at home is paralleled by the shifts and turns of foreign policy, which create a similar impression of a country in a state of drift, her fortunes wholly at the mercy of pressure from England and France. There was initial uncertainty within Scotland immediately after James V's death as to where her best interests lay. James had maintained the alliance with France. When he died the pro-English party led by the new regent and heir presumptive, James Hamilton, earl of Arran, and the earls of Lennox and Angus, were at last free to seek English alliance; but there still existed a powerful pro-French party under the Queen Mother, Mary of Guise, and Cardinal Beaton, and that, combined with Arran's congenital inability to make up his mind, produced the refusal of the Scots to commit themselves finally to the Treaty of Greenwich in July 1543 arranging the marriage of Mary to Edward, son of Henry VIII. That provoked Henry's savage 'Rough Wooing', and the breakdown of possible friendship between England and Scotland. Yet when, in 1548, the Scottish government turned to France, there was still a pro-English group, mainly of lairds in Fife, the borders, and East Lothian. It did not interrupt the alliance with France, which was reinforced when Mary of Guise replaced Arran as regent in 1554, and apparently sealed when Mary queen of Scots married the Dauphin Francis in 1558. But it indicates the divisions within Scottish society, understandable enough at a time when Scottish foreign relations, like so much else, were in a state of flux.

It is an over-simplification, however, to see the changes in her foreign relations as an almost involuntary response to pressure from England and France. When broken down into its constituent parts the same signs of independent thinking that had characterized earlier foreign policy emerge, even if slightly blurred by the absence of a king to give a decisive lead. Both the initial approach to England and the revival of the French alliance in 1548 were the result of positive Scottish policy; and when, in turn, the events of 1559–60 made the French alliance a political embarrassment it was very quickly broken. The fact that the Scots had to summon English aid, because French military strength was considerable, only reflects Scotland's military weakness, not her political strength. Alliances and counter-alliances to meet with particular political situations and crises were a commonplace; and the need for a small power to seek military aid against a greater happened again when the Netherlands turned to Elizabeth for help against Spain, or the Teutonic knights of Livonia to Sweden, when threatened by Russia in the late 1550s. The most interesting aspect of the way in which the Scots dealt with the problem of their relations with England and France is that they averted what looked like the almost inevitable consequence of having a queen regnant. Marriage into the royal houses of either England and France might have meant political annihilation, and was probably intended to mean that by Henry VIII and Henry II. The Scots recognized that Mary must marry, used this as a powerful bargaining counter, and then prevented her marriage from reducing her Scottish kingdom to a satellite state.

It is equally over-simplified to relate the shifts in foreign policy to the fortunes of the religious parties within Scotland. This was an age when growing threat of Reformation did nothing to prevent the Very Catholic King of Spain challenging the Most Christian King of France to single combat to resolve their claims to Milan, to the extreme horror of the papacy; nor did it prevent the same Most Christian King, Francis I, from allying with the infidel Turk against the Very Catholic King and Emperor Charles V, to the extreme horror of most of Europe. Ideological politics were to be a feature of the second half of the century, after the reconciliation of the great Catholic powers at the Treaty of Cateau-Cambrésis in 1559. Hitherto the new phenomenon of religious dissension had not yet become a motivating force in the formation of policy, and the old secular rivalries between European rulers, including the papacy, continued to flourish; the extreme example was the sack of Rome by the Spanish army in 1527.

As in Europe, so in Scotland; the strengths and weaknesses of Catholic and Protestant parties cannot be identified with periods of alliance with Protestant England or Catholic France. Nor did the Reformation 'happen' in 1560 because the political leaders in

Scotland used a small group of religious reformers as a battering ram to push down the crumbling walls of the Auld Alliance. Modern scholars have rightly emphasized that the Reformation was not brought about by an upsurge of 'popular' Protestanism, and that, as far as can be judged, the number of Protestants in Scotland in the 1540s and 1550s was small. But it was a movement that contained influential people, and its development and final success were almost wholly inconsistent with the pattern of foreign relations. It presents us with the paradox that it drew strength from England in the 1530s and 1540s despite diplomatic hostility and war, and it gained ground again in the 1550s, when the need to keep Scotland in alliance with Catholic France rather than the Catholic England of Mary Tudor persuaded Mary of Guise to pursue the remarkable policy of toleration towards the Scottish Protestants.

Intellectual contacts with England, which had virtually disappeared since the time of the Wars of Independence, had already been revived when Wolsey's new college at Oxford tried to encourage Scots scholars of orthodox opinions, like Richardson, and John Major himself to join its ranks. Much more significant was the fact that in the 1530s England offered a haven to those of unorthodox views. The peppery reformer Alexander Alesius (Alane) is the most famous of the men who went to England in James V's reign, leaving it only when the fall of Cromwell removed a sympathetic patron. Alesius was first attracted to reform by his dispute with the martyr Patrick Hamilton. Initially attacking the church from within its ranks, he provoked the same reaction, and rejection, as Luther himself. He was imprisoned, and escaped to the continent. There he opened his attack from without. The first of his extensive writings, produced in 1533, was an attack on the decree of the Scottish bishops prohibiting the reading of the New Testament in the vernacular. This brought early Scottish reforming thought on to the European stage, for Alesius's diatribe brought an answer from the notable and even more peppery Catholic polemicist Cochlaeus, *Pro Scotiae Regno Apologia Iohannis Cochlaei Adversus Personatum Alexandrum Alesium Scotum*, a work known to have graced the bookshelves of Gavin Dunbar, archbishop of Glasgow, the spokesman for the clerical estate when it dissociated itself from the act of 1543 that allowed Scripture to be read in the vernacular. By the mid 1530s Alesius was in England, along with other Scots, the former friars John Maccabeus (McAlpine) and John Willock, George Wishart, and his relative Robert Richardson, now no longer a Catholic reformer. After his return to the continent, he emerged as the Lutheran counterpart to Wauchope, a friend of Bucer and Melanchthon, and prominent in the attempts to reconcile the Lutheran and Roman churches, at Worms in 1540, for example. Through Melanchthon's influence he went to Frankfurt as professor of theology in 1540; his theology may have been sound, but his history was remarkable, for he delivered an inaugural lecture in which he claimed that Germany had been evangelized by the Scots, one of whom was St Boniface. His career was paralleled by McAlpine, who spent some years in England as chaplain to the bishop of Salisbury, and then went abroad to become, again through Melanchthon's influence, professor of theology at Copenhagen. These were among the most outstanding of the many Scots found in this period in the universities of Frankfurt, Heidelberg, Augsburg, and above all Wittenberg, who take the subject of the Scottish Protestant exiles far beyond the confines of England. Nevertheless, England offered these men one place where they could teach and they could write, as it was to do rather later, in the reign of Edward VI, to the most famous of them all, John Knox; and Knox's later career in the 1550s was to be largely associated with the exiles from Marian England in Frankfurt and Geneva.

The Scots scholar abroad had been a familiar figure in the academic life of the continent long before the European universities were rocked by religious dispute. Now, this too hit hard at the old church. Those men who went to England and Europe, rejecting Rome and adopting Lutheran beliefs, seem to have been strongly influenced by the Scottish Lutheran Patrick Hamilton. They had something else in common; they all began as clerics, even priests, in the old church. Hamilton's education in Paris was paid for out of the revenues of the abbey of Fearn; George Wishart was in orders when he went to study in Louvain; even Knox was a Catholic cleric. It was the pre-Reformation church that provided the education at home that opened the way to further study abroad. Those who remained within the church and were receptive to what was happening in Europe had, through that contact, given it its strongest hope of life. But those whom it sent abroad who found themselves convinced by the new beliefs created a rival and very powerful group, with the same appeal to a strongly self-conscious European society as their orthodox counterparts, and the additional appeal of the modern as opposed to the traditional.

It is, however, impossible to quantify the influence of those whose international reputations were maintained abroad, and therefore were a matter of vicarious pride. In the 1540s England's share in offering a bolt-hole for those who had to get out was replaced with something much more crucial. Military intervention, even when given religious justification, was counter productive. The English might regard the Pinkie campaign, in the autumn of 1547, as an effort to free Scotland from the Roman clergy; they at least got another victory out of it, but the Scottish Protestants were scarcely helped by a battle that if anything hardened government opinion against England. But the deliberate English policy of distributing bibles and Protestant literature was very much more effective. England was not, of course, the only supplier of books. Before the English Reformation, Lutheran writings had already been coming into Scotland from the continent, as the 1525 act complained. In 1527 the English ambassador at Antwerp reported that Scottish merchants were taking Tyndale's New Testament to Edinburgh and especially to St Andrews. One of the earliest Scottish reforming works, Hamilton's *Patrick's Places*, was published at Antwerp. Another, John Gau's *Richt Vay to the Kingdom of Hevine*, reflects the importance of contacts with the Baltic; published at Malmö, it was a translation of a Danish Lutheran work. But Wishart's *Confession of Faith of the Churches of Switzerland* found a London publisher in 1548. And England was meeting the need for vernacular bibles. For this reason, the first Scottish translation of the New Testament, made in the 1520s by Matthew Nisbet from Purvey's version of Wycliffe's Testament, remained unpublished (until 1901), and no vernacular bible was printed in Scotland at all until 1579.

The death of James V in 1542 unleashed an immediate demand for vernacular works. The reports of the English ambassador Sir Ralph Sadler tell us of the individual request by the new regent, Arran, and the general enthusiasm for such books, 'marvellously desired now of the people in Scotland'. Later Protestant rumour attributed to James V's bishops the insistence that reading the vernacular bible was a capital crime. That was unfounded, but the act of 1543 which made it lawful for men to read the bible in English or Scots was rightly regarded as a notable triumph. The clerical estate in parliament formally dissociated themselves from the act; Knox produced a wonderful passage extolling the act as 'no small victory of Christ Jesus. . .no small comfort to such as were before held in bondage. . . .Then might have been seen the Bible lying almost upon every gentleman's table. The New Testament was borne about in many men's hands. . . thereby did the knowledge of God wondrously increase, and God give his Holy Spirit to simple men in great abundance'.

As Professor Elton says, 'If there is a single thread running through the whole story of the Reformation, it is the explosive and renovating and often disintegrating effect of the Bible, put into the hands of the commonalty and interpreted no longer by the well-conditioned learned, but by the faith and delusion, the common sense and uncommon nonsense of all sorts of men'.[2] From the beginnings of the Reformation movement in Scotland, demand that the scriptures should be made available to the commonalty in their own language, that they might read and debate, is the single most dominant theme, and the official condemnation of this demand is both the subject of the anti-heretical legislation under James V and of the mockery of satirists, both orthodox and reforming. It turns up in the *Thrie Estaitis*, and in the writings of the rather later court poet Alexander Scott, whose brilliantly simple lines

> For limmer lads and little lassis, lo,
> Will argue baith with bischop, priest and freir

sum up the horrors, for ecclesiastical authority, of what had been unleashed. And it was grist to the mill for the Protestants; it features in the satirical poem by the earl of Glencairn, and is a theme of the extraordinary collection of sacred and scurrilous verse, the *Gude and Godlie Ballattis*, again printed in London. The Bible had become the best-seller of the 1540s.

Scholars and laymen were caught up in the excitement of reforming ideas, the spread of the scriptures and the heady experience of being able to read and interpret them. Novelty and release caused something of an explosion after James V's death. That in itself probably explains why the whole thing collapsed; it was evanescent, without as yet sufficient base, and reaction quickly set in. Knox himself admitted that some of the early enthusiasm was false, the product of the desire to 'make court' to the regent, 'for all men esteemed the Governor to have been the most fervent Protestant that was in Europe'. What the Governor actually was, even he does not seem to have known. But he agreed with the English diplomat Ralph Sadler, who advised him of the need for caution, as his own master, Henry VIII, was showing in his act of 1543 forbidding the reading of the Bible by women, artificers, apprentices, and labourers; this suggests that 'the most fervent Protestant' was taking fright as he saw events slipping out of his control.

[2] G.R. Elton, *Reformation Europe, 1517–1559* (London, 1963), p. 52

Protestant thought in this period was still Lutheran thought, and Scottish contacts were with Germany, Scandinavia, and England; Geneva lay in the future. This may be another reason why so little came of the sudden release of reforming ideas in 1543. It is at least arguable that Lutheranism was not sufficiently different from much of Catholic teaching, and particularly reformed Catholic ideas, to evoke real response. This was the period when efforts were being made to reconcile Rome and Luther. Hamilton's *Catechism* itself shows signs of an attempt to accommodate Lutheran ideas. It drew on the *Enchiridion Christianae Institutionis* of John Gropper, chancellor of Cologne, an orthodox but conciliatory work produced in 1538 under the auspices of Archbishop Hermann von Wied, and also on the Henrician *Necessary Doctrine and Erudition of a Christian Man*, known as the 'King's Book' because of the help given by Henry VIII to the bishops who compiled it. On occasion, the *Catechism* comes remarkably close to the Lutheran position on faith, differing from the Tridentine decree, while it has little to say in explanation of the Mass, and nothing at all on the subject of papal authority. It is true that its subject matter does not actually demand discussion of the papacy, but it is an odd and interesting omission, given the intentions of those who produced it.

Already in 1543 there are indications that some wanted more than current reforming thought had to offer. Sadler naturally put the 'King's Book' at the head of his list of safe and right-minded books which he compiled for Arran. It did not find a receptive audience in Scotland, not because of its association with Henry VIII, but because it was not sufficiently clear and 'thorough' on doctrine. Four years later Knox preached the first of his great sermons, at St Andrews; in it, he apparently attacked the Mass as 'abominable idolatry, blasphemous to the death of Christ and a profanation of the Lord's Supper'. In 1550 he clearly denied transubstantiation, and he was to claim that as early as 1547 he had rejected the Lutheran position. By the mid 1550s there was no doubt about his adherence to Calvinist doctrines; and it was Calvinism, that militant faith which allowed of no possibility of compromise with Rome, that was to gather adherents and become the faith of the Reformed kirk.

The collapse of the movement of 1543 was succeeded by a long and fallow period. In 1544 George Wishart's peripatetic ministry, to Ayrshire, Fife, Lothian, and Perth, shows the existence of local groups of lay Protestants, this time hearing a man who expounded Zwinglian thought. It was such a group, under Norman Leslie, who avenged Wishart's execution by murdering the cardinal in his castle of St Andrews in 1546, and holding out in the castle until it fell to the French in 1547; Knox himself, apparently first won over to the Protestant cause by Wishart, entered the castle in April 1547, in time to be captured by the French and sent to the galleys. His subsequent career in England, Frankfurt, and Geneva, up until 1559, with only one brief return to Scotland in 1555–6, left the Scots without a prominent theological leader within the country. It is therefore perhaps not surprising that the church council of 1552 could congratulate itself on its success in eradicating heresy.

Yet in the same year the act passed on the subject of printing books on the faith, and ballads, songs, and blasphemous rhymes without licence suggests that the council was overconfident. Heresy still lurked in diverse parts of the realm. In the 1540s Alexander earl of Glencairn was already the focal point of a reforming group, which included, it seems, clerics as well as laymen. Erskine of Dun was, similarly, the leader of the Protestants in the Mearns. And Protestanism certainly existed within the major burghs. Signs of it appear remarkably early in Aberdeen, going back to the 1520s; that decade and the next two saw attacks on church property, and concern, by the town council and the king, about Lutheran literature in the burgh, though this early interest in Protestant reform, or at least dissatisfaction with the old church, seems to have died away at the end of the 1540s. In St Andrews itself, the major recipient of Lutheran writings in 1527, the university was deeply split in the early 1530s, in the aftermath of Hamilton's execution, to the extent that the feast of the faculty of arts was suspended from 1534 because some would not attend the Mass and procession; and reformed doctrines were being openly taught in St Leonard's college. The presence of the Castilians in the mid 1540s gave protection to Protestant preachers, and the town and surrounding area became the scene of sermons and disputations. There were riots in Perth and Dundee at an early stage. And in Edinburgh the eventual recantation by the favourers of Luther at Holyrood in 1532 is evidence of the first, and earliest, example of a significant group of the population adopting, at least temporarily, the reformed faith.

None of this amounts to a continuous and clear-cut road to Reformation. But it is a mistake to look for such a road. The three or four decades before the Reformation parliament met are a period in which a few rare souls showed utter confidence and conviction, and a great number of people agonized. Dundee, possibly the most strongly 'protestant' of the burghs, provides us with the illuminating spectacle of the three Wedderburn brothers, sons of a Dundee merchant. The first two were Protestant authors, one of plays highly critical of the old church, which were performed in the burgh, the other, a former priest, probably the author of the *Gude and Godlie Ballattis*. The third brother, likely author of the *Complaynte of Scotland*, remained a Catholic throughout his life. This was an age when certainties were crumbling fast. No section of society escaped. The old church was struggling, within too narrow an area, to re-establish spiritual authority against the highly-informed theological attacks of the academics, and the general criticism and abuse of lesser men, tenants on the land, burgesses in the towns, who found its wealth offensive and its panic when asked to disgorge that wealth unconvincing. It lost out as a landlord in the popular mind because of that panic. The justification for its wealth was eroded as laymen established schools and hospitals, became lawyers, administrators, scholars. It lost out as the maintainer of morals because its own morals were not above reproach. It lost out, finally, as the teacher of doctrine because the laity who could read took the Bible for themselves, and began to interpret it, and those who could not listened to voices other than those of the priests. The sporadic acts of violence, the intermittent successes of Protestant groups, even the sheer difficulty of distinguishing committed Protestants from dissatisfied Catholics, are exactly what one would expect to find in a period of religious, social, and political disturbance. If Rome was not built in a day, neither were Geneva nor Edinburgh. But it may be more difficult to restore an authority that has lost its spiritual and moral force than to establish a new authority with a different ideological base. In the end, it did not matter that the Protestants were few in number. What counted was that they simply had more to offer the various groups in society who had lost the old certainties, and were making new demands, above all the demand for a new certainty. They did not have all the answers. But they were beginning to find better ones than the Catholics.

7

The Reformation

The contrast between the drifting, inconclusive years before 1558 and
the rush to Reformation between 1558 and 1560 is so dramatic, and so
obviously linked to the equally rapid change in the political situation,
that a 'political' explanation for the Reformation seems reasonable.
To divide the people involved into two groups, however, the secular
leaders with their political motives, and the religious reformers with
their spiritual vision, and see the achievements of these years almost in
terms of a stroke of luck for the reformers in that their interests
happened to suit the politicians, is too simple. It underestimates
almost everyone else who played a part, and it overestimates John
Knox. It is not at all surprising to find that political circumstances
explain the timing of the Reformation in Scotland; where was that not
the case? That does not mean that they explain the Reformation itself.
It might be argued that the desire to break with France and ally with
England produced in the secular leaders a political commitment to
Protestantism. It can equally be argued that it happened the other
way round, and that it was the commitment to Protestantism that
encouraged men to turn from France to England at the first possible
opportunity; that opportunity did not come, after all, until Mary
Tudor died in November 1558. Years earlier Lord Methven had seen it
this way round; he gave the 'new apoynzionis' as his primary reason for
the appeal of the Protestant England of Edward VI when he wrote to
Mary of Guise in 1548 warning her of the need for action against
favourers of England. And if the desire for English alliance after 1558
proves 'political' motivation, then Knox's own frantic letters to Cecil
begging for support in 1559 put him into exactly the same camp as the
politicians.

The underlying explanation for the particular course of the Scottish
Reformation lies in the appallingly difficult problem of transforming
a Scotland where a number of influential people were attracted to

the new faith into a Reformed Scotland. Influential people are not enough when there are equally influential people on the other side, and no clear leader, whether secular or religious; hence the importance to the French Huguenots of Condé's decision to put himself at their head. Only in the autobiographical and propagandist pages of Knox's *History of the Reformation* does Knox appear as the Luther, Zwingli, and Calvin of Scotland. In practice, inspiring though he was, he fell short of these towering figures of the Reformation, partly because he was a considerable embarrassment to the secular leaders of the movement. He was still writing to Cecil in November 1559; but once Elizabeth had been persuaded to commit herself, he fell very silent. The author of the *First Blast of the Trumpet against the Monstrous Regiment of Women* — a monstrously turgid work — had done himself as much damage in the eyes of a crucially important contemporary as the author of the *History* was to do himself good in the eyes of posterity. As late as 1561 he was still trying desperately to back-track, producing articles, it was reported to Cecil, which 'hathe mytigated somewhat the rigeur of his booke, referringe myche unto the tyme that the same was wrytten', but there is no sign that Elizabeth ever forgave him. Poor Knox had indeed got his timing wrong. He published his book in early 1558, when, in company with his associates, the English Protestant exiles, he had no reason to expect Mary Tudor to die in the near future. The hostility of her Protestant successor in itself casts doubts on the idea of those who sought political revolution with English backing using the religious reformers to achieve their ends; Elizabeth's support was given despite the existence of Knox.

Similar considerations may have been involved earlier, in October 1557, when Knox had reached Dieppe, on his way to Scotland, and was halted, apparently by the news that the Protestant cause was in decline. This seems an unlikely deterrent for Knox. His own letter on the subject equally suggests that those who had invited him back had second thoughts, because Knox was already *persona non grata* to the regent. On his visit to Scotland in May 1556 he had written to Mary of Guise, at the instigation of the earl of Glencairn and the earl Marischal. His lengthy letter — it runs to 10 pages in print — was written to someone of whom Knox still had hopes, presumably because of Mary's toleration of the Protestants. Mary failed to appreciate the conciliatory intent of a letter telling her that if she did not follow Knox's dictates, 'then shall ye and your posteritie sodenly feill the depressing hande of Him who exalted you'. She dismissed it with some contempt, and ensured Knox's intense hostility. It was during the frustrated days at Dieppe, apparently, that Knox wrote his *First Blast*; in 1558 he wrote again to the regent, a 30-page epistle containing his original letter, with extensive additions in which no punches were pulled. Such a man could be invaluable when the opportunity for concerted action arrived; he was much less valuable in the mid 1550s, when neither side was seeking confrontation. What kept the patchy and regionalized Protestant party alive was not Knox, but little groups of lairds, burgesses, and a few magnates, encouraged by preachers like John Douglas and Paul Methven.

These groups also lacked any secular figure to give a lead. Scotland was not a theocracy; neither was it in any practical sense a monarchy in the 1550s. Authority, such as it was, maintained the old church. But every regent, in every minority, came up against the simple problem that he was not king, which ensured diminished prestige, and forced a temporizing with the political factions of the day. Mary of Guise was remarkably successful in achieving her political aims, alliance with France and her daughter's marriage to the dauphin. The cost was no clear lead for the Catholics and tolerance for the Protestants. It is possible that this policy held them back and minimized their potential danger, for an emerging church may be strengthened by a degree of persecution, or at least resistance, which encourages it to fight for survival.

Certainly there are signs that the Protestant leaders themselves were aware of the need to break the stalemate. Knox in Dieppe fired off three exhortatory letters to the nobility and Protestant brethren, though only the first can have reached Scotland before the lords themselves took action. On 3 December 1557 Argyll and his son, along with Glencairn, Morton, and Erskine of Dun, were the principal signatories to the Band of the Lords of the Congregation. Every magnate in Scotland was thoroughly familiar with the making of bonds for social and political purposes. For the first time this commonplace of Scottish society was turned to religious use; subsumed into the Calvinist idea of the religious convenant, it produced a short and succinct clarion call for the advancement of the new faith, which set a pattern out of which there would emerge, 80 years later, the National Covenant.

Knox in his *History* moves straight from the making of this remarkable band to the invitation to him from the lords, seeking his return: 'before a little. . .letters were directed again to John Knox'. In fact, the letters, to Calvin and Knox, did not arrive in Geneva until November 1558, and, incidentally, provide a moment of almost farcical light relief, for the messenger, one John Gray, having delivered his letters in Protestant Geneva, went straight on to Rome to urge the expedition of the bulls of provision for Henry Sinclair as Catholic bishop of Ross; religious as much as secular diplomacy was shoe-string diplomacy in Scotland!

The Protestants in Scotland had made some advance before Knox was invited to return, and even more before he arrived in Scotland in May 1559. Contemporaries dated the Reformation not from 1560, but from some time in the first half of 1559. One source, a letter of marque of February 1560, picked up by the English at Portsmouth, described Scotland as 'embracing the true religion of Christ and rejecting Antichrist' nine months earlier, in May 1559; the privy council pushed the date back even further to 6 March 1559, a date on which, as Professor Donaldson points out, 'nothing of significance is known to have happened in Scotland'. There is, of course, no 'date' for the Scottish Reformation. But those at the time believed that by the middle of 1559 the balance had significantly shifted. They were right; a fragmented movement was beginning to gain ground and become cohesive.

'Cohesion' in a localized society, temporarily lacking any effective focal point, was at best limited and short-lived. It was created by a small number of magnates and lairds whose commitment to the reformed cause is not in doubt. Glencairn, the earl of Argyll who died in 1558 and his successor, and Lord James Stewart, illegitimate son of James V and future earl of Moray and regent for James VI, were in no sense mere political opportunists. Argyll was the weak personality, who had been so ineffective in the reign of James V. But he became a Protestant, maintained a Protestant chaplain in his household, protected him when he preached publicly in Edinburgh, and resisted the pressure put on him by his kinsman the archbishop of St Andrews. Of all the Protestant magnates, he was probably the least impressive. The adherence of such a man to the reforming movement is therefore suggestive of the extent to which religion as well as politics, perhaps conscience as well as worldly considerations, dictated the actions of those who seized the initiative in December 1557. They were fighting for much more than a political shift in foreign relations and domestic power for themselves. At that stage they were still relatively isolated, supported only by disparate groups of Protestant lairds in the west and in Angus and the Mearns, the latter group led by the remarkable Erskine of Dun, who was prominent in political life in the late 1550s and went on to become one of the first superintendents of the reformed church after 1560.

But no secular leader, however committed, could afford the luxury of the single-mindedness of a Knox. Other considerations crowded in. Leadership, for the magnates, was not based on the power of the pen, the brilliantly compelling oratory. If they, as the great lords of the localities, added religious division to existing social tensions, then they whose duty it was to prevent anarchy, might create it. If they, of all people, opposed established authority within the state, then what an example they would offer their own dependants. Small wonder, then, that the Scottish magnates had reservations about Knox, for Knox and his associates, the English exiles, were beginning to develop theories of resistance which were as much a threat to the nobles as to the crown itself. Both Christopher Goodman, in his treatise *How Superior Powers ought to be Obeyed*, published in 1558, and in the same year Knox, in his *Appellation to the Nobility and Estates of Scotland* and *Letter addressed to the Commonalty of Scotland*, made it terrifyingly clear that if the nobility did not advance God's cause, then they would go beyond them and appeal to the people. Knox himself was to react against the monster he was so willing to unleash; when his own inflammatory preaching produced rioting and iconoclasm, the godly brethren quickly became the 'rascal multitude'. But from the safety of Geneva, and from the ivory tower of theology and political theory, Knox could threaten with almost complete indifference to the practical problems of the exercise of magnate power.

These problems suggest why the nobility look less than wholehearted about religious reformation, and why in the end they appear to have been motivated by the desire for political revolution with themselves as the beneficiaries. In fact, their apparent half-heartedness arose from their initial attempt to bring about reformation without challenging secular authority, and their 'political' revolution was the direct consequence of their failure to do so. Their understanding of the dangers involved in the course they were pushed to take was as complete as Knox's understanding of the course they must take; Knox saw the necessity of that course rather earlier simply because he was script-writer and director from the beginning, but actor only at a very late stage. In August 1559, when the leading Protestants had moved from compromise to confrontation, Lord James and the new earl of Argyll wrote two letters, to the captain of Berwick Sir James Croft, and to Cecil, which put the problem exactly. 'We are sorry', they said in the first, 'to be judged slow, negligent and cold in our proceedings by those whom we most especially favour. You know, sir, how difficult it is to persuade a multitude to revolt of established author-ity'. The second explained why they could not follow Cecil's advice to look to Denmark as their model. In Knoxian terms they accepted their duty to free the realm from the 'tyranny of strangers', and to bring about reformation; for, as they reminded Cecil, 'we have against us the established authority, which ever favoured you and Denmark in your reformations'.

Their initial action, when they made the First Band in December 1557, was therefore an act of considerable courage, and all the more so because, if they had little support at home, they were utterly isolated abroad. England offered no hope. The Scottish Protestants, like Knox and the English exiles, had no reason to suppose that Mary Tudor, the scourge sent by God, would not continue to afflict her land for many years. Elizabeth, whose survival depended on her keeping out of the limelight, was an unknown quantity, and those who hoped for her accession did so more out of desperation than from any certainty about her religious position. The First Band was a decisive step out of the limbo in which Scottish Protestantism had hitherto maintained its nebulous existence; but ideologically and practically there was no alternative in 1557−8 to seeking reformation through persuasion of Mary of Guise and co-operation with her. Lord James Stewart and Erskine of Dun were among the commissioners who went to France to negotiate her daughter's marriage. They may have seen in this marriage an advantage to themselves, in that Queen Mary's continuing absence from Scotland would leave them a free hand, particularly when they were dealing with a regent whom they believed to have some sympathy with their position. Moreover, as long as Mary Tudor lived, there was no doubt about Catholic England, where there was wide-spread conformity by nobility and gentry. But there was some doubt about Catholic France; the growing number of Huguenots gave France at least as much, and probably more, appeal than England to the Protestant nobles of Scotland.

The sensational burning of the aged Walter Myln at St Andrews in April 1558, four days after Mary's marriage to the dauphin, shattered the idea of peaceful advance, even if at this stage Archbishop Hamilton rather than the regent was blamed for an act that was actually out of character with either. Hamilton may have taken fright because of the signs that the Protestants were beginning to organize themselves. Equally, the regent, in the first flush of triumph after Mary's marriage, may have decided that her conciliatory attitude was now less necessary; her policy of strengthening the link with France was accompanied by the desire to bequeath a Catholic kingdom to Mary, and having achieved the first, she could now turn more positively to the second. Yet she returned to her former attitude, riding out the pressure put on her by the Protestants with their petition to her and appeal to the November parliament for reformation, and still offering them some degree of freedom in worship.

In two crucial respects November 1558 was the real turning-point. Mary traded the promise of future consideration of the Protestants' demands for their present agreement to give the crown matrimonial to the dauphin; thus she set the final seal on her efforts to unite France and Scotland. She was a politician of great skill. How far she was also sympathetic to the idea of reform is an unanswerable question. Whether she was as false as Knox naturally believed was in any case now irrelevant, because of the other event of that month. On 17 November Mary Tudor died. The spectre of Protestant alliance with England left Mary of Guise with no alternative; she could no longer afford to indulge the Protestant party.

The new year opened dramatically. On 1 January 1559 the 'Beggars' Summons' was nailed to the doors of the friaries. Inspired by a much earlier English work, the *Supplicacyon for the Beggars* written by Simon Fish in 1529, and drawing on a tract entitled *Querela Pauperum* which had been circulating in Scotland by the end of James V's reign, it called on the friars in the name of the 'Blynd, Cruked, Beddrelles, Wedowis, Orphelings and all uther pure, sa viseit be the hand of God, as may not worke' to give up their patrimony by Whitsun. In the same month Elizabeth's first parliament began to dismantle the Marian settlement, thus reinforcing Catholic fears and Protestant hopes in Scotland. But for the next three months events in Scotland hung fire while the final negotiations leading to the treaty of Cateau-Cambrésis dragged on. The treaty was concluded in April. In May Knox returned to Scotland; Perth and Dundee made public their commitment to reformation; and on 22 May the Congregation of Christ Jesus in Scotland declared to the regent that, having 'served the Authority of Scotland and your Grace . . . so now, with most dolorous minds we are constrained, by unjust tyranny proposed against us. . . . That except this cruelty be stayed by your wisdom, we will be compelled to take the sword of just defence against all that shall pursue us for the matter of religion and for our conscience sake'.

As the death of Mary Tudor had forced Mary of Guise to show her hand, so now did the treaty of Cateau-Cambrésis force the Protestants. A major argument in persuading Henry II to make peace with Spain was the need to combat heresy. France, having lost in Italy, might now turn her attention north to Scotland. It was no empty fear; shortly after the treaty Henry II wrote to the pope about the need to take action against the Scottish heretics. The Scots were not now acting in isolation. The events of 1559–60 were part of a general Calvinist reaction to Cateau-Cambrésis, when growing fears of a Catholic league produced an ideological development from acceptance of ordained authority to the justification of resistance. France as well as Scotland witnessed that change. The Scottish magnates were not acting within the narrow confines of domestic politics, domestic power-struggles, nor concerned only with political revolution. They were one of the Calvinist aristocracies of Europe, and consciously so; they were well aware that the Reformed church of Europe would be strengthened by their victory. Two centuries of insistence that they were indeed a European aristocracy now came to fruition; they had a leading rôle on the European stage.

The regent's wisdom for which the Congregation appealed in their letter of 7 May 1559 did not stay the sword; but neither was the sword much used. The 15 months between the call to arms and the meeting of the Reformation parliament were marked less by fighting than by disruption and civil violence. Already in May 1559 the rioting had begun; in Perth the Charterhouse and the houses of the Black and Grey Friars were looted. The Charterhouse suffered simply because the Perth mob was on the rampage; the friaries were the real object of attack, here and elsewhere in Scotland. The fear and violence that had suddenly flared up, unsettling and undermining society, come to life in little vignettes of evidence. In conservative Banffshire, for example, on 15 August 1559 the Carmelite friars of Banff leased their house and land to George Ogilvy of Dunlugas, the most powerful local laird; their buildings already burned and the friars attacked by night by unknown persons, they were desperately trying to buy protection. And in July 1559 the treasures of St Machar's cathedral, Aberdeen, were packed up and handed over for safe-keeping to the earl of Huntly. Between June and November the burgh of Edinburgh, always the principal sufferer from disorder, was twice occupied and deserted by the Lords of the Congregation; between then and April 1560, when the Congregation finally took over the town, rival councils, Catholic and Protestant, struggled for control. There was sporadic fighting, which produced no decisive result, only the famous boast by Mary of Guise, after a temporary victory by her French troops, 'Where is now John Knox's God? My God is stronger than his, yea, even in Fife'. As early as July 1559 it was reported that 'the manner of reformation is this — they pull down all manner of "freires" and some abbeys which will not receive it — cleanse parish churches of images and monuments of idolatry — and prohibit all masses. In place whereof, the book set forth by the godly King Edward is read in them'.

For the next eight months that more or less remained the situation. The Protestants on the whole were in the ascendant. Town councils, at Ayr, Dalmellington, and St Andrews, for example, were appointing Protestant ministers; Knox was appointed minister of Edinburgh in the summer of 1559, and St Andrews set up its kirk session in the same year. But the French troops were still in Scotland, the regent, although 'suspended' by the Lords of the Congregation in October 1559 and replaced by the 'great council of the realm', still held power. The deadlock was broken when at last Elizabeth agreed to what the Scots Protestants had long begged for: English aid. An English army came north at the end of March 1560 and besieged Leith. By July, mainly because of the crucial part played by the English navy, it was all over; the treaty of Edinburgh was agreed, and the French, as well as the English, withdrew from Scotland. By that time Mary of Guise was dead. This highly talented and appealing personality had pursued a course that in the end proved impossible, but only in the end. So far was she from the monster of hypocrisy and dissimulation of Knox's *History* that even in defeat she retained the respect and perhaps even affection of those who opposed her; it is a remarkable tribute to her, and a profound comment on the nature of the Reformation in Scotland, that when she was dying, on 11 June, there came to her death-bed the Protestant Lord James Stewart and the earl of Argyll, to give her comfort.

The Reformation parliament which met on 1 August 1560 was not the beginning of the Scottish Reformation, but the culmination of the long and difficult process of achieving Reformation. By then, the Protestant party had widespread support among the landowners. The First Band, of December 1557, had five signatories. The bond drawn up at Edinburgh on 17 April 1560 was signed by 7 magnates and 42 others. As is well known, the Reformation parliament itself was attended by over a 100 lairds, most, though not all, Protestant; few lairds had ever attended parliament, but now they turned up in droves, flocking to Edinburgh to demand their right to add their voice in this most crucial issue. The considerations that had prompted people to throw in their lot with the leading Protestants, in the years between 1557 and 1560, cannot now be determined. Motives, sacred and profane, were inextricably linked. Yet in a religious age, political ambition, even political chicanery, will go hand-in-hand with religious conviction, and it is unnecessary, and perhaps unwise, to try to disentangle them in the case of individuals or social groups. In such an age it is hard to imagine that many were able to preserve complete indifference to their hope of salvation; and that was as relevant a consideration as the desire to preserve or destroy the Auld Alliance with France.

Nor was political ambition clear-cut. At the end of the 1550s established order collapsed; the church that men knew, and in which their ancestors had worshipped, was challenged and overthrown. Few who lived through these years would have agreed with Knox's burning enthusiasm for an 'uproar for religion', or an uproar for anything else. Change was a frightening and terrible thing; most men frantically sought reassurance that static and accepted order had not vanished, even if the dislocation of the clergy, the expanding rôle of the laity and the growing self-assertiveness and economic advance of the lairds, meant that the old world had gone for good. The spiritual agony of the clerics of the old church, men like Davidson, was paralleled by the political and religious agony of many laymen. Even the Catholic earl of Huntly temporarily turned to the Protestants. Lord Ruthven, Protestant provost of Perth, 'a man . . . godly and stout', had a moment of doubt when he left Perth in May 1559 and fled to the regent, 'a great discouragement to the hearts of many'. Lord Erskine, said Knox, was the 'chief great man that had professed Christ Jesus and refused to subscribe the Book of Discipline'. Knox's explanation, that he 'has a very Jezebel to his wife', and that he would not give up to the kirk what rightly belonged to it, probably does less than justice to Erskine; it tells us a lot about the great reformer's insistence on absolute commitment to the new church, and nothing about the problems and fears of those trapped by indecision.

The constant reiteration by the Protestants that driving out the French was not revolution, but restoration of Scottish independence, Scottish authority, was not just propaganda, designed to allay the fears of those who, like the burgh of Aberdeen, promised to support them as long as they would not 'interpryss ony purpos aganis the authorite'. Their appeal to the nobility and community of Scotland rings true: 'if religion be not persuaded unto you, yet cast ye not away the care ye ought to have over your commonwealth, which ye see manifestly and violently ruined before your eyes. If this will not move you, remember your dear wives, children and posterity, your ancient heritages and houses; and think well these strangers will regard no more your right thereunto . . . whenever occasion will serve'. God, country, and family: it is an eternal appeal. It was not just a 'political' revolution in 1559—60. It was an attack on a French-dominated government, and a reaction to the real French threat to the Protestants. But Mary of Guise did preserve her daughter's kingdom, her daughter's crown; it was the folly of the daughter, not a revolution against her authority, that was to bring Mary queen of Scots down.

The Reformation in Scotland made as many demands on the spiritual courage of individuals as any other Reformation. But it lacked persecution, and it lacked civil strife. Its leaders bound themselves with 'our whole power, substance and our very lives, to maintain, set forward and establish the most blessed word of God and his Congregation', but when they achieved their reformation they made no effort to displace their kinsmen, friends and dependants, the beneficed clergy and continuing lay adherents of the old church. This was not because of lack of conviction. It was because those who gave the lead were the wrong people, men whose natural leadership was on the whole personal and local rather than political and national, and who were for a short space pushed into something more. If the magnates indeed saw in the Reformation the opportunity to enhance their power, then they behaved with quite remarkable stupidity after 1560, when they neither arrogated more power than they had hitherto exercised in secular affairs nor sought to retain control over the new church. They lost out by that; their reversion to their traditional rôle as local lords, except when forced out again in the aftermath of Mary's deposition, was to make them increasingly isolated, even rather old-fashioned and anachronistic, in the rapidly changing world of the late sixteenth and early seventeenth centuries.

In the Reformation parliament, political and religious issues crystallized. There, in the 100 lairds, lay the real signs of the shift in the balance of power within the state. There, in the Confession of Faith and the three acts on religious issues which comprised the whole business of this parliament, lay the fundamental reason for the Reformation. In Scotland, as in Europe, the leaders of society, both clerical and secular, had recognized the need for reform, whether willingly or not. Reform from within had failed. But reform from without did not succeed because the old church was corrupt or even simply ineffective. It succeeded because its leaders provided a new and compelling answer to the question of what the church was about. It was not, in the last resort, about how many hospitals it ran, how many schoolmasters and lawyers it provided, but about spiritual succour in this life and salvation in the next. When men began to offer a new approach to God, then there was Reformation.

The parliament of 1560 did nothing to establish the structure of the new church. It concentrated on destroying the basis of the old, simply by abolishing the Mass and the jurisdiction of the pope. That concentration shows how far Scottish Protestantism had developed and changed in the decade before 1560. Hamilton's *Catechism*, written in 1552 to meet the threat of heresy, said little about the Mass and nothing about the pope. In 1560 the Mass was a central anathema, and the pope a growing threat. The pre-Reformation papacy was largely irrelevant in Scotland, except in its bureaucratic and legal capacity; and certainly the destruction of the legal basis of the old church involved destruction of the rights of the papacy. But it was more than that in 1560. With the Council of Trent came strong claims for papal authority, and with the Counter-Reformation, the beginnings of the revival of spiritual prestige, and also the tough moral commitment so central to the Scottish reformers. The reigning pope, Pius IV, and even more, his successor, Pius V, were imposing on Rome itself a way of life as morally rigid and 'puritanical' as any kirk session or general assembly ever did in Scotland. Thirteen years earlier it was said of Knox's first sermon that 'others lop at the branches of papistry, but he strikes at the root, to destroy the whole'. In 1560, the very year when even Calvin considered the possibility of an ecumenical council presided over by the pope, provided he was bound by the authority of scripture, the Scottish parliament joined with that earlier lone voice, and did destroy the whole.

The revived papacy was a crucial target for attack. Even more crucial was the statement of faith of the new church. The Scottish Confession is an immensely moving and impressive document, not least because it is entirely positive. With rare exceptions, it avoided dialectic and emotive abuse of papistry; it was never side-tracked from its basic purpose, to explain, in clear and uncluttered language, basic beliefs. It set out its vision of the kirk, both the invisible community of all believers, 'catholik' because it contained the 'elect of all ages, realms, nations, tongues, Jews or Gentiles', and the particular kirks now on this earth. It reduced the sacraments to two, baptism and communion. It denied the doctrine of transubstantiation, but it retained belief in the Real Presence, and managed in a brief phrase to find a form of words that conveyed something of this supreme mystery with an immediacy that far outweighed Calvin's own tortured chapter in the *Institutes*: 'be operatioun of the haly gaist: quha by trew faith caryis ws above all thingis that ar visibill, carnall and eirdly, & makis ws to feid upoun the body and blude of Christ Jesus', in a spiritual union with Christ, 'the verray nurischement and fude of our saulis'. And it ends with a passage on the reprobate and the elect; only those who 'with heart unfenzeitly belief and with mouth bauldlie confess the Lord Jesus' will have forgiveness of sins in this life, and in the next be spared 'the fyre unstauncheabill in quhilk [the reprobate] salbe tormentit for ever, alsweill in thair awin bodyis as in thair saulis', a passage terrifying by modern standards, but still offering more hope than the later fully developed doctrine of predestination would do. The Calvinist church had not yet moved fully to the position where it denied that Christ died that all men might be saved.

In 1560 the majority of the population was almost certainly still Catholic. The high point of the reforming movement had been reached. The next stage would be the long and painful process of establishing the new kirk, the missionary struggle, the squalid argument about money, the row between church and state over rights of political and religious interference. But in the heady days of August 1560 politicians and preachers together produced a statement of militant, aggressive, Calvinist faith which cut through the muddles and uncertainties of the past three decades, the groping through the half-way house of Lutheranism towards a clear alternative to pre-Tridentine Catholicism. The clarity and simplicity of the acts of the Reformation parliament is the measure of their achievement.

8

The Establishment of the Reformed Church

The reformers in 1560, once the Reformation parliament had met, had two major headaches: whether their actions were legal, and how to transform the intentions of 1558–60 into the fact of a reformed church in Scotland. The first question was quickly answered; to the surprise of no one, Mary and Francis refused to ratify the acts of the Reformation parliament. Those who had passed these acts, therefore, were now technically in rebellion. In the long term, the fact that the temporal estates had taken the law into their own hands, and in particular that the lairds had seized a place for themselves, were to have considerable political consequences. But in the years immediately following 1560 the apparent threat to the existence of the new kirk when it had barely reached infancy turned out, astonishingly, to be no threat at all, because neither side, queen or lords, behaved as if a rebellion had ever taken place. Mary's denunciation of the Reformation parliament, coming as it did from a queen who might be nominally regnant in Scotland but preferred to be consort in France, was hardly effective, particularly when France had lost her grip on Scotland. Her own position was radically changed within a few months, when her husband died, in December 1560; she reluctantly numbered her days in France, and eventually returned to Scotland in August 1561. The Catholics of Europe, the pope, the kings of France and Spain, and the earl of Huntly, saw that return as the beginnings of a Scottish Counter-Reformation. But encouraging letters from the papacy, and, more practically, the suggestion from Huntly that she might sail not to Leith and her capital but to Aberdeen, and lead the Catholic revival from the North, had no effect against the blandishments of her half-brother Lord James Stewart, who was her principal adviser in the year before she returned to Scotland, and her own basic ambition to succeed to the English throne. She made a deal with Lord James, by which she became the only Catholic in Scotland entitled to hear Mass; she settled down to write a series of polite and friendly, but ineffective, letters to the papacy which eventually drove it to wash its hands of her; she did make some Catholic appointments to benefices, especially the prelacies, and she continued to refuse to ratify the acts of the 1560 parliament, until herself in desperate straits in 1567; but she never tried to bring back the old church.

Her decision, with hindsight, looks politically wise, if not spiritually wholly honourable. But in Scotland the future of the reformed church was so far from assured in 1560−1 that even politically Mary's action was far from inevitable. Thus, despite the military success of 1560, England still feared a revival of French influence in Scotland, and was to do so for many years, while at the same time being further alarmed by the prospect of Mary's marriage to Don Carlos, son of Philip II. It would be wrong to write off Mary simply as an English sycophant; she had too much sense of her own dignity as a reigning monarch, even if Scotland came a poor third compared to her past as queen consort of France and her possible future as queen of England. But in the last resort, religious considerations, except at the most personal level, and the opportunity to play a part in European politics at least as decisive as that of James V, never outweighed her passion to succeed Elizabeth. Her comparative indifference to Scotland defused the revolutionary situation; it is difficult to be in rebellion against someone who is not particularly interested. Even more important, it gave a semblance of authority to the new church, and provided a breathing space in which it could establish itself.

The real struggle was between the secular leaders of the Protestant party and the ministry of the reformed Church. Long before the famous debate at Heidelberg in 1568 between Erastus and George Withers, the clerical reformers had moved towards the doctrine of the separation of church and state. The earliest hint of the idea that the secular magistrate should defend but not control the church is found in Henry Balnaves' treatise on *Justification by Faith*, written in 1548. On 6 May 1559 the 'professouris of Christis Evangell' had warned the regent to 'understand yourself, maist nobill princess in Christis kingdome to be ane servand and na quein, hawand na preheminence nor authoritie above the kirk'. The general message was very clear. It was not particularly directed against Mary queen of Scots, who manifestly could not fulfil the rôle of 'godly prince' and was therefore irrelevant. It was the political leaders who had been at the head of the reforming movement who were now asked to give up that lead and accept a rôle in which they would follow the instructions of the ministry, would support God's work on earth — and specifically would finance it — but would not guide it. It was too much for those who had risked a great deal in the crisis years, and it would certainly be too much for King James.

From the church's point of view, it was offering the secular powers a wholly positive place. The Calvinist godly magistrate, the man who would uphold and defend the Kirk, supplementing ecclesiastical discipline with the authority of the state, was indeed a man with a high calling. Despite the theocratic tendencies of the Scottish reformers, the rôle of the secular magistrate was never played down, any more than it was by Calvin in that more manageable theocracy, Geneva. Undoubtedly this had an appeal, especially to Knox's 'princes and judges', the nobles who had given a lead before 1560, and would continue to do so, at least politically, because of the absence of an effective monarch until the early 1580s when James VI took over government. It gave them a new ideological basis for their exercise of power, adding a crucial religious dimension to their traditional social rôle. Men like Lord Glamis, Archibald earl of Angus, John earl of Gowrie adopted and endorsed this ideology. The flood of religious bonds which were a prominent feature of the years between 1557 and 1560 inevitably died away once the immediate crisis was over. But in their political and social bonds, the promise of mutual assistance in all their lawful actions might now be rendered as godly actions, and the bond between Colin earl of Argyll and James earl of Morton, for example, began with the undertaking to advance 'Goddis trew religioune'.

This kind of expression was a reminder that the nobility did not merely see itself as the junior partner of the ministry in advancing God's religion. From the point of view of royal or aristocratic magistrates, the rôle ascribed to them could all too easily degenerate into the subservient position of being bullied by the church, over both money and long-established principles, and even threatened by such extremists as Knox and Goodman with a challenge to their authority if they should not meet the kirk's demands. The new church got off to a flying start in 1560 when, in April of that year, the Great Council of the Realm commissioned the work that became the First Book of Discipline. It was a remarkable and impressive document. But it immediately opened up the cracks; it was not endorsed by parliament, almost certainly because of its sweeping demand for enough of the church's patrimony to be handed back by the laity to maintain schools and universities, hospitals and the poor, and to pay stipends to ministers of between 100 and 300 merks, to exhorters of 100, and to readers, whose office was part-time, of 40. In theory, it was an immensely noble vision. In practice it was an ill-thought-out and arbitrary claim, giving no room for negotiation and no consideration to practical problems.

Money and the church, whether it is the church demanding or the laity grudging it, is always an emotive subject. The laity remember 'Consider the lilies', the church the widow's mite. Lay greed is always an element in the problem, but the Scottish aristocracy were not uniquely selfish. It is, for example, very difficult to argue convincingly that they were guilty of self-interest in advancing the cause of reform because a revived Catholic church might have reclaimed her patrimony; the ability of the English landed classes to welcome Mary Tudor's restoration of the old church with tears of joy while hanging grimly on to former church property casts doubt on such an argument. Indeed, in Scotland the reverse was the case. The laity had made considerable inroads into church lands in the 30 years before the Reformation. A new, vigorous kirk was the real threat to those lands. Many of them were held on the pre-Reformation ecclesiastical title of commendator and were therefore not hereditary; the council ordinance of September 1561 forbidding men to go to Rome to seek curial authority for feus of church lands suggests the doubts many felt about their titles. Moreover, the lands which had been alienated by the church were now hopelessly entangled with secular property, and teinds were a property right, often leased to tacksmen. The situation was highly complex, in which uncertainty bred fear. The claims of the First Book of Discipline must have confirmed these fears; the demands of the kirk added uncertainty about possessions and place in the world to uncertainty about religion and spiritual safety.

In the long run, the state was by no means unsympathetic to the need to provide for the church. The immediate problem was not just the refusal of a self-interested laity to support the institution it had helped to create. It arose because, remarkably, the Reformation did not destroy the structure of the old church. The monasteries were never dissolved; the little communities of monks were allowed to die out in their own time, at once a grimmer and a gentler fate than that of the English monks. Nor were holders of benefices, major or minor, turned out before 1573. Even if they refused to conform, as at least half of them to a greater or lesser extent did, they still retained the major portion of their revenues, and those who did conform were not bound to serve the kirk. This was the almost inevitable result of the political and social circumstances of the Reformation. The absence of a strong and committed monarchy meant that political support was diffused. It came from a section of the nobility and gentry whose careful appeals to the kinsmen and dependents who did not follow them into the reformaing movement before 1560 were hardly likely to give way to tougher action afterwards. Natural reluctance to give up their revenues, the appalling problem of assessing what should be given up, and the bonds of kinship and lordship not broken by religious division, all militated against the demands of the kirk to take the required revenues for itself and do with them as it saw fit.

Yet no one doubted that the new church must be financed. In 1562 an unsatisfactory compromise was arrived at: the Thirds of Benefices, which left two thirds of the revenues in the hands of the unreformed clergy, and gave the remaining third to the crown for the maintenance of the kirk. It was a remarkable imposition on a Catholic monarch. Yet she did, it seems, honour her obligations up to a point, despite the kirk's endless griping and criticism about her use of the money for her own interests, from playing cards to getting married and baptizing her son. This arrangement dragged on with piecemeal attempts at solution; Lindsay of Balcarres' attempt to establish the principle that the ministers' stipends should be first charge on the teinds largely failed in 1596, but the idea was revived and given parliamentary backing in 1617. The tacksmen who held the teinds naturally had to be compensated, being given extensions of their leases, and the solution was as yet only a compromise, unlike the wholesale solution thought up by Charles I, whereby the crown proposed to annex all kirklands and teinds, and did so in such an arbitrary and ham-fisted way that it was a major precursor to the revolution of the late 1630s. But there is another side to this problem. It is worth repeating that after the 1560s no minister was ever left in such desperate straits as the pre-Reformation parish clergy. Various commissions of laymen and ministers were set up to inquire into low stipends, and some were raised as a result. It was possible for the reformed clergy to do well. Dr W.R. Foster's analysis of the testaments of 81 ministers from the commissariat courts of Edinburgh, Dunblane, and Brechin between 1600 and 1638 show that even in the first decade of the seventeenth century the average net assets were £1,244, and by the third they had risen to £3,777, falling off in the fourth, but still remaining at just over £2,000. And in 1611–12 eight ministers were summoned before the privy council for the crime of 'ockery' – that is, charging more than 10 per cent interest. It took a long time for the finances of the kirk to be put on to an acceptable footing; but Sir Benjamin Rudyerd's complaint to the English parliament that many English vicars had only £5 per annum, while James had settled ministers in Scotland with stipends of £30 sterling (£360 Scots), indicates that even before Charles's radical solution the ministry was enjoying what would be regarded as a reasonable competence for a professional man.

If money was one issue which caused tension between church and state, so also was the vexed question of ecclesiastical patronage. In 1560, while the kirk, its eyes raised to heaven, proposed to abolish patronage, the crown stepped in and took over almost the whole lot. It could do so simply by asserting its right to the patronage of religious institutions, and as 86 per cent of the parish churches were appropriated to these institutions, there was very little left for anyone else. But the crown never insisted on exercising all its rights, and the situation changed when James's act of 1587 annexed the temporalities of the benefices; from then on, he began to erect temporal and hereditary lordships from former ecclesiastical lands. This removed one social anomaly, the post-Reformation lay commendator, and patronage was granted to the new lords as a property right along with the lands, thus extending the number of lay patrons. Even so, there was less chance for potential Scottish equivalents of the earl of Huntingdon, who used his ecclesiastical patronage to establish puritan ministers in Yorkshire, Lancashire, and Leicestershire. By the time the nobility did begin to get their hands on patronage, the Act of Conformity of 1573 had long been in force. Even the great Catholic lords, like the earls of Huntly and Errol, were unable to use it as a method of re-establishing Catholic priests. The real problem for the church was simply that it did not have complete control of the ministry, and particularly of those nominated to bishoprics once the office had been formally restored by the Convention of Leith in 1572. Crown and nobility continued to interfere.

In these two matters, the kirk did not get what it wanted from the state. At the same time, the state found itself under attack from the church on a completely new scale. In 1563 parliament showed a willingness to underwrite the tough and uncompromising morality of the reformed church, but this was far from enough. Pressure from the kirk went on relentlessly. In 1596, when the king asked the assembly that any offence he gave might be dealt with in private discussion with the ministers, the assembly replied with a series of public criticisms of the king, the queen, and the royal household. The same assembly went on to broaden its onslaught against the 'universall coldenesse and decay of zeale in all estatis. . . .Adultereis, fornicatiouns, incests, unlawfull marriages and divorcements . . . excessive drinking and waughting; gluttonie, which is no doubt the caus of the dearth and famine; and gorgeous and vaine apparrell, filthie and bloodie speeches. . . . Universall neglect of justice both in civill and criminall causes, as namelie, in giving remissions and respits for blood, adultereis and incests'. This last point was an attack on the long-established principles of the bloodfeud, with its support from the king in the form of pardons to the criminal who had made compensation, by a kirk for whom crime was a sin against God. The comfortable days of the pre-Reformation era when the state could criticize the church had gone. Now even nobleman and monarch came under the vastly critical eyes of the kirk and were found wanting. Godly magistrates they might try to be, as the kirk insisted; but human sinners they too often were, as the kirk endlessly reminded them.

Even more dangerous was the kirk's assumption of its right to decide who was godly and who was not on specific occasions; it might uphold 'godly' rebels against 'ungodly' authority. It is a measure of the kirk's growing power that this was less a feature of the reign of the ungodly princess Mary than of that of the godly prince James VI. Thus in 1584, when the leading Presbyterian nobles, the Ruthven raiders, were in exile after they had lost control of the king, they were admonished by James Melville, a minister and the nephew of the great reformer Andrew Melville, that they should return to Scotland and fight off their political opponents, 'as becomes valiant warriors and capteanes of the Lord's army'; this was nothing less than incitement to armed rebellion. James VI's own troubled dealings wtih that inconsistent spitfire the earl of Bothwell were immensely complicated by the measure of support for Bothwell from the kirk; the temporary alliance of Bothwell with the northern Catholic earls indicates an element of stubborn perversity in the kirk's relationship with the crown. The kirk also added considerably to the king's difficulties after that most mysterious episode of 5 August 1600 known as the Gowrie conspiracy; the leading ministers in Edinburgh publicly proclaimed their disbelief in the king's version of the death of the kirk's most favoured magnate.

Conflict between church and state crystallized into two issues in the 1580s and 1590s: the king's hostility to the kirk's insistence on adding a fourth court, the presbytery, to the three that had existed from the beginning, kirk session, synod, and general assembly, and thus another link in its chain of control; and the kirk's hostility to the king's insistence on having bishops with a seat in parliament. In the 1580s the government's attitude changed according to who was in power: Lennox's government helped to set up the first 13 presbyteries in 1581, and the Arran régime denounced them in the 'Black Acts' of 1584. The 1590s was the critical decade. It opened badly for James with the passing of the 'Golden Acts' of 1592 − the colour representing the joy of the kirk after its earlier defeat in the 'Black Acts'. Yet the crown's loss was less severe than it looked. Presbyteries were already in existence anyway, and the office of bishop, though no longer recognized by assembly or parliament, was not statutorily abolished. Moreover, James retained one vital weapon, the right to summon and determine the time and place of the general assembly. He used it with great skill, paying the expenses of moderate ministers to ensure their attendance, and turning up himself to lobby and negotiate, and organizing business so that contentious issues were left to the end, thus giving him the chance to manipulate the commissioners.

At the end of 1596 an anti-papist riot in Edinburgh gave him his opportunity to strike hard at the kirk. He held the ministers and citizens responsible and threatened to withdraw his government; the frantic burgh, faced with considerable loss of revenue, paid a fine of 20,000 merks, and showed considerably less enthusiasm for the vocal and critical ministry. Thereafter, James broke the monopoly of Edinburgh and St Andrews, centres of Presbyterian influence, as meeting-places of the assembly and began to summon it in Perth, Dundee, and Montrose, where the ministry was more conservative. By 1600 he was strong enough to appoint three parliamentary bishops; by the end of the reign, there were 11 bishops, and diocesan episcopacy had been restored. He was right to see clerical representation in parliament, and control of nomination to church office, as essential to him. In 1621, in the dramatic fight over the Five Articles of Perth, by which he sought liturgical and doctrinal changes, such as private baptism and private communion for the sick, the only estate in parliament to vote solidly for him was the clerical estate of the 11 bishops. In general, neither king nor kirk got all that they wanted. James managed to eliminate the extreme Presbyterians, Andrew Melville and his followers, but not the presbyteries. His church was an uneasy mixture of limited episcopacy and growing presbyterianism.

'Church' and 'state' are convenient and necessary terms, but too monolithic. It was never the case that the two lined up like opposing armies. At all times the church found support from within the state. Lennox had created presbyteries. James's great secretary and chancellor Maitland of Thirlestane was much more in sympathy with the Presbyterians than was the king, and he was the statesman of influence at the time when the council of 1586 declared presbyteries acceptable. In the 1590s the parliament that passed the Golden Acts, and men like Stewart of Blantyre or Lindsay of Balcarres, again show strong support for the church, the latter despite a major row which brought him a public rebuke from the pulpit in 1597. And in the parliament of 1621 there were more people who voted against the Articles, or abstained, than voted for them. If the state was not a monolith, then neither was the church. The Calvinist church was utterly clear about doctrinal unity, and on that point James and Melville were at one. It saw itself as the universal church, containing the 'elect of all ages, realms, nations, tongues, Jews or Gentiles', and the visible churches on this earth. But there was no such clarity, or even demand, for unity of polity. Distinctions as well as parallels can be found when comparing the polity of the Scottish church with Reformed churches abroad. The Genevan model could hardly be made to fit exactly into the very different social, geographical, and political structure of Scottish society, and in fact the Scottish polity, with its hierarchy of courts, came closer to that of France. Parallels can also be found with Lutheran churches, the office of super-intendent, for example, being characteristic both of Lutheran and Calvinist organization.

Not until 130 years after 1560 did bishops finally disappear from the kirk. On the whole, the delay was caused more by political pressures than by divisions within the church, but there was no time when at least a minority voice did not call for an episcopal rather than a presbyterian polity. It is too easy to assume that Scotland was solidly presbyterian from the beginning, England solidly episcopal. There were advocates of both forms of polity within the churches of both countries. There was a strong and articulate group of English presby-terians, like Thomas Cartwright and John Field, who maintained close contacts with the church in Scotland, but the episcopal party had the advantage of royal backing from the start, even if Elizabeth had to accept that her first bishops were Calvinists. In Scotland, the anti-episcopal ministry always had a much stronger and more central rôle, but it was not exclusive.

Diversity of opinions can be seen from the beginning. The early reformers drew on wide-ranging experience of all the reformed countries of Europe, and contained within their ranks — even within the ranks of the six authors of the First Book of Discipline — radicals, like Knox and Willock, conservatives, like John Winram and John

Douglas, and even men who were still strongly influenced by their early Lutheran beliefs, such as Erskine of Dun. This diversity, as much as the political, social, and economic problems surrounding the establishments of the new church, may explain the comparative lack of attention given in the First Book to the general polity of the church. It had plenty to say about individual congregations and the qualifications and means of election of individual ministers; about the place of elders and deacons and their relationship with the ministry; and about its vision of basic education for all – of both sexes – and higher education for those whom it would profit, so that Scotland would be blessed with an educated ministry and a laity who could be taught to understand the faith. But its section on superintendents, though lengthy, was a late addition. And there were only five references to the General Assembly, though the first assembly had met in July 1560, and in December 1560 the second ratified the book; there are only passing references to the other courts of the church. It was a blue-print for a religious society; given the problems faced by those who compiled it, it was inevitably less comprehensive as a blue-print for a church polity.

It is not surprising that the polity of the kirk was not wholly thought-out from the start. The kirk had two pressing needs. One was to get itself established at all, and understandably it did that within an existing and accustomed framework. Hence the early assemblies were modelled on the greatest secular assembly, parliament, with its three estates. The fact that the magnates were not noted for whole-hearted attendance of parliament *en masse* had the inevitable consequence that neither did they flock to the assembly. But it was a natural starting-point, and only gradually, as the clay feet of the aristocracy became clear, and as the kirk became stronger, did there develop the desire for an assembly in which the laity were present, but, as in the Second Book of Discipline, could vote only if they were there as elders or elected representatives of the lesser courts. The second need was to establish itself as an institution clearly distinct from the old church. A great deal of early Protestant thought, both in Scotland and in Europe, reflected this need. Ordination, for example, was not rejected outright either by Calvin or by the French church; both took the position that it should be temporarily omitted because it might be seen as superstitious, but should be restored after a judicious interval. Language was carefully and consciously changed; thus 'parish' gave way to 'kirk' or 'congregation'.

The long debate over bishops derived from the church's awareness that any institution produces leaders and led, and its fear of a reversal to the state of the old church. Hence the exaggerated violence of the attack on the pre-Reformation bishops, and the careful searching of Scripture, which led to Calvin's stress on the scriptural use of the word bishop, and also presbyter and pastor. Bishops who governed churches were not there by divine command, but by the human and expedient need to have a 'president' in the assembly, and that use of the word bishop was, for Calvin, a 'corrupt signification'. Moreover, opinion hardened, partly as a reaction to the signs of abuse. Even that great reforming magnate Alexander earl of Glencairn tried to seize control of the archbishopric of Glasgow through the nomination of his dependent John Porterfield in 1571, and the nominations to St Andrews and Glasgow by the regent in the name of the crown led to a strong reaction in the subsequent assemblies. Yet the issue was not always clearcut. Beza denounced bishops in his letters to Knox in 1572, and to Lord Glamis in 1575–6. But even Andrew Melville returned from Geneva in 1574 with something of an open mind, which was to be closed within the next two years by his experience in Scotland: the dilapidation of the bishoprics, the assembly's difficulties in controlling bishops and forcing them to fulfil their duties as visitors, and the obvious interest of the crown, all made the rejected past look very present. The Second Book of Discipline, produced and adopted in 1578, was therefore a clearer statement about the nature of the church and its organization, both in general, and in the detailed account of the offices within the church, than the first had been. Early attempts to fit a wide range of ideas, drawn from Luther, Zwingli, Bullinger, Bucer, Calvin, Beza, and other reformers, and from experience of other polities, into a Scottish context gradually but inevitably gave rise to a clearer vision of what was actually needed, and would best advance the kirk in Scotland.

Here, then, was a church that was substantially underfinanced; whose polity evolved slowly and often gropingly, sometimes in the face of considerable opposition from both Regent Morton, who wanted a church modelled on English lines, and James VI; that to begin with simply did not have enough people to provide a ministry throughout the country; and that, even as numbers grew, had the problem of establishing itself within local communities where religious change brought not only welcome, but also indifference, fear, and open hostility. Yet the impact of the kirk on society was not something that became familiar only in later centuries; from contemporary records comes a tremendous impression of strength, not weakness, even in the first half-century of its existence. It is a remarkable success story.

This success can partly be explained by good fortune in never having to face a sustained challenge from the Catholics. The possibility of Counter-Reformation was feared for almost a century after the Reformation, and on the face of it with some justice in early days. The number of powerful Catholics in Scotland fluctuated, but could be as high as one third of the nobility and gentry, as an English report claimed in 1600. George earl of Huntly, grandson of the earl who had offered Mary support for a Catholic revival, entered into negotiations with Philip II in the late 1580s and 1590s, portraying himself as the man who would indeed advance God's work by restoring the old faith; the new ideology was not only used by Protestant magnates. Even in Edinburgh there were still more Catholics than Protestants in 1565, and Mary's private chapel looked very like a Catholic parish church.

But such strength was more apparent than real. The Catholics after 1560 were caught by the problem that had beset the Protestants before: the difficulty, in a localized society, of creating a general movement out of disparate groups. Ayrshire Catholics might be protected by the Catholic earls of Cassillis and Eglinton, Aberdeenshire Catholics by Erroll and Huntly, and those in the borders by Lord Maxwell. But these things ran in parallel lines. Ayrshire was the scene of the only organized attempt to revive Catholic worship, with the public celebration of Mass at Kirkoswald and Maybole at Easter 1563, presided over by Archbishop Hamilton, and protected from disruption by an armed force led by Kennedy lairds. But it was a localized event, and nothing came of it. The only occasion when more might have happened was in 1561, with Huntly's offer to Mary; but he was turned down, not only by Mary, but by the Catholic earl of Atholl, whose geographic position would have given him the chance to unite with Huntly and crush the intervening Protestants of Angus. Political circumstances never favoured the Catholics, as in 1558–60 they had favoured the Protestants, or at least forced them into more than local action. The Catholics remained wholly regionalized, and so they remained weak.

This is one reason for the lack of persecution in Scotland. Another is that in such a society personal ties were strong enough to maintain social bonds, even in an age of religious division. In 1610, for example, Alexander Douglas, Protestant bishop of Moray, wrote a moving letter to King James pleading that the Catholic laird of Gight should be left in peace because he was ill: 'I wad humbly craiff your Hieness that he might keep his health in sum uder church', for, after all, 'the papists, I perceive, are not universally of ane corrupt disposition'. Moreover, the kirk itself, despite its obsessional fears of the 'Catholic under the Bed' expressed in assembly after assembly, took the highly intelligent line of exhortation rather than persecution of leading Catholics. Catholic earls were plagued by godly men, as the kirk politely and relentlessly sent ministers into their households to resolve their doubts. Occasionally they fought back. In 1575 the earl of Atholl made it quite clear that the offer of ministers willing to sit up through the night with him in an effort to resolve his doubts was unacceptable; he required a night's sleep and more time. Yet Atholl did conform. Even that persistent sinner George earl of Huntly was three times reconciled to the kirk, and once absolved by the archbishop of Canterbury, before finally managing to have himself buried a good Catholic. The day-long party in the burgh of Aberdeen which the kirk organized to mark his second reconciliation in 1597 — an event that bears no relation to the idea of a kill-joy church — is a good illustration of what the kirk was after. It was the ecclesiastical equivalent of the publicity that surrounded the end of a secular feud. If the kirk would join with God in rejoicing over any sinner that repented, it would certainly do so with a maximum of noise when the sinner was such a catch. It knew very well that Huntly's reconciliation was unlikely to mean more ministers, more kirks, more money, although it made plantations of kirks a condition of receiving Catholic magnates back into the fold. Much more important was the public triumph of the God of Scotland over the God of Rome in the case of the greatest man in the locality. The personal importance of the Scottish magnate, and the belief inherited from Calvin and Beza in the efficacy of the conversion of a single noble, combine to explain the patient and gently ruthless pursuit of the Catholic nobility.

The kirk's success, however, depended on far more than weak opposition. Its dazzling self-confidence and its impressive refusal to compromise were tremendous sources of strength. A church with no money and not enough ministers, which publicly criticizes the king, and demands that merchants do not trade with Catholic countries, cannot be considered weak, even if the king fought back and the merchants did not give up their trade. Its utterly clear image of the society it wanted to create, according to God's word, infuses every page of the two Books of Discipline. From the beginning, there was to be no compromise over the ministry. If no suitable candidates offered themselves as ministers or superintendents, then rather than have men incapable of preaching the word, there would be no appointment;

thus they introduced the offices of reader and exhorter, initially as a temporary measure, and kept under scrutiny by the assembly in order to ensure that, even for the sake of expediency, these lesser officers did not exercise a full ministry of the word and sacraments. Nor was there any compromise over the pre-Reformation bishops who conformed and were prepared to work for the new church, like Adam Bothwell of Orkney, Robert Stewart of Caithness, and Alexander Gordon of Galloway. If they were to be absorbed into the ministry, it was not as bishops, even if that would have offered an appealing continuity to the puzzled souls of their dioceses.

This was a new church, not a revised version of the old. It did have a strong sense of continuity with the past — the past of the early church (though not the Celtic church of legend). But it was a complete break with the immediate past in its distaste for hierarchy, both in the original Greek sense of priest-rule, and in the more familiar connotation of acknowledged and unchanging status. Its initial three-fold order of ministers, bishops or preachers, elders, and deacons or distributors, and the later four-fold order including doctors, which was derived from Calvin, and also from Bucer and Bullinger, was in no sense hierarchical, for all were exercising a ministry, and all were answerable to the courts of the church. In practice, no society has ever succeeded in eradicating hierarchy, and the kirk was no exception. Nevertheless, the principle of parity was followed as far as possible, within the ranks of the kirk itself. No matter how much any individual minister became top-dog in his congregation, he was not proof against the assembly's regular castigations of the ministry for lack of zeal. One of the notable early reformers, Paul Methven, was publicly deposed for adultery in 1562, and left Scotland for the gentler haven of the ministry of the church of England. Erskine of Dun himself, as superintendent of Angus, was under fire in the 1562 assembly for failure to do more — in the two years since the Reformation — to eradicate popery and establish godly ministers and elders. Even turning up late to preach on Sunday did not escape the notice of the assembly. Tight control, and the insistence that this time the ministers of God would do God's work, is seen even before 1560: Christopher Goodman, when he became minister of Ayr in 1559, was given no time off to pursue his career as a scholar of European distinction, and was allowed only eight or nine days absence at a time, with a locum put in for the duration.

If society, on the whole, responds to commitment, and becomes indifferent to lack of it, then the approach of the new church gave it a head start. It could be an exhausting business, and the assembly was always faced with the problem of those who found it too much. The unfortunate commissioners sent to root out recusancy in Aberdeen and Moray — one for each area — were only two of those who had to admit that the assembly's mission might be divine, but they were but human; both asked to be relieved, in 1570 and 1572. But this sense of urgency compares sharply with the state of the old church, and with its partial and demoralized survival after 1560. In human terms, the kirk's sense of urgency could be cruel. Its refusal to follow one classic path, that of absorbing older ways of worship, and transforming them, was no doubt necessary: it is an easier path from paganism to Christianity than from one form of Christianity to another, and the kirk regarded Catholicism as worse than any form of paganism. But any former papist reconciled to the kirk was required, under pain of apostasy, to throw out all religious objects, rosaries, crucifixes, images of saints, the things that bring a sense of comfort and well-being at least to some, and are hard to jettison. Echoes of older beliefs which had been assimilated by the medieval church, if only as a veneer, are heard in the 1616 assembly's attack on those who went on pilgrimage to wells, trees, and old chapels, and put up bonfires. Inevitably, the ordinary parishioner was far more vulnerable than the rich and powerful to this kind of onslaught. The pathetic case of Isabel Umphray, warned by the Elgin kirk Session not to frequent the Chanonry kirk (by the 1590s used only for private prayer), 'or to pray on her bairn's grave', is one example of what must have been a common situation. Every Reformation produces its Isabel Umphrays, wholly remote from the great doctrinal changes, conservative, confused in heart and mind, denied traditional, and, to them, harmless comfort.

To the modern mind, there is, in the end, something deeply unattractive about the crusading zeal of the new church. Calvin's oath that he would uncover the truth about a group of citizens holding a dance in a private house in Geneva, 'even at the cost of my life', diminishes rather than enhances the image of one of the greatest of religious reformers, because it is tinged with the ridiculous. The sheer quantity of cases of sexual offence before the kirk sessions make the kirk's moral attitude more boring than impressive, and in any case reflects its failures, not its successes. The abolition of saints' days is understandable, as is the kirk's sabbatarianism, but it was socially harsh on a working population. A gentler parliament did reinforce the church's laws, in a series of acts banning games and sport on Sundays and transferring Sunday markets to weekdays, but in 1598 it redressed the balance by declaring Monday to be a day of rest for all servants, so that they might use it for 'handling of thair armour and in uther lauchfull gaimes and pastymes procureing habilitie of body quhairby all personis myndis and bodyis may be recreate'. Equally harsh, socially, and a good deal more doubtful in religious terms, was the abolition of Christmas and Easter; the idea that the birth and death of Christ should be celebrated continuously is an unsatisfactory alternative, reflecting obsessive fear of popish custom. No wonder Richard Maitland of Lethington, supreme exponent of the idea of the 'good old days', wrote a lament beginning 'Quhair is the blyithnes that hes beine', and commenting bitterly that 'all merines is worne away'.

Moreover, as time went on, the kirk's zeal became increasingly directed against the lower orders, and the God of respectability began to tarnish its own high standards. The deposition of the prominent reformer Paul Methven in 1562 is very different from the treatment of James Douglas, elder and provost of Elgin, whose punishment for adultery in 1585 was not the humiliating public penance of the stool of repentance during the Sunday service, but the task of repairing the north windows in the church, which almost cast him in the rôle of public benefactor rather than sinner. It was the same preoccupation with respectability that encouraged a secular authority, the town council of Old Aberdeen, to banish Catherine Lyne in 1610 for the appalling crime of referring to Alexander Forbes, baillie, as 'suetie hat, clipit brekis and blottit hips'. Discipline, so much associated with the Calvinist church, to Calvin himself provided 'the very sinews of religion'; but it was doctrine and the preaching of the Word that gave the church its real unity. In the individual parts of the church, however, Geneva, France, Scotland, discipline was crucial as the visible sign of the fulfilment of God's purpose while the church struggled to establish and assert itself. But as the highest in society held aloof, and the lowest kicked against it, it was the middling classes, the lairds, burgesses, and ministers, who accepted discipline with enthusiasm, and began to use it for purposes inevitably more self-interested than the church had initially intended. A high ideal, and the reality of social and political life, between them gave rise to middle-class respectability.

Yet this in itself was a source of strength. The godly society of the seventeenth century was much narrower and more rigid than the godly society of the sixteenth. In the sixteenth century, unlike the seventeenth, the kirk was not yet strong enough to impose its will wholly on society. More effectively, it reflected, and gave a lead to, social developments; its vision of a sanctified society was in tune with the conscious and unconscious ambitions and changes within secular society.

To the nobility who joined its ranks, however unsatisfactorily from its own point of view, it offered a new and inspiring image of themselves. Their awareness of being a European aristocracy was underwritten by a church that saw itself as one of the leading parts of the church universal. The programme devised by James Melville for the Ruthven Raiders at Newcastle in 1584 would have left no time for the normal aristocratic pursuits, with its demands for four sermons a week, common prayers, bible readings and psalms at every meal, lectures on doctrine, and one week's abstinence and public humiliation every month; it was therefore hardly practical. Yet the general appeal to a nobility 'whom God hes callit to be counsellours to their King, fathers of his peiple and defenders and meanteiners of his Kirk in this cleir light of the Gospell' added a new ideal to the long-established old one, while concentration on the Old Testament had its own attractions for what was still an aristocracy with an essentially military ethos.

The lairds in the localities equally found their already established position enhanced by a church that called on them to take an active part in its work. The new dignity of elder, with its aura of vocation, had great attraction for people who had long had an independent voice at home and who were now using it in national affairs. The insistence of the reformers that churchmen take no part in the business of the world not only removed the clergy from government and the law, but also did so at a time when the clergy's place was already substantially challenged by the laity, and in particular by the gentry. The extraordinarily close and formal links set up by the kirk between centre and locality through its courts, from assembly to kirk session, was a model to which a local gentry increasingly involved in central government could respond. Moreover, the changing position of the laity in society depended on lay education. From the church's point of view, the value of education lay in a highly-trained ministry, and a laity educated in religion. But because, unlike the old church, it wanted education for all, it also met the secular needs of the lairds, for whom education and especially legal training were now the path to advancement in government.

In the towns, the leading burgesses who had begun, in the century before the Reformation, to take over provision for schools and hospitals found that the new kirk, which called upon them to do so gave civic pride a religious dignity. The 160 'faythful brethren of Edinburgh' who in 1562 supported the kirk session resolution to raise funds for a hospital on the site of Blackfriars yard came mainly from the wealthy merchants and lawyers, and are an early and notable illustration of an appeal that went beyond the spiritual. Likewise, in the rural areas, the insistence of kirk sessions that they had responsibility for the poor, and, more generally, the church's creation of an office — the diaconate — with specific duties on behalf of the poor, had the attraction that the church did now fulfil the rôle expected of it. Moreover, as men began to look more frequently beyond their localities, the traditional forms of the bond of kindred slowly began to weaken. The new and tight organization of the kirk session, as it took over some of the functions associated with kinship and lordship, accelerated that process; it also reflected it.

At the end of the sixteenth century men looked back to a long period of trauma in society. There had been a spiritual revolution. There had also been social and political unrest; if Scotland had no wars of religion, it had endured six years of civil war after the deposition of Mary in 1567, and in the late 1580s and early 1590s the north-east was torn by one of the most dramatic feuds of the sixteenth century, between Huntly and Moray. It has been argued in various contexts, English and European, that the immediate aftermath of upheaval produces a heightened search for stability. The great triumph of the kirk was that its combination of doctrinal certainty, discipline, and effective organization offered, more than anything else in Scotland, the hope of stability. When the authors of the First Book of Discipline turned to consider the polity of the church, they distinguished between the necessary and the merely profitable. Necessity involved simply this: 'that the word be truly preached, the sacraments rightly administered, common prayers publicly made; that the children and rude persons be instructed in the chief points of religion, and that offences be corrected and punished. These things, we say, be so necessary, that without the same there is no face of a visible kirk'. That sentence shows a remarkable ability to see the essentials. It also shows a remarkable ability to respond to the aspirations that existed in late-sixteenth-century Scottish society.

III

Renaissance Scotland: The Reigns of Mary and James VI

9

The King's Government

Even the best of the innumerable biographies of Mary queen of Scots leave unanswered crucial questions about her reign. Much ink has been poured out on the subject of the murder of Darnley, and Mary's guilt or innocence. But it was not this murder which brought her down. A considerable section of the political nation of Scotland appears to have been hanging around the house or gardens of Kirk o' Field on the night of 10 February 1567, while the queen danced at Holyrood, and the earl of Moray 'looked through his fingers'; only Darnley's own family, the Lennox Stewarts, had any desire for his survival. Much more relevant to Mary's personal position were the three massive political mistakes she made. The first was marriage to Darnley. It has been convincingly argued that this was indeed a political marriage, designed to provide the queen with an ally against the ruling clique, her half-brother James and her brilliant secretary William Maitland of Lethington, the Scottish 'Michael Wylie' of Machiavellian politics; but given Darnley's wholly unsatisfactory personality, her choice of ally, no doubt encouraged by Darnley's own place in the English succession, shows political ineptitude of staggering proportions. The second mistake was almost a mirror image of the first; the marriage to Bothwell was made not because of romantic rape, that drama used *ad nauseam* by historical novelists, but because her political options were even more restricted than they had been when she married Darnley in 1565: this time, escape from Moray's influence possible only by throwing in her lot with a man whose intelligence far outweighed Darnley's, but who was politically isolated, and was the subject of European scandal. It was the Bothwell marriage, not the Darnley murder, that cost Mary her international reputation; France, Spain, and the papacy finally gave her up. Her third misjudgement was her flight to England after she lost the battle of Langside in May 1568. Her presence in Scotland in the year of her enforced abdication in July 1567 had at least provided a focal point for what became a strong party seeking her restoration, including 9 earls and 18 lords. Her absence, although it did not mean the immediate collapse of that party, left it at an immense psychological disadvantage. The three years of stalemate that followed were broken when in 1571 four of the leading Marians changed sides; the fall of Edinburgh in April 1573 was only the belated last act in a struggle whose outcome had not, for some time, been in doubt.

The problem Mary poses is more than a personal one. Neither her passions nor even her political follies wholly explain the collapse of a reign, which for four years had been surprisingly successful, into the two-year melodrama of 1565–7. Too much spotlight on the queen, too little on the other major political figures, means that we do not yet fully understand the rôle played by Moray and Maitland of Lethington as the motivating force of Mary's government before 1565. That in turn affects the question of what the queen wanted when she sought to put Darnley into Moray's place, and why Moray rebelled against her. But these are certainly not questions purely about Scottish internal politics. J.H. Elliott has looked back from the general crisis of the mid seventeenth century to that sixteenth-century decade of revolutions, the 1560s, when the Scots joined the Vaudois, the French, the Corsicans, the Dutch, the Moriscos, the English, and the Swedes in revolt to a greater and lesser degree. Knox himself was deeply aware of the contemporary situation; he told Mary that her realm was 'in no other case at this day, than all other realms of Christendom are'. It was not an age in which people could feel any security about events at home or abroad.

Hindsight makes it clear that Mary's return to Scotland heralded neither counter-Reformation nor a revival of the Auld Alliance. Without the benefit of hindsight, the Scots could not be entirely confident that she would never try to revive the old church, and the English government kept an exceedingly anxious eye on affairs in Scotland; hence its support for the marriage of Mary to the earl of Arran, and indeed the idea of marriage between Mary and Robert earl of Leicester, favourite of Elizabeth and close political ally of the earl of Moray. More generally, Mary's return to Scotland came at a time when Protestants throughout Europe had recovered confidence after the fears created by Cateau-Cambresis of a new assault on heresy; Henri II's death and the success of the Scottish Protestants had given grounds for optimism. It was dented by the outbreak of war in France; but it was the years 1565–7 – precisely the period of Mary's own crisis — that brought real panic. In the summer of 1565, when Mary married Darnley, France and Spain once again came to terms at Bayonne; rumours of a Catholic league, involving the Scottish queen along with the French king and the pope, were rife. Alba's march up through Europe in 1567 at the head of a Spanish army intent on the *Reconquista* of the Netherlands confirmed all fears. In that context, Mary's marriage to the Catholic Darnley, the ousting of the leading Protestant, Moray, and the scandal of Rizzio, the secretary who wrote her letters to the pope, all take on a much wider significance; while Moray's reaction to the marriage, his part in the Rizzio plot, and his recovery of power after Rizzio's death, cannot be seen only in the context of personal ambition, or even concern only with Scottish affairs. Nor should the emotional spectacle of a girl bullied into abdication by brutal means obscure the fact that this 'girl' — almost 25, and a reigning queen for six years — had a European rôle which made her potentially very dangerous indeed, should she regain power and the interest of the Catholic powers.

If the prestige of the monarchy was weakened by the last years of Mary's rule, it was further damaged by the civil war that followed. The minority government of the infant James VI was less clearly a government than a party: the king's party, as opposed to the queen's. The personal standing of the earl of Moray, regent from 1567 to 1570 provided some semblance of royal authority, but even that was lost when he was murdered in January 1570. His successor, Lennox, was chosen by Elizabeth, after five months of stalemate which paralysed Scottish politics; he lasted little more than a year before he too was killed. His successor, Mar, also lasted for only a year, though he at least managed to die of natural causes. The problem was that, to many, the deposition of the monarch, whatever her shortcomings, was wholly unacceptable; attacks on sovereignty were always a very difficult matter, and never more so than in this age of uncertainty. Political, not religious, considerations now divided the nation. Mary had a strong body of support even after her flight to England; so much so that in 1571 this dreary period was enlivened by the 'creeping parliament' of Edinburgh, when the king's supporters huddled into a house on the Canongate to avoid being fired on from the castle, held by the Marians, who a month later held a dignified parliament in the normal place, the tolbooth. This was, however, the last occasion on which the queen's party showed any signs of strength. By the summer of that year several of its leaders had defected. In May 1573 Edinburgh castle fell to the king's party, providing a second moment of light relief with an extraordinary example of Elizabethan parsimony: some of her troops — aided by the Scots, who extracted payment for it — had to crawl around the foot of the castle rock, picking up cannon-balls for re-use.

From 1572 until 1578, when he lost office as the result of a political *coup*, James earl of Morton was an immensely powerful and able regent. Even thereafter, the *coup*'s leaders, Argyll and Atholl, showed such remarkable inability to use the power they had seized, that his influence remained dominant, until a second coalition against him ensured success by executing him in 1581. Thereafter the régimes dominated by James's early favourites, Esme Stewart, duke of Lennox, and James Stewart, earl of Arran, were as unstable as any minority government. When Lennox was ousted, for a variety of religious and political reasons, in 1582, the king was held for a year by the Ruthven Raiders. It was only with Arran's downfall in 1585 that the reign of James VI himself can be regarded as having begun. It was a very low point for Stewart kingship.

The problems created for James by political realities were matched by problems of political theory. Great care was taken to educate the king, and George Buchanan, one of the greatest scholars of Europe, was naturally appointed James's tutor. It meant that the man who was one of the most noted exponents of a political theory that put considerable restrictions on royal power, and created for 'the people' — in practice the aristocracy — a constitutional right to depose a king, was now training the king. He failed; James was not convinced.

The idea of such a restriction on monarchy was not new. Major, without a political axe to grind, had argued in 1520 for an elective monarchy answerable to its subjects. But it had new and dangerous implications in the circumstances of the late sixteenth century. These implications had been seen by Mary; her famous reply to Knox's harangue, after 15 minutes of stunned silence, that 'I perceive that my subjects shall obey you and not me', shows that she was as aware as Knox of the new and unresolved problems created by the Reformation. The shattering of the religious unity of the west, and the developing idea of the 'nation-state', meant that the power of the secular ruler was, at least in theory, immeasurably enhanced, as heads of individual states and leaders of reform or defenders of the old faith. In practice, it forced bizarre choices on to rulers; Elizabeth, while strenuously upholding royal authority in England, supported the Netherlands against their lawful ruler in the 1580s, as she had the Scots in 1560 and after 1567. It also forced a radical re-assessment of royal authority by those who were threatened by it. Luther himself had clung desperately and unrealistically to absolute order in a world whose order he had helped to destroy: 'The princes of this world are Gods, the common people are Satan. . . . I would rather suffer a prince doing wrong than a people doing right'. Lutheran reliance on the backing of secular authority gave that claim some point. This was not the case with the Calvinists. Calvin himself tried to avoid the issue, but the political circumstances of Scotland in the 1560s, and France in the 1570s, forced others to be less reticent.

Both Buchanan and the Huguenot writers based their theory on the idea of an ancient constitution, under which the final authority was not that of the king. But there was a significant difference in their answers to the question of where ultimate responsibility did lie. Francois Hotman's *Franco-Gallia* argued for the estates. Beza's *Du Droit des Magistrats sur leur Subjets* gave this thesis a dangerous twist by emphasizing that the right of resistance lay with the magistrates, for this apparent moderation made it easier to accept. That idea was taken up in the most influential of all the Huguenot writings, *Vindiciae contra Tyrannos*, probably written by Philippe du Plessis-Mornay, and developed into a fully-articulated theory of contract between king and people, and between king, people, and God. The king's power was conditional on his acceptance by both God and man. The Huguenots were writing after the Massacre of St Bartholomew of 1572, when they could no longer maintain the idea that they were challenging not the monarchy but the 'malign influence' of the Guise family. There was no doubt that they were now resisting legitimate authority; but the change from fighting with swords to fighting with pens was a measure of their weakness. Buchanan was in a different case. His 'ancient constitution', and his examples of the deposition of the early mythical kings, like Mary, monsters of vice, was written to give intellectual justification to successful resistance. The rebellion of 1488 could be transformed into a great constitutional act. Even more important, so could the events of 1567.

Yet Buchanan's theory was not such a threat to royal authority as the Huguenot challenge. In a letter written to the English in 1571, and in his extensive statements of his theory, *De Iure Regni apud Scotos* (1579) and *Rerum Scoticarum Historia* (1582), Buchanan produced a different solution to the problems of where power lay. 'The people' was a convenient but meaningless concept; it was not with them, nor with estates and magistrates, but, much less formally, with the 'nobilitie of

Scotland [who] hes power to correct thair kingis . . . a part may do als wele as the haill'. Buchanan was one of the most influential scholars and theorists of his day, well known to the Huguenot writers, and used not only by the Scots but also by Leicester to justify his support of the Netherlands in the 1570s. Yet in the end all his theory came down to was a highly formalized and scholarly account, in beautiful Latin, of political reality in a society where, for acceptable political and social reasons, the aristocracy had considerable power.

James's theory of divine right, argued out in his academic treatise, *The Trew Law of Free Monarchies*, published in 1598, and in his practical manual of king-craft, *Basilikon Doron*, produced for his son Henry in 1599, was not an assertion of autocracy against a rising tide of 'democracy'. He was more fortunate than his mother in the period of his rule. The inevitable reaction to years of challenge to long-accepted beliefs and the collapse of traditional order in church and state was a search for the restoration of that order, by men like Montaigne, and Jean Bodin, who answered the Huguenots with the call for strong monarchical power as the best hope of restoring order. James was far too traditional in his approach to kingship in Scotland to see in strong monarchy a denial of the political and social importance of 'the people', or in practice the magnates; Buchanan's deposers of tyrants remained James's natural counsellors. His eyes were focussed on different problems. The threat posed by Buchanan and the Huguenots in the 1570s was overtaken in the 1580s by the claims of the counter-Reformation papacy, whose revival as a moral, political, and spiritual force was in no doubt; the right of popes to depose rulers, advocated most influentially by Cardinal Bellarmine, might be put into practice by assassins, and the theory was answered by James, among others, in his *Apology for the Oath of Allegiance*, written in 1607 as part of his policy towards English Catholics. Meanwhile in the late 1590s James was winning his battle against the Melvillians, who had taken over the old papal claims for the separation of spiritual and temporal powers. It was to them that the king's political theory was addressed. To Melville, who had told him that 'Thair is Christ Jesus the King, and his kingdome the Kirk, whase subject King James the Saxt is, and of whase kingdome nocht a king, nor a lord, nor a heid, bot a member', James could reply that 'Kings are called Gods by the propheticall King David, because they sit upon God his Throne in the earth'.

Hence the violence of language in the first part of *Basilikon Doron*, 'A King's Christian Duty towards God', when James unleashed his fury against the 'vaine Pharasaicall puritanes', is not matched in the second part, 'A King's Duty in his Office'. The threat to the state came from those who 'began to fantasy to themselves a democratic form of government . . . and yet will judge and give law to their king, but will be judged nor controlled by none'. From the leaders of the church, James turned to the leaders of secular society, certainly attacking, in brilliantly pithy prose, 'their feckless arrogant conceit of their greatness and power', but at the same time emphasizing the supreme importance to the state of the men who were 'your arms and executors of your laws'; and this awareness of their local rôle was matched by a desire to involve them in central government: 'delight to be served with men of the noblest blood that may be had . . . [for] ye shall oft find virtue follow noble races, as I have said before in speaking of the nobility'.

The political theorists had not undermined the ideological basis of James's kingship. Neither, in practice, had the civil war and dissensions of his minority weakened his political power. The very fact that he regarded the kirk as the greatest danger shows that he did not feel politically threatened. In domestic terms, his assumption of power was as welcome as that of his predecessors; indeed for a society that had endured 40 years of upheaval without a king, it was probably especially welcome, for it offered some hope that at last the troubled years were over, and established authority restored. The absence of major crises, other than the problems caused by Huntly in the late 1580s and 1590s, and the brief drama of the Gowrie conspiracy, suggests that James was right to feel confident.

It was generally a different world from the political upheavals and fears of a Catholic revival that had caused the chaos of the mid 1560s. Mary had been the weak link in a chain of Catholic powers who might threaten the Calvinist communities of Europe. James was the unchallenged Protestant king of an undoubted Protestant country. In European terms, he reverted to the attitudes of his predecessors. Like James III, the first king discussed in this book, James VI, the last, turned to Scandinavia for his wife; in 1589 he married Anne, daughter of Frederick II of Denmark. Economic and political ties with the Baltic, important in the late fifteenth century, had become increasingly valuable in the sixteenth, as trade-links were opened up and developed, and as the Reformation provided common interest for two northern countries. And James's enjoyment of debate, during his otherwise romantic visit to Denmark in pursuit of his bride, with Lutheran theologians, the astronomer Tycho Brahe, and

Hemmingius, with whom he discussed demonology, is a notable royal example of a cultural contact that had earlier led Scots academics to the university of Copenhagen, and Scots merchants to absorb and transmit to Scotland Lutheran influences.

Even the English succession — of which, again, he was confident — did not deflect his belief in himself as an independent monarch of European vision. The outlines of the policies he pursued after 1603 were already laid down in the 1590s. Kingship in England enhanced but did not create his rôle in Europe; he was already *Rex Pacificus*. Thus Elizabeth's frantic bullying failed to prevent his friendship with Spain; indeed, his reluctance to take strong action against the earl of Huntly and his associates in the north may have had something to do with their usefulness in keeping open a back-door to Spain. 'Methinks I do but dream' was Elizabeth's scathing comment, and James made no attempt to awaken her. At the same time he carefully cultivated the United Provinces; this was probably as much for economic as ideological reasons, but it gave the Dutch hope of a more committed protector than the cautious and non-Calvinist Elizabeth. In the event, the hope was never realized. In 1604 he ended the Anglo-Spanish war; as king of Scotland, he was not at war with Spain. He used his pen, not his power, to maintain his image as the great upholder of the Reformed church. Thus the prophecy of the Lion of the North who would destroy Babylon, which gave his English subjects and European Calvinists such hopes of him, was not fulfilled by James. He was too much a Scottish king, combining a personal distaste for war with the traditional Scottish insistence on being involved at the negotiating tables, but not the battle-grounds, of Europe.

His high opinion of his own kingship had its inevitable effect at home. He was a remarkable combination of the man of informality, and casual and friendly approach, admirable in a Scottish ruler, and the king whose lofty ideas subsumed and expressed the self-confidence of his kingdom. The very fact that this first British king since Alfred to write books about the nature of his office was doing so not to harangue his subjects but to contribute to the great European debate was itself a matter of pride. The same instinct for effective self-advertisement, and the same taste and skill, are seen in his coinage. Since James III's 'imperial' silver groat, Scottish coinage had had an impressive history; the work of Dr Ian Stewart has shown that, in contrast to English coins, Scottish issues showed complete awareness of the styles and idiom of Renaissance Europe, just as their architecture and music did. Dr Stewart has drawn particular attention to James's use of his coins to state his political concepts. Some emphasize 'divine right', with mottos such as *Florent sceptra püs regna his Iova dat numeratque* ('sceptres flourish with the pious, God gives them kingdoms and numbers them'); and the familiar tag *Nemo me impune lacessit*, which in James's reign had real political point, appears for the first time. Such coins were a retort to the first issue of the reign, the 'ryal' of 1567–71, which showed a naked sword with a hand pointing to it, and carried the motto *Pro me si mereor in me* ('for me, against me if I deserve it'): a good statement of Buchanan's theory.

He did, of course, have political problems, which arose from the rapidly changing nature of his government. He was himself highly conservative. He relied, or wanted to rely, primarily on his nobles; 'mean men' (middling men) were in his eyes those who should deal with routine administration, and financial affairs, which barely interested him. His appointments to offices reflect this; before 1584 only three earls had held the office of treasurer, and always during minorities, but, despite his comments on 'mean men', James appointed three earls to this financial position during his personal rule. Moreover, the nomination of councillors shows his anxiety to bring the magnates in; in 1593, for example, their reluctance to attend was countered by the demand that any noble should sit on the council 'quhen thai happin to be present', and in 1598 it was stated that there should be a council of 31, 'quharof sextene salbe erlis and lordis'. The 1593 arrangement named certain persons 'to be still resident, attending . . . his majestie'. The first three names on whom this burden fell were the duke of Lennox, the earl of Mar, and the earl of Montrose. By magnate standards, these three had a good record of attendance on the council; Mar's and Montrose's names appear on about 40 of the 160 sederunts between 1587 and 1592, while Lennox's is on 35 for the period 1589–92. Between March 1593 and March 1594 Lennox and Mar turned up on 15 of the 27 meetings, but in the following year they managed only 9 and 11 respectively out of 38; Montrose came only seven times in these two years. It was an uphill struggle for the king.

It is impossible to give any precise interpretation of his motives. Personal preference cannot be discounted. The notorious favourites of the English James I have their slightly more respectable parallels in the Scottish James VI; letters signed 'your Dad, James R', so familiar an aspect of James's relationship with Buckingham, first appear in the 1590s to the earl of Huntly. James's passion for hunting, already a comment in 1584, was likely to be shared with his aristocratic friends.

It may also have been a matter of political expediency. Involving the magnates in central government strengthened the links with localities and that would have made sense to any Scottish king. Certainly James saw in co-operation with Huntly and Argyll the best hope of controlling the Highlands, even though the council disagreed. But there is enough urgency about James's attitude to suggest something more. It is possible that the traditional James wanted a counterbalance to the new breed of lay lawyers and administrators who were transforming his government, both at the centre and in its relationship with the localities.

This was not, of course, a sudden process. Even after a century of increasing lay participation there were still many aspects of James's government that looked distinctly familiar. His famous letter, written at the height of a temper that made him almost incomprehensible, castigates a string of government officials, from the exchequer, household, session, and treasury, for failing to turn up at his summons: 'I have been Fryday, Setterday and this day waithing upon the directioun of my affairs, and nevir man comand'. That graphic description of the casual and personal nature of government suggests that Scottish government was only beginning to lumber belatedly towards some degree of bureaucratic order.

Yet in some ways the change, once firmly begun, happened fast. In 1621, for example, parliament issued a detailed list of fees due for the letters and writs issued by the various 'civil service' departments, thus formalizing what had presumably been a haphazard business hitherto. Moreover, although accident of survival may to an extent distort the picture, there does seem to have been a scramble for position at court on a new scale. The diplomat James Melville, himself as involved in the scramble as any, wrote savagely about the conflict between the king's council and the king's chamber, describing the council's attack on the evils done by those of the chamber who forced the king to subscribe 'sindre hurtfull signatours and commissions, and gat past for themselves and their frendis the best and maist proffitable casualties'. A slightly more objective voice is that of Richard Maitland of Lethington, himself a successful courtier and royal officer, and father of two of the leading politicians of the late sixteenth century. His poem on patronage at court laments the passing of the days when kinship counted; now, when he went to court, 'thinkand I had sum freindis thair/to help forwart my busines', he discovered that 'kyndnes helpis not ane hair', and only when he put gold and silver into his kinsman's hand did he call him 'kyndlie cousing', and promise speedy assistance. As yet, analysis of patronage and office-holding under James VI remains to be done. But these accounts, though obviously exaggerated, do give an impression that the court of James VI had much in common with those of Elizabeth and James I, and that in Scotland the level of pressure on the king was greater than ever before.

This pressure can be associated with two interrelated developments: the proliferation of offices, and the demand of the laity to hold them. The first was mainly the natural result of the growth of government business. The office of master of the requests, for example, came into existence in the early sixteenth-century. It was much more limited in scope than the English or French offices with the same title, for in Scotland there was no auditorial function; Scottish masters of requests were clerks of council and king's secretary. The office became firmly established only in the minority of James VI. Its development in the early seventeenth century shows the other force at work, the ambitions of the laity. The absence of the king after 1603 added the duty of transferring petitions between king and council, and, after 1617, the master of requests was included in the councillors who classified petitions, and he claimed the right to present them to parliament. This led to a row between the master, William Alexander, earl of Stirling, and the secretary, the earl of Melrose, lawyers who had risen to the peerage through royal service, 'new men' both. As typical members of Jacobean government, and in their struggle over their powers, they show what change had taken place: it was a new phenomenon when lesser laymen sought offices and squabbled over them.

The lawyers, most of whom pursued a dual career in law and government, were the people who above all created the new milieu of professionalism and definition. In their legal capacity, the senators of the college of justice mounted an impressive attack on the amateur lay standards of the past. In 1579 a complaint about the choice of 'young men without gravity knowledge or experience', who bought and sold justice, led to the insistence that the king's nominees be men who feared God, were of good literature and understanding of the laws, of good fame and of sufficient living; they were to be examined by the other judges and, if not qualified, rejected. The first nomination thereafter, John Lindsay of Menmuir, was made in 1581 in precisely these terms. In 1593 restrictions on the crown were taken a stage further; vacancies were not to be filled for 20 days, to allow time for proper selection, and to present pressure from courtiers, and then the king would prevent three candidates for selection by the court. When that happened in 1596, King James appeared in person, to deliver a typical harangue about his affection for the court and love of justice; the judges, having listened, took the precaution of having a secret ballot. What was demanded of would-be judges was no easy test. In 1605 it was agreed that judges would be chosen from the six most learned advocates, the principal clerks of session, lords of parliament and their sons, and knights worth £2,000 per annum. They were required to discourse in Latin on a legal text, and to hear an action, describe the issues involved, and give an opinion. Their insistence on wealth was based, reasonably enough, on the desire to have judges who would be less tempted to take bribes, as the 1579 act had said. But that insistence, the demand for legal training, and the closing of ranks after 1605, had another and very far-reaching social effect: it established an exclusive, wealthy, and very powerful professional caste within Edinburgh.

They were of course dealing with people who saw no reason to change their own approach to justice. Helping one's kinsman, in a court action, as much as in the private settlements of the localities, was an acceptable and indeed expected course. The letters of a late-sixteenth-century senator of the college of justice, Patrick Waus of Barnbarroch, show very clearly what pressures the judges were under; he was the recipient of a number of letters from lords supporting their kinsmen, begging him to pursue the course of true justice, and assuring him that such a course would inevitably lead him to find in favour of the kinsman. It was a blatant attempt to use personal connexion, in a society where personal connexion offered most men their best hope of security. It looks sinister only to a society where personal connexion is no longer so crucial. The objection, in so far as it existed at the time, was not that it was wrong, so much as that it might undercut the business of the professional lawyer — and his fee. Hence the insistence, in an act of 1555, that although friends might accompany men to court, advocates must also be present. Hence also the fact that Waus left £8,000 on his death in 1597.

Though lawyers might find traditional expressions of kinship frustrating and irritating, it is quite clear, at the same time, that they never forsook the ideal. Instead, they transferred it into their own world, and established legal kindreds, dynasties, within the new professional élite at Edinburgh. The clerical dynasties, Drummond's 'church-race', is paralleled by the foundation of legal families in Edinburgh by the end of the sixteenth century, Hays, Colvilles, Kers, Hamiltons. The most famous of James's government officials, Thomas

Hamilton, Lord Binning, later earl of Melrose and finally earl of Haddington, was the descendant of a cadet branch of the Hamiltons of Innerwick, who four generations earlier had moved into Edinburgh and gone in for law. Hamilton's father and two of his brothers became lords of council and session. Hamilton himself, the success-story of the family, made his mark in government in the 1590s. He was one of the Octavians — the small group appointed in 1595 to manage James's financial affairs — and became lord advocate, president of the court of session, and, as secretary, James's right-hand man in Scotland during the last decade of the king's life. It is a curious comment on the achievements of these early lawyers that the connexion of kin was to survive into modern times as a more relevant consideration within the legal families of Edinburgh than in its original home in the localities.

It is difficult to attribute the profound change in late-sixteenth-century government, the final take-over from clerics by educated laymen drawn from the gentry and burgesses, to James's policy, or even particularly his inclinations. The origins of the change go back into the fifteenth century; the emergence of men like William Maitland of Lethington, Sir James Melville of Halhill, the great lawyer Balfour of Pittendreich, and George Buchanan, keeper of the Privy Seal as well as king's tutor, poet, and European scholar, who were all prominent in the 1560s, show that it was under way long before James VI took over government. James's attitude has a certain ambivalence. Temperamentally, he was a man who saw kingship in its highly academic and its highly personal guise. He understood very well the art of managing men, and gave a lot of time to it. As he took a personal part in the assembly of the kirk, so he did also in the secular institutions of government, attending council and parliament regularly. But he did not share the interests of his administrators in the sheer slog of government. He needed civil servants, as any king did, but he was no Philip II or Elizabeth. He may have reacted against the increasing professionalism of his 'new men' in Scotland, just as in England he was to make full use of Robert Cecil's talents without ever having affection for him. He had a distaste for being managed. The dominant politician and government servant of the first decade of his personal rule was John Maitland of Thirlestane, younger brother of Lething-ton, and secretary and chancellor. He probably owed his fall from favour to the fact that he had managed too well. He had built up considerable personal power at the cost of alienating individual magnates, and he had a more favourable view of the Presbyterians than the king. James's reaction to the chancellor who had been the guiding hand of his government was to comment in grim jest after his death that 'he would no more use chancellor or other great men [in his financial affairs] but such as he might convict and were hangable', and to keep the office vacant for four years until 1599, when he appointed the earl of Montrose.

A particular example of the different approach of king and lawyer-administrators is seen in the act about feuding of 1598. This was the first attempt to break down the system of private settlement and arbitration. But of the three kinds of conflict covered by the word feud in sixteenth-century Scotland, civil dispute, murder on one side, and murder on both, only the second was taken out of the hands of local lords and brought firmly under the control of the lawyers. For the other two, the king added his weight to the actions of friends and kinsmen of the parties at feud to bring about a settlement. Again, it was the traditional order, for which James stood, against the new order of the lawyers. The point is reinforced by the speed with which James's council, dominated by these 'new men', tightened up and extended legislation against feud after the king's departure to England.

That example also shows how important it was for the king to be personally present. Despite James's famous boast to the English parliament in 1607 about ruling Scotland with a pen, he actually ruled Scotland much more successfully before 1603 than afterwards. The royal presence was critically important in parliament. Like his predecessors, James wanted an authoritative parliament. One way of achieving this was to make it look impressive. In 1587 penalties were laid down not only for absentee members, but also for absentee heralds, macers, and trumpeters; at the same time it was agreed that 'every estait sal have thair severall apparrell in semelie fassioun conforme to the patroun thairof quhilk the kingis Majestie sall caus mak'. The king's majesty's ideas and sense of colour led to a dazzling 'Riding of Parliament' in 1606, when the citizens were treated to the sight of crimson and scarlet silks, and velvet, ermine, and furs, as the estates of this 'Red Parliament' processed solemnly through the streets of Edinburgh into the parliament house.

But an authoritative parliament could, in the late sixteenth century, be a dangerous one. If no one wanted to repeat the dramatic events of 1560, when a parliament had acted without royal authority and done so successfully, nevertheless the late-sixteenth-century parliament had that precedent behind it, and a new rôle as one of the ideological battlegrounds of the state. Certainly it asserted its authority. It was in this period, even before it had become clear that taxation was now to be regular, that the estates began to object to attempts by the government, under both regent Morton and James VI, to use conventions that were little more than privy councils to raise money. In 1583 a small convention at which only one burgess was present did vote the king money for his immediate needs, but insisted that his larger demands be referred to a larger convention or a parliament; and in 1586 another small convention turned down his request for money for the expenses of pleading Mary's cause.

The demand for proper representation can hardly be separated from the new interest of the lairds and burgesses. The burgesses' position in parliament was of course recognized. That of the lesser barons and lairds was much more anomalous after the failure of James I's shire election act of 1428. It became a major issue with the dramatic appearance of over 100 lairds in the Reformation parliament, illogically demanding a place in terms of the 1428 act. Attendance thereafter fluctuated, but the threat of such an influx was always present. This situation was resolved in 1587, when in response to the petition presented to parliament in 1585, the 1428 act was revived, and provision made for the annual election of two representatives from each shire (apart from Kinross and Clackmannan, which had one each). Those who could vote and were elegible for election were freeholders who held land of the crown worth 40s. of auld extent; the fact that this qualification excluded the feuars, who had to wait for almost another century before getting the vote in 1661, may indicate social tension between established landed families and the new group of proprietors, many of whom had risen in the world because of transferring their tacks and rentals to hereditary feus. Certainly the desire for official recognition in parliament, even if only through representatives, seems to have come from the lesser barons, who were apparently responsible for the 1585 petition. It is unlikely that it was the king who sought to bring them in, to provide himself with support against the magnates. James's attitude to the magnates was rather to object to their non-attendance and to put pressure on them to turn up. His interest in the 1587 act was more probably the need to control and harness the voice of the lesser barons and lairds; indeed, he made them pay £40,000 for the privilege of shire elections, which surely shows where enthusiasm for the act really lay.

Where the king did take a lead was in the strenuous attempts of the 1580s and 1590s to control parliamentary business. This was done in two ways. When Scottish parliaments met, they habitually elected a committee, the lords of the articles, drawn from each of the estates,

which deliberated over the details of legislation before it was passed b
the full parliament. Control of that committee was crucial, and Jame
sought to get it by bringing in the officers of state as non-electe
members. It was a new device, and one that was resented; in 1617, th
king was forced to agree that there would never be more than eigh
officers of state on the articles. The other method was to censor th
business that came before parliament. This was done by the simple
means of insisting, in 1594, that petitions for that parliament must b
given to the clerk register within three days, and that for the future
four from each estate should meet 20 days before each parliament to
receive petitions and articles and sift out frivolous material. All
petitions were to be signed, and those regarded as acceptable were to
be printed in a book and put before the lords of the articles. The only
exception to this rule was the king, who could raise any matter at any
time. Control of parliament by the crown was not, of course, new. But
James raised it to a new level, and did so undoubtedly because of the
threat from the kirk which might well be reinforced by the unwelcome
appearance of a vocal group of lairds, the section of society from which
the kirk drew its greatest support. It is small wonder that James
demanded tighter control, and demanded also the restoration of a
clerical estate which he could influence, and which he achieved up to a
point in 1600 with the creation of three parliamentary bishops. As
long as he was in Scotland, his control was, except in 1592, reasonably
successful. After 1603, he still maintained it, but with considerable
effort, and sometimes only by a hair's-breadth, as the vote against the
Five Articles of Perth made clear in 1621.

James VI was an undoubted success as king of Scotland. His high
opinion of himself had sufficient grounds for it to be accepted by
others. His independent foreign policy, and in particular his refusal
to be brow-beaten by Elizabeth, combined with his position as her
most likely heir, gave him considerable prestige. He was personally
popular, as the description of him by the English diplomat Henry
Wotton shows. He was intelligent and likeable, easy-going but capable
of sudden and ruthless action when necessary; he trod on few toes, save
those of the kirk. He offered Scotland stability because he was the first
adult king since James V's death in 1542, and because he was the first
king since James III to have an heir growing up in his own lifetime, and
also a second surviving son, for Henry was born in 1594 and Charles in
1600.

Inasmuch as professionalism and efficiency look more impressive
than amateurism and casualness, his government can also be termed a

success. The period of transition from cleric to layman was over. The ultimate expectations of the 'new men' were the equivalent of those of the king's former ecclesiastical servants; where churchmen had looked for bishoprics, the laity looked for earldoms, and many got them, in the flood of creations from 1600 onwards. In the field of civil law, they achieved a new degree of centralization, although criminal law still remained a local matter; the attraction, even the mystique, of paying for professional expertise offered in technical language did increasingly outweigh the amateur, commonsense justice offered in the local courts. Desire for stability made the government of James VI attractive. Yet it was not wholly successful. It never forged the close and effective bonds between centre and locality that existed through the courts of the kirk. But it impinged more directly than before because it introduced regular taxation. People in the localities were suddenly jolted out of their relative isolation.

10

The Local Community Disturbed

In 1586, and again in 1599, the kin-groups of which Sir John Murray of Tullibardine was the head came together and drew up bonds in which they accepted Sir John as arbiter in all their disputes, supported by the counsel of certain named kinsmen. A similar agreement was drawn up by Patrick Lord Drummond and his kin in 1588. In the same period, the sensational murder of the earl of Moray in 1592 was the climax of several years of feud between Huntly and Moray in the north, when Moray challenged Huntly's pre-eminent power. Several families, notably the Macintoshes of Dunnachton and also the Grants of Freuchy, whose ancestors had once been dependents of an earlier earl of Moray, seized their chance to reject Huntly's lordship, which they resented. It was only when they were attracted back into Huntly's service that the stalemate between the two earls was broken, and Huntly's victory assured; but it had been at the cost of several years of intermittent feuding which disturbed the north-east, and a murder at the end which made the affair a national drama. Both these things, the pacific bonds and the bloody feud, make it seem that nothing had changed.

It had; and the change can be seen even in these events. The very fact that the Murray and Drummond kindreds made bonds at all suggests a new degree of formality which reflected that of the central courts, and also indicates that some men felt the need to give greater weight to traditional concepts by committing to writing what had hitherto been unwritten. There is also a strong possibility that the 'local' feud of Huntly and Moray was from the beginning very much more, for Maitland of Thirlstane seems to have had a part in inciting Moray to challenge Huntly, and thus destroy the long-established balance of power in the north. The king's refusal to take action against Huntly after the murder shows again how conservative he was; his inactivity was not just because of his personal affection for Huntly, but also because he understood the value of the traditional rôle of the magnates. People like Maitland naturally saw it differently; the new concept of what government was about depended on more involvement in the localities.

The new pressure put on the localities looked arbitrary and unnecessary. Scotland was still not at war, and there was no obvious reason at home to justify taxation. Yet regular taxation began in 1581, and thereafter was levied in increasing quantities every few years. The first four levies were relatively small, but the tax of £100,000 imposed in 1588 for the king's marriage shifted the whole business on to a new scale, and set a pattern for the future. In 1566 James's birth cost the country £12,000. In 1594 the approaching birth of the queen's first child was held to justify a tax of £100,000, an increase that was more than the rate of inflation. The demand in 1612 for a tax of £240,000 finally transformed resentment into opposition; Michael Lord Burleigh claimed that the king had intended to ask for no more than £10,000, and was sacked from the council for his temerity. Nine years later James went further and introduced a new form of taxation, on annualrents, whereby he levied 5 per cent on all interest on loans, this time hitting the burgesses. This tax was forced through a hostile parliament, but that was only the first hurdle. Whereas collection of previous taxes seems to have been reasonably efficient, the 1621 tax was still being collected in the early 1630s. It was not a happy precedent for Charles I's efforts to continue the tax on annualrents, and indeed raise the rate. Reaction to taxation can be traced back to 1587, when a memorandum presented to the estates expressed the fear that James would tax 'sa oft as he pleases upon collorit causes'; James's extravagance and endless lack of money were all too well known. Suspicion of the government's motives even led to the tragic refusal of the shires around Edinburgh to co-operate in the council's genuine attempt to organize poor relief in the terrible famine year of 1623. For perhaps the first time the government might have been able to do something about famine by breaking down local barriers. It failed. When the nobles and gentry of East Lothian met to consider the council's proposals, they rejected them because the council's idea of assessment was 'odious' and 'smellis of ane taxation.'

The second area of trouble was legal. The justice of the feud was undermined by Edinburgh lawyers, at first unwittingly and then deliberately. The principles of compensation had been taken over into the courts, and already in the early sixteenth century judges were beginning to take on the mantle of the head of kin or lord by assessing compensation themselves. In doing so, as Balfour of Pittendreich's account of 'assythment' (compensation) in his *Practicks* makes clear, they were in no sense attacking the methods successfully used in private settlements, but they were formalizing them and increasingly associating them with the justice of the courts. In the late sixteenth century the new interest in bureaucratic efficiency produced legislation insisting that royal remissions would be given only when the treasurer had seen and registered letters of slains from the injured kin. This was reasonable enough, but it altered the rôle of the government from one of co-operation with a kind of justice, which depended on flexibility and lack of professionalism, to one of direction and intervention. Even more damaging was the attitude of the lawyers reflected in the act of 1598, which asserted their right to replace the justice of the feud in cases of single murder. None of these things, nor the attack on the feud by the kirk, had an immediate effect; not until the convenanters were firmly in control, with ·Johnston of Warriston symbolizing in his person the combination of legal and clerical attitudes, did the private settlement cease to be a potent force for restoring order. But the seeds of decline were sown in the late sixteenth century.

At the same time, beginning in a small way in 1581, the government tried to introduce new commissions to deal with petty crimes, social abuses such as slaughter of fish and mixing of wines, and also price-fixing in time of dearth. This was extended in 1587 to commissions that would draw up indictments, and either bring criminals before the justice-ayres or, in lesser cases, try them themselves in courts held four times a year in the principal burghs. Occasional references to lairds becoming king's commissioners, even in 1586 and certainly in 1587–8, suggest that some attempt was made to implement the idea, but it was clearly difficult to find people to do the work; little came of it, although in 1593 commissioners were named as among those with a local responsibility for putting the acts on vagrancy into effect.

The idea was revived in 1609, and followed up in 1610 with a comprehensive scheme for commissioners from each shire, drawn from magnates, lairds, provosts, and bailies. The council clearly intended to keep shire commissioners closely in touch with the centre; every local list included the chancellor, the treasurer, privy councillors, and senators of the college of justice, along with the archbishops of St Andrews and Glasgow, who divided the country between them, and some of the greatest magnates, Montrose, Lennox, and Hamilton, who were involved in several shires. Finally, in 1617 there was a massive act setting out in great detail the powers of the justice, and widening them to bring them into line with the English model. But this was a violent intrusion of a foreign idea on to local communities with no tradition of such an office. It is not, therefore, surprising that despite the council's efforts, less than a quarter of the Scottish shires had justices of the peace at James's death. Those who were appointed spent their time arguing over their jurisdictions, using their offices to settle old scores, or being made fools of. The burghs were particularly touchy about the shire J.P.s, and in 1612 the council had to set up a commission to deal with the problem and try to force co-operation. From June 1612 to December 1613 the council was burdened by the quarrel of two Perthshire lairds, Patrick Butter of Gormack, J.P., and Patrick Blair of Ardblair; what was clearly a local and minor feud was complicated by Butter's ability to summon Blair for contempt of the justice's court, and for carrying firearms, to which Blair not unreasonably replied that Butter was doing the same thing. The council upheld the J.P. It can hardly have improved local relationships, and was certainly more provocative than a private settlement by a local lord would have been. The whole problem is summed up in the row in council in 1611 between Thomas Hamilton and George Gladstanes, archbishop of St Andrews, who burst out in a fury 'that the institution of the Commissioners of the peace wes verie recent, without any warrand of law, and it wes no reasoun that that Commissioun as ane sone sould overschaddow and obscure all the uther jurisdictions of the kingdome, and that the realme had had many hundreth yeires bene weill governed withowt Justices of the Peace'. This spokesman for tradition was not a leader of any local community. He was as much a royal servant, a 'new man' as Hamilton. But he seems to have been more aware than the centralizing missionary lawyers of the council that traditional attitudes were not easily broken down.

Government efforts to find new solutions to areas that were increasingly regarded as 'old' problems had some success in the borders. What made the crucial difference, however, was the co-operation of the English and Scottish governments, even before 1603; a joint commission was set up in 1597 as a result of the dramatic rescue from Carlisle castle of 'Kinmont Willie', hero of one of the great ballads, and border thug in the eyes of both governments. After 1603 the borders found themselves policed by a force led by Sir William Cranstoun; the very real problem of border violence was brought under some control.

The highland problem was much less soluble. The government's belief in the highlands as the 'headache' area, which can be traced back for at least two centuries, had now hardened to the point where lack of interest and understanding were almost absolute. The effect of the new governmental approach on this area was much more destructive than on the borders. The original solution put forward for both highlands and borders was the 'general band', by which landlords were given formal responsibility, under heavy financial cautions, for their dependents and tenants; it did have the merit of invoking the traditional and acceptable principles of personal kinship. But in *Basilikon Doron* James gave the highlands no more than a brief reference which showed only the extent of his indifference. Because the king was in general terms traditional enough to maintain the authority of the magnates in the localities, he was more amenable than his council, particularly after 1603, to the idea that when a clan was particularly troublesome, like the MacGregors, the most effective way of dealing with them was to invoke the earl of Argyll. But both he and his government seemed to assume that the MacGregors were offensive only in the government's eyes, and failed to appreciate that their neighbours in the highlands might also find them intolerable; it was a particular comment on the extent to which the government now assumed that the highlands were wholly lawless, and that the whole burden of maintaining any degree of order lay with it. This attitude was unpleasantly tinged with the 'colonialist' assumption of the need to impose civilization on the uncivilized.

Such an attitude underlay the other major efforts of James and his government to deal with the highlands. The first, which was closely paralleled in James's Plantation of Ulster, involved sending men from the lowlands to settle in the highlands in order to introduce an acceptable level of order and culture; hence the 'gentlemen adventurers of Fife' went to Lewis, in 1602 and again in 1605/6, to meet with at best strong resistance and at worst murder. The second was formulated by the Statutes of Iona of 1609, which tried to insist that highland chiefs should come to the lowlands at regular stated intervals, and (in the re-issue of 1616) learn English as a qualification for inheritance. This was the age when the bloodfeud was visibly beginning to be undermined as an effective system of justice in the lowlands, while in the highlands it was a subject of pride in the achievements of the kin. The idea of division was further heightened by the failure of the kirk to establish itself in the highland area, despite the efforts of the bishops of the Isles, John Carswell and Andrew Knox. Yet the highlands were not an isolated society; they were a very proud one, with an awareness of their place in the history of their country, not least the fact that it was Dalriada, the Gaelic west, that had given Scotland her kings, and indeed the well-thumbed king-lists which now provided the basis of lowland political theory. Isolation was forced upon them by the ferocious language and policies of the lowland government, increasingly supported by the lowland people. As the prospect and then the reality of the English succession affected him, the lowlander found his contact with the different culture of the west an increasing embarrassment. Thus the gulf widened, to the detriment of both lowland and highland society.

The impact in the lowlands of the new kirk with its increasingly strong hierarchy of church courts, in contrast with the relative failure of the government to introduce a secular parallel, linking the wide judicial powers of the council to new local courts, presents something of a paradox. Expectations seem to have differed. The church was responsible for men's souls. It offered certainty to those who would accept it – and clearly there were many – after generations of doubt; it behaved as a church was expected to behave, after generations of inadequacy among the parish clergy. But in secular life there were no such obvious problems. On the whole, breakdown of order had been more quickly and efficiently coped with by local men than by the government in Edinburgh. The literate gentry who moved into Edinburgh and began to make money in government and the law were, in a way that is impossible to define precisely, opening up a gulf between themselves and the local community from which they had originally sprung, and could be seen as betraying the ethos of that community as they rejected its traditional ways of doing things and sought to impose their new ideas. The gulf must have been offensive at least to some who were not interested in changing their rôle in life but were certainly not prepared to be seen as backwoodsmen. The Campbells of Glenorchy strenuously asserted that they were more than just local lairds with their chapel organs and formal gardens at Finlarig and Balloch, their mid-seventeenth-century collection of royal and family portraits, some at least painted by the first great Scottish portrait painter, George Jamieson, their foreign travel, their rearing of horses; and they were a crucial link between centre and locality in the government's onslaught on the clan Macgregor. How could men like these regard themselves as other than the cultured and successful backbone of Scottish society, with far more relevance to the community than the Edinburgh lawyer-administrators? Indifference rather than direct opposition seem mainly to have characterized the reaction of those who maintained the old order. It did not make for government success.

The government's problems went far beyond the imposition of its ideas and taxes on reluctant localities. The late sixteenth century was a period of considerable and concentrated economic distress, which is of course a major factor in government unpopularity, particularly governments that impinge directly — as the Scottish government was beginning to do — on the lives of those who suffer. It could be blamed for adding to distress, perhaps even seen to cause it, with its savage taxation and its brutal depreciation of the currency. In 1582 a pound of silver produced 640 shillings; in 1601, 960. The exchange rate with England stood at £6 Scots to £1 sterling in 1565; by 1601 it had dropped to £12. The government made £100,000 out of depreciation between 1583 and 1596; recalling old money and reissuing new was profitable for it and inflationary for everyone else. The historian and minister David Calderwood described it as sucking the blood of the poor.

The problems of the late sixteenth century, as population grew and costs soared, were in fact completely outwith the control of a government that had neither the policies nor the means to cope. Population is impossible to assess. Informed guesses put it at somewhere around, or just under, one million. In comparative terms, that number appears favourable. As Dr Ian Whyte's recent study of seventeenth-century agriculture has shown, it meant a density of 11 people per square kilometre compared to 44 in Italy, 34 in France, 36–40 in England, 37 in the Low Countries and 27 in Ireland, and less sparse only than Norway. But whether these figures mean that the Scottish population was not pressing heavily on resources is doubtful. Contemporaries were impressed not with absolute numbers, but with the rise: they did not quantify it, but did comment on it. Sir Thomas Craig of Riccarton even explained it: 'our women do not indulge themselves with wine, exotic foodstuffs and spices from distant lands, so harmful to the womb, hence the more readily do they conceive'.

One of the best and simplest comments on the horrors of inflation comes from the pen of Richard Maitland of Lethington:

> Now we have mair It is weill kend
> nor our foirbearis had to spend
> bot far less at the yeiris end
> and never hes ane mirrie day

Wages certainly rose rapidly, by four or five times between 1560 and 1600; the mason's 15s. in 1560 was 60s. in 1600, and the barrowman's 5s. went up to 25s. But this was of little comfort when prices rose faster. The 2d. loaf of bread of the first half of the sixteenth century cost 6d. between 1560 and 1580, and 12d. between 1580 and 1600; a boll of one of the main food crops, oats (a boll being a unit that fluctuated regionally but was probably on average *c*. 140 lb.) rose from 10s. before 1560 to 65s. at the end of the century. Soaring prices, more people, bad harvests, the need to import grain regularly from the Baltic, Scotland's 'emergency granary', made the second half of the sixteenth century, and particularly the last decade, something of a nightmare. Between 1550 and 1600 there are 24 years of scarcity (local or national) mentioned in the sources, when people starved to death. They also died of plague, especially during the two concentrated outbreaks of 1584–8 and 1597–1609.

Despite these checks on population growth, the overall rise combined with recurrent famines intensified the problem of vagrancy; indeed the legislation of 1574, 1579, and 1592, and the council's references to vagrants and paupers give the impression that Scotland was now overrun by rootless bands, thieves and beggars, a constant threat to ordered life. The new kirk saw poor relief as one of its most basic obligations in its creation of a godly society. The government latched itself on to the organization of the kirk, using the parish as the basic unit for poor relief, and indeed for the J.P.s who had a duty to deal with vagrants. Its Poor Law of 1574 was modelled on that passed in England in 1572. It laid down savage penalties for able-bodied masterful beggars. Only 'cruikit folk seik impotent folk and waik folk' could beg. The list of those who could not is massive, including jugglers, wandering minstrels, and 'taill tellaris', those who claimed skill in palmistry and 'utheris abused sciences', and even 'all vagaboundis scollaris of the universiteis of sanctandrois glasgow and abirdene not licencit be the rector and Dene of facultie . . . to aske about almous'. An attempt was made to create an effective system for identifying and helping those genuinely in need, the poor, the sick, the old. Each parish was to draw up a list, and its inhabitants were to be assessed for poor relief by deacons and elders or some other overseer. But harsh treatment even of those people was inherent in the insistence that poor relief be given only to those who belonged to the parish. Those who did not would be given a testimonial and sent 'fra parochyn to parochyn quhill they be at the plaice quhair thay wer borne or had thair maist commoun resort and residence during the last sevin yeris'.

And recognition that this act would itself increase the number of vagrants produced the final provision that since the stocks and prisons would now be more in use, some of the money collected for the genuine poor would be diverted for the maintenance of the prisoners. Its acknowledgement that the wandering poor are a 'sklander to a cristiane commoun welth that has ressavit the evangell' does not make it other than a grim law. It differs significantly from the English act in making no attempt to provide work for able-bodied beggars. Indeed, its refusal even to consider that 'able-bodied beggars' might sweeten life indicates that here at least church and state were at one, reflecting the condemnatory face of Calvinism.

This age of economic distress was also the age of the first great persecution of witches. References to witchcraft before the Reformation are tantalizingly few. It is not altogether clear why in 1563 witchcraft was included among the business of the pre-Reformation courts, which now had to be subsumed into the jurisdiction of either the state or the new kirk; when the assembly petitioned the council to deal with the problem, it did not include witchcraft as one of these matters. Dr Kirsty Larner, whose knowledge of Scottish witchcraft is unrivalled, has argued from this that the church's rôle in creating a witch-panic was less than that of King James, whose visit to Denmark in pursuit of his bride in 1589 introduced him to a country already indulging in witch-hunts, and to men who were thoroughly familiar with full-blown continental demonology. It is perhaps unlikely that James was entirely unaware of Bodin and other continental writers on witchcraft before 1589, but certainly he seems to have taken little interest until a group of witches at North Berwick, with whom his bête-noire Bothwell was supposedly associated, paid him the compliment of claiming to raise storms to destroy him at the command of their master, Satan, who regarded him as 'the greatest enemie hee hath in the world'. The North Berwick trials were a marked turning-point in Scottish witch trials, because they introduced the demonic pact for the first time, and it is indeed the case that the persecution lasted almost exactly as long as James's interest: that is, until 1597, the year when he both encouraged it by writing the *Daemonologie*, his attack on the sceptics Reginald Scot and Johann Weyer, and discouraged it by revoking the standing commissions on witchcraft. Possibly the *Daemonologie* was the intellectual signing-off by a king who was beginning to have doubts; it completely accepts the demonic pact, but it shows hints of unease about accusations of witchcraft in practice.

The kirk's interest, however, also seems to have been strong. Knox himself preached against a witch at St Andrews, who was 'set upe at a pillar before him', prolonging her suffering before she was eventually executed. And Erskine of Dun's witch-hunt throughout Angus and the Mearns in 1568−9 was no small matter, involving at least 40 accusations. The kirk had a considerable number of obsessions; the assembly continually badgered the state to take action on a range of matters that undermined the Christian community, from swearing and gluttony to incest, adultery, and murder. The problem of witchcraft was exactly the same as the problem of other crimes and vices; until the state acted, there was little the kirk could do. Certainly it howled loudly in 1598 when the secular magistracy lost its zeal for hunting out witches, just as the ministers of Holland were to do rather later. Even without the demonic pact in its full form, the Protestant church set its face firmly against the possibility of benign magic, insisting that all supernatural manifestations were by definition of the devil. The almost complete absence of persecution in the highlands, where the church's grip was weak, further suggests that the rôle of the kirk was a crucial factor.

There is no simple explanation for witch-persecution. The Reformation and Protestant theology are not enough, for it is equally a feature of Catholic countries. Essentially, this nightmare fantasy seems to be the kind of reaction of any disturbed society seeking stability, whether religious, economic, or political, and thus rending the unorthodox, be they witches, Jews, or heretics. Moreover, it was precisely in this decade of economic trouble that the resentments identified as underlying accusations of witchcraft − the refusal to help a neighbour, the beginnings of poor-relief which undermined the obligation to give personal help, the greater inability to help because of bad harvests and rising prices − existed in Scotland. Reaction to economic instability is perhaps the one factor that may be ascribed to all the periods of witch-hunts, the 1590s, the 1620s−30s, and the 1640s. In the 1590s it combined with the attitude of the kirk, and was sparked off by the attitude of the king and the lawyers who tried the cases. To the modern observer, it presents the paradox of a society, and indeed a king, priding themselves on their knowledge, their intellectual rationalism compared to the past, and yet showing intense and hideous obsession with superstition. But it is perhaps precisely their enthusiasm for the educated approach, the search for certainty in religion, and the dark things done in its name, that produced the demonic pact where before there had been only magic, both black and white. It was not a failure of intellect that made James VI claim, in

Basilikon Doron, that the death of James V's sons in infancy, leaving 'a double curse behinde him to the land, both a Woman of sexe and a new borne babe of aige to reigne over them', was God's punishment on a king of immoral life. It was, rather, an intellectual approach lacking technical information.

Amidst the general gloom of a society bedevilled by its own imaginings, and by the very real problems of price-rise and famine, two groups stand out as exempt from the sufferings. On the land, there were some with plenty to eat, and enough money to build and adorn their houses. The payment of rents in kind might make life even harder for the tenant, but it did not significantly cut the standard of living of the landlord. The comments of the English water-poet, John Taylor, who came to Scotland in 1618, suggest a pattern of life that may have meant that even in the bad years before 1600 the gentry were relatively cushioned against dearth; one such he describes as a man who will:

> weare no other shirts but of the flax that growes on his owne ground and of his wives, daughters or servants spinning; that hath his stockings, hose and jerkin of the wool of his owne sheepes backes; that never (by the pride of his apparrell) caused mercer draper, silkeman, embroyderer or haberdasher to breake and turn bankrupt; and yet this plaine homespunne fellow keepes and maintaines thirty, forty, fifty servants or perhaps more, every day releeving three or four score poore people at his gate; and besides all this can give noble entertainment for four or five dayes together, to five or six Earles and Lordes, besides Knights, Gentlemen and their followers, if they be three or four hundred men and horse of them; where they shall not only feede but feast, and not feast but banket. . . . Many of those worthy housekeepers there are in Scotland, among some of whom I was entertained; from whence I did truely gather these aforesaid observations.

And even before the levelling-off of the price-rise, shortage is hardly suggested by the household account of Campbell of Glenorchy in 1590, which lists 90 beeves, 20 swine, 200 sheep, 424 salmon, 15,000 herring, 30 dozen hand fish, 325 stones of cheese and butter, wheaten bread — and 1 sugar loaf and a small amount of spices and sweetmeats. The large household which reflected status was still eminently possible in Scotland in the 1590s.

But it was more than that. Whether the greater availability of money consequent upon rapid depreciation was the significant factor is only a guess. But certainly money was now spent on a great deal of building of very high quality, reflecting a desire to increase comfort and cut a dash. In Kirkwall (Orkney) the earl's palace stands as a lovely monument to an attitude to building that had nothing to do with defence, and everything to do with taste and gracious living. Further south, it is impossible to ignore George marquis of Huntly, who carved his name in vast letters along the fine series of oriel windows he added to his castle at Huntly, and put above his door not just his coat-of-arms, which would have been ordinary enough, but those of king and pope, and above them the symbols of the passion and the statue of St Michael, thus providing himself with an entrance of unrivalled dramatic impact. Most remarkable of all is the Italianate façade incorporated by Francis earl of Bothwell into the heavy fourteenth-century castle of Crichton; this delightful architectural extravaganza, the final addition to a basically plain and massive keep, already made more civilized by the impressive mid-fifteenth-century hall built by William Lord Crichton, is the great visual expression of the aristocracy's image of itself as men of taste, travel, and culture. This was an age when what might almost be regarded as the Grand Tour began, so much so that in 1579 the government was expressing concern about the dangers of corruption in religion for the youth of the realm passing 'beyond sey'. The letter of John earl of Gowrie, written in a fine Italic hand from Rome during his holiday abroad in the 1590s, and containing dashes of Latin and Greek, must have reassured them; it contained a lengthy and bitter account of the burning of a man of true faith by the Roman heretics. On the whole, travel to France and Spain did not affect the religion of the nobility; it did very much affect their architecture. And the same interest in building is seen among the lairds, this time with the concentration on developing the native style, the tower-house. Basic and simple designs were transformed into L-shapes and Z-shapes, or incorporated into new buildings; and this is the great age of the sometimes magnificent painted ceilings which adorned many houses. In the north-east, the Bell family of masons were probably responsible for a number of impressive lairds' houses, notably Crathes, Midmar, and Castle Fraser, which testify to pride of ownership and prosperity. Their greatest achievement is the supreme example of what a Scottish tower-house could be: the perfectly proportioned, beautifully embellished, almost fairytale castle of Craigievar in

Aberdeenshire, built in the early years of the seventeenth century.

That pinpoints the extent to which Scottish society and economy were in a state of transition. The leaders of rural society gained from food renders which enabled them to lord it over large households, and thus emphasize their pre-eminence, and there was therefore little incentive for them to depart from conservative attitudes. The advantages of that approach, which was served by a primarily agricultural and pastoral economy, is seen in greatest detail in Scotland precisely at the time when that attitude was breaking down. Rents in kind were no longer able to sustain the expectations of aristocracy and gentry; the developing money economy created a strong counter-force. Luxury goods, the services of masons, had to be paid for in cash.

Within the towns, and especially within the capital, the 'vigour and vitality' contrasted sharply with the countryside. Sir Thomas Craig castigated his fellow-countrymen as men who 'choose to live in idleness, nay even in poverty, than to apply themselves to any gainful trades; because by dealing in them they falsely reckon the honour of their birth to be impaired and stained'. But there were some who did not worry about the honour of their birth, or else used trade to increase their honour. The Edinburgh merchants John Sinclair and George Baillie who bought themselves country estates are only two examples of men who had scarcely been idle; and Craigievar was built for a man who had made his money in trade, William Forbes — 'Willie the Merchant'. Moreover, although the scale was limited, James VI's reign was a period of industrial development. The cloth-making industry made progress in the north-east, although the attempt to attract Flemings over to train the Scots in new methods was unsuccessful; the Flemings who came were miserable, and the Scots hostile. Glass-making was another matter; the Venetian brought to Scotland was more acceptable than the Fleming, and the Scots began to produce enough glass to begin to export it, and alarm their competitor Sir Robert Mansell, the English glass monopolist. The Society of Brewers, established in Edinburgh in 1596, represents another attempt to replace imports with native production; previously, even such Scottish brewing as there was produced only ale in limited quantities, and beer had been imported, but now hops were brought in from England, and Scottish beer could be made.

There were staggering individual success stories. Nathaniel Udward, son of a provost of Edinburgh, was cordially hated by his native burgh, partly because he insisted in living in Leith, and partly because he became the great Scottish monopolist; linen, brick, tile-making, soap, ordnance, saltpetre, and salt all came into the hands of this 'rolling stone now heir now thair leiving upoun projects', as the burghs bitterly described him. Above all, there was Sir George Bruce, whose coalmine at Culross, using German techniques to solve the drainage problem caused by the water of the estuary, became one of the tourist attractions of the day, visited by Lord Howard de Walden and James VI. The low rambling 'palace' at Culross — so called because it housed the king in 1617 — with its attractive rooms, fine painted ceilings, and general air of comfortable domesticity, and the impressive Bruce tomb in the parish church, are a lasting comment on the advantages to one Scottish laird of the life of an industrialist rather than a country gentleman.

Bruce's 'palace' is not the only example of success within the towns; stone buildings of the late sixteenth and early seventeenth century stand in a number of east-coast burghs, in Crail, for example, and further inland in Falkland, as evidence of prosperity in urban life. More generally the appearance of new towns and the apparent growth of population suggest that the reign of James VI was something of a 'boom' period for the Scottish burghs. On the west, Glasgow was clearly expanding, moving steadily up the 'league-table' of tax contributions to reach fifth place in 1585, and the burgh tax lists show also the increasing importance in the east of Dysart, Kirkcaldy, and Anstruther. None of this turned Scotland into a country with an advanced economy; there was still far more conservatism than innovation. But there was enough to make the late sixteenth century notably different from the past. The king himself did not wholly encourage or even accept developments at home. In *Basilikon Doron* his comments on the merchants and craftsmen read like the eternal layman's moan about prices and quality; indeed, at exactly the time when efforts were being made to replace imports with Scottish manufacture, James begged for more imports, 'so shall ye have best and best cheape wares'. A decade later, a sudden rush of interest in Scottish trade led him to demand that the export of timber be banned, leaving a no doubt embarrassed council to remind him that none had been exported within living memory. Yet James's mercantilist ideas were not merely the simplistic theorizings of the layman. The idea of national wealth was gradually emerging in sixteenth-century Europe. James's approach suggests the dawn of the idea that there was a 'national economic policy' that could be pursued. Muddled and sometimes even wrong-headed application of that idea only reflects the fact that naturally people were slow to take it up. It was nevertheless a dramatic advance when for the first time a Scottish king thought in such terms.

His parliament, and even more his council, were of course heavily concerned with economic matters. But the merchants themselves had stronger voice than before, partly through their own attendance at parliament, partly, perhaps, because of their close links with the Edinburgh lawyers on the council, and above all, because they now had a formal organization. The Convention of the Royal Burghs, whose origins go back at least to the fourteenth century, was very powerful indeed by the late sixteenth. It was an exclusively merchant body, whose authority was underwritten by parliament in 1578 and 1581, and on the whole it was listened to rather than directed by the government. In 1579 parliament and council agreed with the Convention to ban the export of raw wool and the import of English cloth, not this time on the old grounds of the need to bring in bullion, but to protect the clothworkers, hit by poverty and unemployment. The inevitable fall in customs revenues made the government think again, but it was not until 1598 that the council lifted the ban.

The Convention organized the Staple at Campveere, keeping up the pressure for privileges, and it dictated the pattern of foreign trade. To the traditional trading partners there was added Spain; despite objection by the kirk, imports of wine, luxury goods, and iron were brought in from Spain, in exchange for 'a collection of dull but worthy (Scottish) merchandise', as S.G.E. Lythe describes it. There was also much more trade with England; it was only the English merchants' fear of allowing the Scots in, rather than Scottish reluctance, that put any barrier in the way of an obvious area for expansion. And the most notable advance came with the exploitation of the woodlands north of Stavanger, as the increase of population in Norway encouraged farmers to cut down timber and reclaim land. For some 200 years after *c.* 1580 trade in this timber was known as *Skotterhandel*, as Scottish ships from Montrose to Dunbar, and mainly from the Fife burghs, moved in to carry timber not only back to Scotland but also to Europe. Subsequently the Dutch joined in the carrying trade, but Scottish shipping remained dominant; and the Scots began to finance timbermills, to settle in Norway, and to intermarry. It is a remarkable example of the enterprise that the Scottish merchants could show.

Yet despite evidence of enterprise and ingenuity, this most Calvinist of countries offers, at least in the early years after the Reformation, little support for either the brilliant thesis of Max Weber, who saw in the Calvinist ethic the inspiration for a new spirit of capitalism, or the counter-argument by R.H. Tawney which saw the Calvinist cart drawn along strange paths by the capitalist horse. Usury was certainly given legal approval, in the act of 1587 which set the interest rate at a maximum 10 per cent, but that was far less because of Calvinist thinking, which was still ambivalent, than because of pressure from the merchants, and the forcing up of interest rates as the Baltic merchants demanded coin in exchange for their grain exports to Scotland. The ministers accused of 'ockery' in 1612 show Calvinist clerics as well as Calvinist merchants trying to make gains from the fact that usury was now accepted, but neither can be easily associated with a Calvinist ethic. Nor is it easy to see much thrift in a merchant class busy enhancing its already favourable lifestyle, where it could, with houses such as the elaborate urban equivalent to the Italianate Crichton, Gladstone's Land in Edinburgh, and buying its way into the ranks and attitudes of the country gentry. Even more difficult to relate to the Weberian idea of individual effort and individual conscience is the combination of the collectivism of the Convention and the kirk's insistence on conformity. The Udwards and Bruces were the small minority of individuals who broke through these fetters, and were not necessarily liked for it. Both the state of economic life in Scotland and the often conservative attitudes of the merchants meant that in terms of the Weber thesis, they began a very long way back.

But it is difficult to discount it altogether. In the mid eighteenth century two Scotsmen, James Stewart of Coltness and John Millar, colleague of Adam Smith, were among the earliest exponents of the idea that the revolution of the seventeenth century came about because of a class struggle in which 'the wealth of the industrious will share, if not totally root out the power of the grandees'. They were writing in a century when, as Professor Smout suggests, Calvinism, while not the primary cause of economic growth, ensured that 'when the opportunity came for that growth, after many other pre-conditions had been fulfilled, the Scots would be a nation psychologically well equipped to exploit the situation to the full'. This is based on the long-term effect of the Calvinist vision of universal education, and the insistence on the idea that the godly life, rewarded in heaven, was evident in this world in piety, industry, and frugality.

It is unrealistic to seek for clear signs of that effect as early as the first half-century after the Reformation. It is probably unrealistic to deny altogether that the seeds were there. More immediately, if Scotland was not yet a capitalist society, it was certainly a changing society. There was a great deal more poverty and therefore a much wider gulf between those in the towns and the countryside with wealth and those without than there had been a century earlier. It would be wrong to suggest that the whole of James VI's reign was a period of unrelenting hardship for the population on the land. The horrors of the 1590s gave way to two decades of much more stable economic conditions, when people may have felt that life was more secure, and probably attributed this wrongly to the government, instead of rightly to the accident of climatic conditions. But it is not only the colossal disaster of 1623, the worst famine year of the seventeenth century, that reminds us how precarious life was for most people. Even in the better years, the gulf between the economically secure and insecure was being further widened by the breaking-down of traditional bonds, by no means yet substantially undermined, but visibly affected by the new attitudes of the government, and by the formal organization, based on the parish, of things that had formerly been based on personal connexion. Neither was as yet acceptable or effective enough to provide psychological or material security.

11

Cultural Achievements

In the early 1580s a verse-letter written to Robert Hudson, one of the musician poets of the court of James VI, described how:

> If Ovid wer to lyf restored
> to see which I behould
> he might inlairge his plesant taels
> of formis manifould
> be this which now into the court
> most plesantlie appeirs
> to see in penners and in pens
> transformed all our speirs
> and into paper all our jaks
> our daggs in horns of ink.

The immediate context of this letter, as Helena M. Shire has shown, is the rescue of the king from the Ruthven Raiders, and the point is the importance of poetry at James's court. It contrasts sharply with Dunbar's complaint, a century earlier, that the poet was a lowly figure. But it might be used as a comment on a more general change in attitude, which had now reached the point where literacy was an end in itself. It was the mark of the cultured man, who could move easily from the things of the world − his career, the running of his estates, his trading − to the things of the mind, history, languages, law, the arts, sciences, mathematics, medicine. It was no longer enough for kings and nobles to be read to, as Gibert Hay had advised; they read for themselves − and they wrote also.

The impact on the law was considerable. Modern Scots law is regarded as having originated with the publication in 1681 of the *Institutions* of James Dalrymple, Viscount Stair, the first 'serious attempt to erect Scots law into a philosophical system'. But Stair could draw on a long tradition. From the reign of James I the Auld Lawes — the huge muddle of legal treatises, including the lawyers' bible *Regiam Maiestatem*, their practical handbook *Quoniam Attachiamenta*, various assizes, and bits and pieces accurately if unhelpfully described as *Fragmenta Collecta* — were the subject of an increasing number of manuscript collections and commissions set up by parliament with the intent 'to codify them. These commissions achieved nothing until the late sixteenth century. The first lawyer to produce an account of the substantive law of Scotland was a cleric, John Sinclair, pre-Reformation senator of the college of justice. Sinclair's *Practicks* were quickly followed by the comprehensive *Practicks* of James Balfour of Pittendreich. He and Sir John Skene of Curriehill were leading spirits in the new scheme for codification. Balfour's work provided a wealth of information about the current state of the law, based on both the Auld Lawes and case-law. Skene did much more. He produced an edition of the acts of parliament and a magnificent legal dictionary, *De Verborum Significatione*, a goldmine whose riches extend far beyond the strictly legal; and he edited *Regiam Maiestatem*, producing for his contemporaries an impeccable pedigree for their law, for he attributed it and much else besides to that Scottish Justinian, David I. The fact that his editing is now heavily criticized only means that his techniques were not those of the modern scholar, and that he worked to a pre-conceived idea; yet his achievement in the 1590s and 1600s may be measured against the fact that the Auld Lawes still await a proper modern edition. The third outstanding lawyer of this generation was Sir Thomas Craig of Riccarton, pupil of the great French lawyer François Hotman, and author of two massive works, both of which have some claim to be considered 'philosophical': *Jus Feudale* was his academic analysis of feudal law, and its relation to the social conditions of his day; *De Unione Regnorum Britanniae* was something more, written, as its title suggests, to explore the possibility of uniting the laws of England and Scotland, and doing so with an erudition and historical approach that made his work one of the greatest contributions to the debate on law raised by the union of the crowns. The writings of these men show that for some the legal profession involved more than simply the practice of law; these were the great academic lawyers, for whom a sense and understanding of the past was as important as their technical knowledge of their modern law.

A sense of the past now had a very specific purpose. In the 1560s an English writer produced a lengthy treatise on the king's two bodies, designed to show that the subordinate monarch Mary could succeed to the English throne. This massive work ends rather charmingly with the prayer that Elizabeth would produce many children 'and make frustrate all this my discertation'. But it became increasingly obvious that she would not. As the prospect of the English succession took hold of men's minds, so the need to assert Scottish independence and sovereignty became more pressing. Buchanan himself was led, in pursuit of this need, to take up the unpopular subject of the highlander, and to produce an account that gave the Gaelic part of Scotland a respectability and justification as part of the unified nation. It was this that brought him to his sensational discovery of the common origin of the Celtic languages, and its division into two broad types, the Belgic and the Celtic — more or less equivalent to the P- and Q-Celtic recognized by scholars today. His own interest in his achievement was that it enabled him to glorify the Gaelic-speaking Scots at the expense of the subservient Welsh, a soothing consolation for a man whose *History* was attacked by the Welsh antiquary Humphrey Lluyd before it was even published. He himself infinitely preferred the harmonious sounds of Latin to the 'harsh sounds' of Gaelic, but he extolled the Tacitean virtues of a people uncorrupted by wealth and worldly ambition, with their primitive discipline and, more important for his political theory, their continuing practice of electing their chiefs and making them answerable to their councils. No other writer followed Buchanan in making the highlands an integral part of the assertion of the ancient and free Scottish kingdom. But men like Craig, in his *Scotland's Sovereignty Asserted*, and Hume of Godscroft, the historian of the house of Douglas, also took up the general battle with Lluyd and William Camden on the early history of Scotland. Their belief in that history was maintained throughout the seventeenth century. No less a person than Sir George Mackenzie, the lawyer who founded the Advocates Library, which was the basis of the later National Library of Scotland, strenuously and even hysterically upheld the account of Boece, on which all later writers depended, partly on the grounds that Erasmus had described Boece as a 'person who could not lie'. The antiquity of Scottish kingship was a myth. But out of this myth had come one remarkable intellectual achievement.

The other great theme to which men in post-Reformation Scotland turned their attention was the apocalypse. The reformers could claim that they had replaced a corrupt church with one that fulfilled God's purpose for mankind. But they had created a religious revolution that undermined natural and traditional attitudes, and set men on the quest for new assurances. So they had to justify themselves by filling in the details of their case. This depended on explaining their relationship with the early church, and the extent to which the church of Rome had departed from the lines laid down by the early church. The Reformation could then be seen as God's direct intervention in human affairs, when he overthrew Antichrist – identified by Luther and Knox with the papacy – and enabled men to create a new and godly society. The emphasis in Reforming thought was therefore primarily on the past rather than the millenarian future; and the histories of Knox and Calderwood, for example, concentrated on the manifestation of the divine will in the present, as men of faith struggled to establish his church. The concept of the ultimate victory against Antichrist was of course a part of apocalyptic thinking; the idea of the 'godly prince' who in the last age of the world would fulfill God's ultimate purpose by destroying Antichrist naturally appealed to King James, whose early interest encouraged him to write, by 1588, two works, the *Paraphrase on the Revelation of John* and *Ane Fruitfull Meditatioun . . . of the 20 Chapter of Revelation in the forme of ane sermon*. But it was the historical approach that produced one of the most remarkable examples of the educated Scottish laird, John Napier of Merchiston. His fame today rests on his invention of logarithms. But to Napier that discovery was as much a by-product of his real purpose as Buchanan's discovery of the common origin of the Celtic languages. In his *Plaine Discovery of the Whole Revelation*, published in 1593, he identified emperor with papacy, and saw the struggle with Antichrist finally being resolved by those seven kingdoms – the seven horns of the beast – that had survived from the 10 ancient kingdoms. One of the seven was Scotland; and his mathematical genius was pressed into service to explain the date of the Scottish Reformation in terms of the prophecy that after 1,260 years a tenth of the Antichristian city, Rome, would fall. This was the man whose 'fertile brain also explored the possibilities of tanks and submarines as well as the mysteries of alchemy', and also the use of salt as a fertilizer and improved methods of mine-drainage.

The towering figures of Buchanan and Napier are accompanied by a host of other scholars, men like Timothy Pont, the first Scottish cartographer, and his successor the cartographer and musician Robert Gordon of Straloch, and a considerable number of highly educated laymen. The king's sad little complaint, 'They gar me speik Latin ar I could speik Scots', and his early library – which became the basis of the Royal Library after James went to England – both testify to the careful attention paid by those in control during the minority to the proper training of a late-sixteenth-century king. George Keith, earl Marischal, founded Marischal College at Aberdeen, thus providing the burgh with its second university, while the Frasers of Philorth tried to establish a third northern university in the burgh of Fraserburgh, although this, given the competition, not surprisingly failed within a decade. Most astonishing of all was the lawyer's son George Bannatyne, who stayed in Edinburgh during the time of plague in 1568, when merchants and lawyers fled the town, and compiled his five-volume collection of Scottish poetry, 'the main source of our knowledge' of a century of writing. And there is the attractive story of Andrew Melville and his nephew James, visiting George Buchanan in his last illness, and finding him 'sitting in his chaire, teatching his young man that servit him in his chalmer to spell, a,b,ab; e,b, eb, etc'. Perhaps the only reservation to the idea of a literate laity lies in the staggering illegibility of many of the private letters which were now becoming commonplace, and the practice of using messengers to explain verbally the writer's mind; that suggests that some at least were following the new fashion with difficulty!

The pre-conditions for the increasing literacy of the laity remain as puzzling at the end of the sixteenth century as they had been a century earlier. But by now the reformers were beginning to create a milieu in which it was becoming more possible to be educated. Inevitably, the situation still varied widely. The reformers' dream of education for all could not be realized. In the First Book of Discipline they echoed Luther's appeal to the nobility and town councillors of Germany to accept responsibility for the education of the youth of the realm, and their demand for the church's patrimony was in part designed to provide education; in the rural parishes, the ministers were to instruct children in the catechism, while in the towns, grammar and Latin were to be taught. The reformers followed the great reforming educationalists of the continent, Sturm at Strasbourg, for example, and Cordier at Lausanne; like them, they linked education to both home and school, and were strongly opposed to children being educated away from home, a belief that may underlie the different pattern of Scottish and English education in the following centuries, for Scottish education, even for the wealthy and academically able, remained primarily local education, both at school and university. The reformers pressed for schools in every parish, and put a premium on differing levels of ability; any child of intellectual ability should proceed to higher education, while others, having acquired the rudiments of education, should be trained in some craft. They laid down detailed plans for the amount of time to be spent at the various stages of education, and for a radical change at the universities, where specialist teaching was to replace the 'regenting' system whereby one man was responsible for the whole of a student's university course.

They did have an existing structure on which to build, in the song- and grammar-schools of pre-Reformation Scotland. The reformers may have extended the idea of education as a basic element in producing a godly society, but they did not invent it; the real distinction is that they wanted an educated laity, whereas the pre-Reformation church had offered opportunities to those who could not afford education by inviting them into their ranks. The song-schools existed primarily to produce choristers with a smattering of elementary Latin for the church. The grammar-schools were the 'academic' schools, and the presence of masters like Henryson and Ninian Winzet indicate that standards could be very high. But they were almost entirely associated with the burghs, and with a career in the church. Yet at least two familiar figures of the post-Reformation world of education and letters owed their early training to Scottish grammar schools before 1560. One was the chatty chronicler Robert Lindsay of Pitscottie, author of the immensely readable and racy *Historie and Cronicles of Scotland*, written in the 1570s, and combining two traditions, the oral and the literary; he does not seem to have gone to university, and it was on the basis of school education, apparently, that he could call himself 'ane young scholar' who certainly knew Latin and probably French. And the man who revolutionial university education in Scotland, Andrew Melville, was educated in the 1550s at Montrose under Thomas Anderson, staying on to benefit from the teaching of Greek by Pierre de Marsiliers, brought to Angus by Erskine of Dun; thus he was able to stagger his masters at St Mary's college, St Andrews, by reading Aristotle in Greek. We have a description of that school from Andrew's nephew James, who was a pupil in the early 1560s, where the teacher was now the minister William Gray. His account of the gentle approach of Gray, and the kindness of his educated sister, who reminded him of his mother, suggest that at least at Montrose there was a master whose ideas of how to teach had much in common with the enlightened theories of Roger Ascham and Montaigne, in a century of harshness; and there he studied the catechism, prayers, and scripture, learned Latin and French and read works of Linacre and Erasmus, and was also taught archery, golf, fencing, wrestling, and swimming. School education both before and after the Reformation was much more patchy than it was later to become; in the country-side few schools existed at all, and in the burghs standards depended on the luck of the draw, for not all schoolmasters can have been Henrysons. Nevertheless, it was possible for children to be well taught.

The impact of the reformers on the universities was much more dramatic. The influence of Boece on Aberdeen, and the astonishing flowering of humanist scholarship at Aberdeen and Kinloss, made the north an exception. But Alexander Hay failed to introduce the teaching of Greek and the oriental languages at St Andrews in the 1540s. That left the remarkable situation that Greek was taught not in the universities, apart from Aberdeen, but in the non-university town of Edinburgh, where Edward Henryson, protegé of Ferrerio and Bishop Reid, was appointed to give public lectures in 1556. The most poorly endowed of the three universities, Glasgow, was sinking into complete decline in the mid sixteenth century; in the 1550s this small university attracted only 53 students.

Yet Glasgow was the starting-point of the great Melvillian reforms, for Melville was reluctantly persuaded to return from Geneva in 1574, not as the leading advocate of Presbyterianism, but as principal of a dying university. Already, at the age of 29, he was a scholar of great distinction, as a linguist, philosopher, and poet, educated at the Royal Trilingual College in Paris, and at the law school in Poitiers. Only when he went to Beza's Geneva did he develop the interest in theology that created the basis for the rôle of the great reformer for which he is best remembered; but he came back to Scotland to attack not the bishops nor the state, but the low standards of education, as Dr James Kirk's work on the university of Glasgow emphasizes. The most profound influence on Melville was not Beza, but the man who revolutionial education, Pierre Ramus; indeed, when the convinced Aristotelian Beza drove the anti-Aristotelian Ramus out of Geneva, Melville followed him to Lausanne, and the link was broken only with Ramus's death during the Massacre of St Bartholomew. Ramus had swept away the artificial, highly formalized bonds that fettered the teaching of rhetoric and logic; they had become a barrier to understanding, in this age of questioning and controversy, the ideas that were difficult enough to articulate even in the vernacular. Rhetoric was now no longer an end in itself, but a means of communication, the 'art of discoursing well'. Logic was simplified; easily communicated, classified logic was the key to all learning. Ramus's straightforward techniques, his use of mnemonics as an aid to learning, were applied to all scholarship, languages and sciences as well as philosophy, which was now down-graded from its hitherto pre-eminent position.

The Scottish universities in the 1570s — for success at Glasgow led to success at St Andrews and Aberdeen — were violently woken up by Ramus's great pupil, the man who set out 'to schaw that Aristotle could err, and haid erred, contrar to St Androis axiom Absurdum est dicere errasse Aristotelem'. The traditional curriculum, traditional methods of teaching, reluctant scholars like Peter Blackburn at Glasgow, all went down before the onslaught of Melville. The metamorphosis of the universities into colleges of specialist teaching, where for the first time Ramist methods were used, and the startlingly novel introduction of compulsory Greek in the first year was followed by Aramaic, Syriac, and Hebrew, while metaphysics were discarded as unprofitable, had a dramatic effect. Indeed, Melville's Glasgow seems to have influenced the new foundation, Trinity College, Dublin, established in 1592.

Andrew Melville and King James were both scholars; and the famous debate at Falkland in 1596, where Melville plucked the king's sleeve, calling him 'God's silly vassal', has the flavour of lively academic debate, which both protagonists may have enjoyed, despite the very deep issue that divided them. On the other hand, there is no doubt about the king's general hostility to Melville; it was primarily an attack on Melville when, in 1597, James, with some of the councillors and the commissioners from the assembly, declared that doctors and regents of the universities were banned from sessions, presbyteries, and synods. He had grounds for his hostility. After Melville had moved from Glasgow to St Andrews he was accused of encouraging disputation on the question of the right of subjects to depose their kings, in which it was argued that although succession was lawful, all kings should be elected. Hobbes's answer, in *Behemoth*, to the question about the 'fits of rebellion' which afflicted the states of Christendom was that 'the fault . . . may be easily mended, by mending the universities'. It looked very applicable to the Scottish universities of the last three decades of the sixteenth century.

It did not last. Melville's educational reforms were frustrated, as much as his attempt to free a Presbyterian church from royal control. In the early seventeenth century Aristotelianism and regenting were brought back to the universities; only the thorough-going reforms of the eighteenth century finally brought regenting to an end. Conservatism was once more prominent; the university of Glasgow refused to subscribe to the National Covenant of 1638. Yet the Melvillian university was an exciting place, attracting even sons of the nobility to include in their educational programme, as well as their private tutors and education abroad, a spell at the universities at home. This was the period of the foundation of the university of Edinburgh, which was the one Scottish example of the 'tounis college', following the example of the great city colleges hinted at in the First Book of Discipline, which had been established at Strasbourg, Lausanne, Geneva, and elsewhere; and under its first principal, Robert Rollock, Edinburgh adopted Ramist methods from the beginning. From the universities came the educated ministry on which the church depended. And George Strachan, who went to Paris in 1592, studied in various Protestant and Catholic universities in France, went on to Rome, and was last heard of pursuing linguistic learning in Persia, is perhaps the best comment on what had happened in Scotland, where scholars still as cosmopolitan as their predecessors now found inspiration in the universities at home.

James's own contribution to the universities was to offset militant Presbyterianism by insisting that the catechism *God and the King* must be read in the schools and universities, and decreeing, in 1617, that the town college of Edinburgh should be known as 'King James's College'. He had little chance, in fact, to give any sort of lead; the Melvillian reforms were well established in the 1570s, during his minority, and the new university came into being in 1583, when he was not yet his own master. What he did achieve was the transformation of his court into a brilliant cultural centre. Mary's court had been adorned by the master-poet Alexander Scott, who can probably be identified with the man of that name who, while studing law in Paris in 1540, was also *'joueur de fifre'*, and went on to become canon of Inchmahome, organist, and poet and exponent of *musick fyne*, the part-writing of sacred and secular music. But the great age of the court opened with the arrival of Alexander Montgomerie, a distant kinsman of the king, and a member of the family of Montgomery of Hesilhead, a cadet branch of the Montgomery earls of Eglinton. Under the king's direction there was a 'flyting' between the newcomer and the established court poet – indeed, apparently the only court poet – Hume of Polwarth, whom Montgomerie ousted from his 'bardic' chair in the 'chimney nuike'.

Thereafter, 'beloved Saunders, maistre of our art', presided over a circle of court poets which by 1583 had been established by James as the 'Castalian band'. For the first few years, these poets and the king indulged in the 'writing-game', the use of verse in fun, such as the 'epitaph' composed for Montgomerie when drunk. The Castalian band took its name from the spring in Mount Parnassus dedicated to the Muses, with Apollo represented by the king — as du Bartas was tactful enough to say. It was created for the deliberate purpose of developing poetic theory and practice, advancing Scottish 'poesie' by combining its own native traditions of alliterative poetry and flyting with the poetry of England and the continent, and translating foreign prose and poetry. It was a collective enterprise. James himself, in his *Essays of a Prentice to the Divine Art of Poesie*, written in 1584, and the *Reulis and Cautelis of Poesie* of the following year, supported the use of Scots, 'for we differ from thame (the English) in sindrie reulis of poesie', and encouraged the alliterative style, devising rules for rhyme, rhythm, and stanza formation, while exhorting Scots poets to be open to foreign influence. William Fowler, a man of burgess family, later secretary to James's queen, Anne of Denmark, and uncle of the great mid-seventeenth-century poet and historian William Drummond of Hawthornden, was persuaded by the king to translate Petrarch's *Trionfi* and Machiavelli's *The Prince*. Robert Hudson produced his translation of du Bartas' *Judith* in 1584, with a preface including sonnets by his colleagues, the king, and Fowler, as James's *Essays* had been prefaced with sonnets by Montgomerie, Thomas and Robert Hudson, and Fowler.

The Castalian poets lasted into the seventeenth century, some of them following James to England; but the greatest period was the first decade, before the Catholic Montgomerie was forced to leave the court in 1590, and Scots 'poesie' was increasingly submerged by English influence. In that first period, it is pleasant to speculate on the effect on James himself, the lonely and browbeaten youth, who was only beginning to gain influence in political and ecclesiastical affairs. In 1584 John Stewart of Baldynneis' New Year's gift to the king was a 'propyne' of verse, which must have given more than formal pleasure, for when Stewart looked forward to James's great political future, 'deserving now ane Doubill croune and moir', the double crown had a poetic significance as well as being an indication of James's likely succession to the English throne. As Dr Shire points out, the poem 'crowned' the poet-king, as Petrarch had been 'crowned' in Rome in 1341, and Conrad Celtis by the emperor in 1487. James was no Petrarch; his poems, and his laboured epic on the battle of Lepanto, show how far he was from the master-poets of his court. But he was the centre and *raison d'etre* of that group, and as such deserved recognition, even if couched in terms of elaborate flattery.

These men, and others like them, James Lauder, musician at the courts of Mary and James, and Andrew Blackhall, canon of Holyrood before the Reformation and minister of Ormiston after it, combined both poetic and musical talent. There is little evidence of music treated academically in post-Reformation Scotland, although Lauder is recorded as having examined in music at Edinburgh in 1593. Nor does there seem to have been much interest in 'music speculative'. There are few hints of the Platonic idea of music as the means of expelling the disturbances of body and soul, and lifting man's mind to God, the idea taken up by the great neo-platonist Ficino; the high level of discussion, following Augustine's *De Musica*, of the relationship between the senses, reason, and God in terms of hearing and rythmical proportions, seems to have passed the Scots by. James paid a passing tribute to 'music speculative', echoing Ronsard with his phrase 'the tuichstane . . . of all is Musique'. And Blackhall may have been aware of it; his setting of the Helicon tune for four voices, for Montgomerie's great poem 'The Cherrie and the Slae', was intended to produce 'four-part perfection' in universal harmony. Otherwise, Scottish music was 'music practical', much influenced, as it had been since James V's reign, by French part-songs and sonnets, until the end of the century when English influence became strong. It was not surprising, in a circle dominated by a king who was a scholar but no musician, and a poet, Montgomerie, who was a considerable musician but not academically trained.

The court was not the only centre for Scottish music. The great musical development of the sixteenth century is that associated with the kirk, and indeed follows the theological move from Lutheranism to Calvinism. Luther's famous claim that the devil should not have the best tunes reflects his enthusiasm for music, shared by Calvin and other early reformers. In his music Luther retained the main elements of the Mass, and drew on Latin hymns as well as vernacular songs. *The Gude and Godlie Ballattis* were in the Lutheran tradition; they retained their popularity, running through a number of editions between the early 1540s and 1621, although they were never officially accepted by the kirk. Post-Reformation music followed Calvin, who rejected the entire corpus of Latin hymns. Only what was Biblical was to be used in public worship. That meant the psalms.

The Scottish psalter of 1564 was commissioned by the Assembly which, in 1562, lent the printer Robert Lekprevik £200 for the work; it drew on the psalters compiled in the previous three decades by the great French musician Clement Marot, household official of Francis I, by Calvin himself, who, although not a musician, contributed five psalms to the Strasbourg psalter of 1539, and by the English Thomas Sternhold, John Hopkins and William Whittingham. The 1556 Genevan psalter, produced by Whittingham for the English congregation in Geneva, has been described as the parent book of the Scottish psalter. More immediate was the 1561 edition, which included 87 new psalms by William Kethe, among them the Old Hundredth. It has been regarded as unfortunate that the Scottish psalter drew heavily on England and Geneva, for if the devil did not have the best tunes in the sixteenth century, the French certainly did. The great French psalter of 1562, the work of Marot and Beza, has endless variety in metre and stanza, and hence a degree of individuality which contrasts with the comparative monotony of much of the English and Scottish psalters; in this psalter, the ancient modal system was giving way to the major and minor keys of modern music. In fact, its influence was not negligible; indeed, some of the English and Scottish psalms ran into difficulty because of the attempt to fit their words to the French tunes. There was considerable interchangeability; the first line of the Old Hundredth is found in psalm 134 of the French psalter, and its component parts turn up in various combinations. Moreover, Whittingham's great psalm 'Now Israel may say' is worthy of inclusion anywhere; Calderwood's description of 2,000 people singing this psalm in the Royal Mile, to welcome back John Durie after his banishment, has an emotive force that is almost terrifying.

The original intention was to provide tunes for each psalm. The 1564 psalter contained the 150 psalms, including 21 new versions by Scottish writers, six by Robert Pont, minister of Dunblane, and 15 by John Craig, Knox's fellow-minister at St Giles, of which three are still in use today. Of these 150, 105 had proper tunes. The first common tune does not appear until 1615, but by then it was already called old, and it has been suggested that it dates back to the mid sixteenth century, when the first Sternhold-Hopkins psalter was brought to Scotland, in an edition without music. It is immensely simple, and therefore both appropriate and very moving as the introduction to many people of their part in public worship.

The apparent attack on polyphonic music may not have been wholly successful. James earl of Moray, an enthusiast for church music, invoked the services of one of the canons of St Andrews, David Peebles, telling him to depart from the 'curiosity of music' — that is, polyphony — 'and sa to make plaine and dulce'. Yet Peebles' tunes, which appear in the manuscript written in 1566 by Thomas Wode, vicar of St Andrews, were set in four parts, apparently as Moray wished. James Melville describes how he learned the 'gam, plean-song [that is, the tenor line, which was the melody] and monie of the treables of the psalms, wherof sum I could weill sing in the kirk'. Thus although the tunes were not harmonized until the editions of 1625 and 1635, it seems that harmony was known earlier, despite the antipathy of the reformers to the elaborate music of the Catholic church. The real difficulty was that simplicity was essential for the successful introduction of congregational singing; thus harmony was probably little used, and where it was, the congregation sang the melody, trained singers the contra-tenor, treble, and bass parts. The tradition thus created produced, over two centuries later, the famous description by Burns of the psalm-singing in the *Cottar's Saturday Night*, followed by the amazing line: 'Compared with these, Italian trills are tame'.

The reformed kirk is widely regarded as having had an adverse effect on the cultural life of Scotland. It did move in on the world of literature, taking over control of the printers and imposing censorship. It is probably because of this that Bannatyne's manuscript was not published, although Bannatyne lived in Edinburgh, moved in legal circles, and knew printers. In 1568 the kirk banned publication of a volume described as 'ane psalme booke' because 'in the end . . .was found printed ane baudie song callit "Welcum Fortoun" '; this may have been the *Gude and Godlie Ballattis*. But it was not until the late sixteenth century that the kirk began to set its face against drama. And from the period of the first 60 years of its existence come some of the most vigorous Scottish ballads, like 'The Laird o' Logie', 'Kinmont Willie', and possibly even the extant version of 'Chevy Chase'. A church as committed to the idea of education as the reformed kirk cannot be regarded as wholly philistine. Nor was a kirk that encouraged music; only in the mid seventeenth century did music decline. The reconciliation of the earl of Huntly in 1596 has already been cited in support of the view that it is the church of the seventeenth century, not the sixteenth, that created the image of harsh antagonism to enjoyment of the things of the world, including the cultural things. With its own magnificent achievement, the psalter, the kirk felt, with Calvin, 'the great force and power [of music] in moving and inflaming the heart of man to invoke and praise God'. The kirk did not only remind men that they were sinners. In the end, it is a matter of speculation, even that dangerous thing imagination; but when, in the uncertain world of the Reformation, men sang for the first time that great clarion-call of faith, the Old Hundredth, when they were bidden to 'sing to the Lord with cheerful voice', when they came to the words

> His truth for all times firmly stood
> And shall from age to age endure

it is difficult to believe that they were not inspired by a new awareness of a God who was more than the terrible and vengeful judge.

Epilogue: Scotland after 1603

James VI's departure for London in April 1603 amidst scenes of great emotion looked like the high point of Scottish pride. The Scots had given their 'auld enemeis' a king, and thus provided the final answer to the aggression of Edward I, Edward III, Henry VIII. James, through the medium of his coinage, allowed himself a pardonable boast, with the smug little motto *'Henricus rosas regna Jacobus'* (Henry [VII united] the roses, James the kingdoms). It was all very gratifying. It also created an immense problem: absentee kingship. It is a remarkable tribute to James's ability as king of Scotland that he succeeded as well as he did. He had certain advantages denied to his son. He was known to the Scots, and interested in them. The fact that he returned only once, in 1617, has given rise to the myth that in his enthusiasm for the English crown he forgot all about his northern kingdom. It was quite the reverse. He went to England determined to maintain the interests of that kingdom; in his moving speech to the English parliament of 1607, his last appeal for the union for which he had pressed at the expense of his popularity, he begged a hostile house of Commons to consider the problems of a country 'seldom seen and saluted by its king'. He had a dream of a united nation, in which Scottish merchants, Scottish lawyers, Scottish councillors, would play a full part. He failed; the English merchants were determined to keep out the beggarly and importunate Scots, and the English and Scottish lawyers were, on the whole, sufficiently satisfied with their own traditions. He did not even succeed in retaining close personal ties; after the first decade, when he surrounded himself with Scots, the resentment of the English courtiers forced him to send them home. Yet he kept his channels of communication open, writing endless letters to his council and demanding information from it; these flowed between Edinburgh and London with new speed, because of the efficient postal service that he set up, cutting the time for the round trip to a fortnight in reasonable weather conditions. And at the end of his life, in ill health and worn down by the frustrations of his English rule, he turned back to his original kingdom. In 1621, when his English parliament was obsessed with the burning issue of foreign policy, and frustrated by James's refusal to give a clear lead as the defender of the Reformed church, the king was heavily involved in pushing his ecclesiastical policy, the Five Articles of Perth, through a reluctant, even hostile Scottish parliament.

Yet he could do no more than survive; his departure imposed a new, and in the long run, intolerable strain on a society already suffering from the undermining of traditional structures and the development of new structures as yet uncertain and inadequate. The removal of the court left a vacuum in political, social, and cultural life; and there was as yet no group or individual to replace the focal point that had so abruptly disappeared. The extensive list of James's peerage creations begins in 1600, but is mainly related to the period after 1603. The king's attempt both to reward and to enhance the prestige of his government officials, Seton, Hamilton, and many others, was understandable enough. But a *noblesse de robe* which lacked the power base of the older aristocracy in the localities was not yet a substitute for either king or aristocracy; while for the older nobility, one part of their dual rôle within the state, which had always depended on personal rather than institutional contact with the monarchy, was cut away.

The outlying areas of the kingdom, the highlands and borders, were affected in different ways. James's belief that, as the 'middle shires', the borders would cease to be a problem, encouraged him to relax the policy of strong government control which had had some success since the 1590s; by the end of the reign, falling revenues from the estates of the earl of Northumberland indicate how misplaced James's confidence was. The highlands suffered more, for James's indifference became hostility; his passion to show the English that in language, geography, and manners the two nations could be one allowed of no tolerance for that part of his older kingdom that could not be squeezed into his model.

Indifference to highland culture was not matched for the lowlands, but the effects were roughly similar. The Castalians, Fowler, Robert Aytoun, and others, went to the English court, and gained a high reputation among the metaphysical poets. But they were now writing in an essentially foreign medium, for James's Anglicizing policy was not confined to the highlands. The translation of *Basilikon Doron* into English, in time for it to be rushed on to the London market in 1603, and become, inevitably, a best-seller, marked the changed attitude of a king who had once extolled Scots 'poesie'. He did, rather inconsistently, criticize one of the Castalians, William Alexander, for his 'harsh verses' written in the English fashion rather than the smooth manner of the Scottish Castalians. But his general policy led to the point when, in 1617, interpreters were declared no longer necessary at the port of London, because English and Scots were now 'not so far different bot ane understandeth ane uther'. What he had created was a three-tier system, with Gaelic at the bottom and English at the top. The culture of his Scottish court did not immediately disappear; it moved 'from court to castle', the castles of men like William Mure of Rowallan. But it was diffused and uncertain; Mure wrote partly in English, Drummond of Hawthornden wholly so. Vernacular poetry was no longer the poetry of the fashionable world. The ballad, rather than the poetry and music of the court, became the mainstay of Scottish cultural life. It was not until Burns that the legacy of the brilliant age of the makars was seen again as more than the popular poetry of the common folk, and made literary history.

James's ecclesiastical policy remains a matter for debate. Recent work on the English church has shown that James's enthusiasm for Calvinist theology within an episcopal polity created a more settled church than had existed under Elizabeth, or would exist under Charles I. In Scotland, James's initial success in crushing the Melvillians, whose leaders were brought to England, imprisoned in the Tower, and then exiled, probably encouraged a false sense of security. His proposal to introduce statues of the Apostles in the chapel at Holyrood was a bad tactical error; the development of episcopacy from limited parliamentary bishops to full-blown diocesan episcopacy was not effectively challenged, but neither was it acceptable; and the opposition, not only in the assembly of 1618, but also in the carefully managed parliament of 1621, shows that control of both church and state by king and councillors was now precarious. Professor Donaldson has stated that 'James left a church at peace', but it was too delicate a peace to survive the accession of James's son. It required a man who understood Scottish attitudes, and knew how to temporize. That was true of James, but could not be true of his successors. The staggering ineptitude of Charles's act of 1625 immediately illustrates the extent of the problem; it was designed to find a comprehensive settlement for the kirk, but it broke all precedents, and indeed principles, by revoking not just minority grants but all grants dating back to 1540, and it was in any case passed by a king who, being almost 25 at his succession, had not had a minority in any but the most brief and technical sense. Such a mistake would never have been made by James.

Social and political change is not, except in very rare circumstances, a sudden and dramatic thing. Yet James's accession to the English throne did mark a significant change, even if it was not immediately obvious. Scotland in the late fifteenth and sixteenth centuries had been intensely outward-looking, self-consciously aware, indeed proud, of her receptiveness and contribution to the political, economic, religious, and intellectual life of Europe. The personal union of the crowns meant that her frontiers narrowed, as English interests began to restrict her freedom of action; her trade, for example, was to be significantly affected by English wars, and the pattern of her political life largely determined by the basic fact that her king was king of England. Even before 1603 the one institution within Scotland that seemed to offer assurance and stability in a world where changing government attitudes and economic crises had opened up cracks in the old order had been the kirk. The king, not wholly at one with his 'new men', had succeeded, despite the pressures, in restoring and enhancing the prestige of personal monarchy. Now, he too was gone. The most natural and supreme part of the old order was lost; as the crisis mounted in the seventeenth century, after his death, there was little left to halt the realization of the ultimate Calvinist dream, the creation of a theocracy.

A Note on Further Reading

A *Primary Sources*

Scottish historians have been well-served by editors. The major record collec-
tions in print are: *The Acts of the Parliaments of Scotland*, eds. T. Thomson
and C. Innes (Edinburgh, 1814–75); *The Register of the Privy Council of
Scotland*, eds. J.H. Burton *et al.* (Edinburgh, 1877–); *Registrum Magni
Sigilli Regum Scotorum*, eds. J.M. Thomson *et al.* (Edinburgh, 1882–1914);
Registrum Secreti Sigilli Regum Scotorum, eds. M. Livingstone *et al.*
(Edinburgh, 1908–); *The Accounts of the Lord High Treasurer of Scotland*,
eds. T. Dickson *et al.* (Edinburgh 1877–); *The Exchequer Rolls*, eds. J. Stuart
et al. (Edinburgh, 1878–1908); *Calendar of State Papers relating to Scotland*,
eds. J. Bain *et al.* (Edinburgh, 1898–). The nineteenth-and twentieth-century
publishing clubs have added a wealth of material so vast that only a small
selection can be itemized. The Bannatyne and Maitland Clubs published
the major chronicles of the sixteenth century, *A Diurnal of Remarkable
Occurrents in Scotland* (1833), *The Historie and Life of King James the Saxt*
(anon., 1825), David Moysie, *Memoirs of the Affairs of Scotland, 1577–1603*
(1830), and Sir James Melville of Halhill, *Memoirs of his own Life* (1827).
They also printed the Catholic bishop of Ross, John Lesley's *History of Scotland . . . from the year 1436 to the year 1561* (1830), and the Scottish Text
Society published the translation of Lesley's Latin history (1890–5), as well
as Robert Lindsay of Pitscottie, *Historie and Cronicles of Scotland* (1899–
1911). The Scottish History Society produced John Major's *History of Greater
Britain* (1890). The works of the great scholar George Buchanan were
published by T. Ruddiman, *Omnia Opera* (1715), and are presently the
subject of a major enterprise at the university of St Andrews; meanwhile,
Buchanan's *History* exists in the translation by J. Aikman (Glasgow, 1827–9),
and *De Jure Regni apud Scotos* in D.H. MacNeill, *The Art and Science of
Government among the Scots* (Glasgow, 1964). Legal sources are the province
of the Stair Society, including *The Practicks of Sir James Balfour of
Pittendreich* (1962–3); and a comprehensive guide to legal texts is given in its
Sources and Literature of Scots Law (1936). There is also a fascinating
collection of letters to a senator of the College of Justice, *Correspondence of Sir
Patrick Waus of Barnbarroch, 1540–97*, ed. R. Vans Agnew (Edinburgh,
1882). The Spalding Club publications are invaluable for the north-east:

notably *Illustrations of the Topography and Antiquities of the Shires of Aberdeen and Banff* (1847–69), *Miscellany of the Spalding Club* (5 vols., 1841–52) and *Extracts from the Council Register of the Burgh of Aberdeen* (1844–8). Records of Aberdeen and other major burghs were published by the Scottish Burgh Record Society, along with the *Records of the Convention of the Royal Burghs of Scotland* (1866). Other economic sources include *The Rental Book of the Cistercian Abbey of Coupar Angus* (Grampian Club, 1879–80) and *The Ledger of Andrew Halyburton, Conservator . . . in the Netherlands*, ed. C. Innes (Edinburgh, 1867); and observations of foreign observers – usually critical, sometimes scurrilous – have been collected in P. Hume Brown's *Early Travellers in Scotland* (Edinburgh, 1891). The 'Fraser Books' (all published in Edinburgh) provide a great deal of material on aristocratic families: W. Fraser, *Montgomeries, earls of Eglinton* (1859), *The Lennox* (1874), *The Douglas Book* (1885), *Family of Wemyss* (1888), and others. Royal and diplomatic correspondence is found in the Scottish History Society editions of *The Letters of James IV* (1953), *Flodden Papers* (1933), *Foreign Correspondence with Marie de Lorraine (Balcarres Papers)* (1923–5), *Scottish Correspondence of Mary of Lorraine* (1927), *The Warrender Papers* (1931–2). Also *The Letters of James V*, eds. R.K. Hannay and D. Hay (Edinburgh, 1954), *State Papers of Sir Ralph Sadler*, ed. A. Clifford (Edinburgh, 1809), A. Teulet, *Relations politiques de la France et de l'Espagne avec l'Ecosse au xvie siècle* (Paris, 1862), and *Letters of Queen Elizabeth and King James VI* and *Correspondence of King James VI with Robert Cecil and others* (both Camden Society, 1849 and 1861).

The Reformation has of course produced a flood of material, beginning with that great work of self-propaganda, John Knox's *History of the Reformation in Scotland*, ed. (and translated into English) W.C. Dickinson (Edinburgh, 1949); it is also published (in Scots) in John Knox, *Works*, ed. D. Laing (Edinburgh, 1846–52). Then there is the *Autobiography and Diary of Mr James Melville* (nephew of the great reformer Andrew Melville) (Wodrow Society, 1842); and two histories of the reformed kirk, one by a presbyterian minister, David Calderwood, *The True History of the Church of Scotland* (Wodrow Society, 1842–9), the other by an archbishop, John Spottiswoode, *History of the Church of Scotland . . . to the end of the reign of James VI* (Spottiswoode Society, 1847–51). Earlier reforming literature published by the Scottish Text Society includes John Gau, *Richt Vay to the Kingdome of Hevine* (1887) and *The Gude and Godlie Ballattis* (1897), and the Scottish History Society produced the plea for internal reform, *Commentary on the Rule of St Augustine by Robertus Richardinus* (1935). *The Catechism of John Hamilton, Archbishop of St Andrews, 1552* was edited by T.G. Law (Oxford 1884). *The First Book of Discipline*, ed. J.K. Cameron (Edinburgh, 1972) and *The Second Book of Discipline*, ed. J. Kirk (Edinburgh, 1980) are essential reading for an understanding of Scottish reforming thought; both contain excellent introductions. The Bannatyne and Maitland Clubs published *The Booke of the Universall Kirk, Acts and Proceedings of the General Assemblies of the Kirk of Scotland*, ed. T. Thomson (1839–45), again an essential source. The Scottish Text Society is the major source for literature of the period: *The Bannatyne Manuscript* (1927–32), *The Maitland Quarto Manuscript* (1915) and *The Maitland Folio Manuscript* (1919–27), *Hary's Wallace* (1968–9), *The Works of Sir David Lindsay of the Mount* (1929–36), *The Complaynt of Scotland* (1979), *Satirical Poems of the Time of the Reformation* (1893–8), *The Poems of Alexander Montgomerie* (1886–7), *The Basilicon Doron of King James VI* (1942–4), and much else. *Trew Law* and *Basilikon Doron* are printed in *The Political Works of James I*, ed. C.H. McIlwain (Harvard, 1918; reprint 1965); the *Daemonologie* was published in Edinburgh, 1597, and London, 1603. Also, *The Poems of William Dunbar*, ed. W.M. Mackenzie (Edinburgh, 1932); F.J. Child, *The English and Scottish Popular Ballads* (Boston, 1857–9; reprint 1957); and the anthologies by J. and W. MacQueen, *A Choice of Scottish Verse* (London, 1972) and R.D.S Jack, *Scottish Prose, 1550–1700* (London, 1971).

B *Secondary Works*
There are various aids to scholarship, all useful and some invaluable. In particular: *The Scots Peerage*, ed. J. Balfour Paul (Edinburgh, 1904–14), a mine of information, but to be used with caution; I.B. Cowan, *The Parishes of Medieval Scotland* (Scottish Record Society, 1967); I.B. Cowan and D.E. Easson, *Medieval Religious Houses, Scotland* (London, 1976); D.E.R. Watt, *Fasti Ecclesiae Scoticanae Medii Aevi ad annum 1638* (Scottish Record Society, 1969); C.H. Haws, *Scottish Parish Clergy at the Reformation* (Scottish Record Society, 1972); J. Durkan and A. Ross, *Early Scottish Libraries* (Glasgow, 1961); C.J. Larner *et al.*, *A Source-book of Scottish Witchcraft* (Glasgow, 1977); G.S. Pryde, *The Burghs of Scotland* (Oxford, 1965); G. Brunton and D. Haig, *Historical Account of the Senators of the College of Justice* (Edinburgh, 1832); D. Macgibbon and T. Ross, *The Castellated and Domesticated Architecture of Scotland* and *The Ecclesiastical Architecture of Scotland* (Edinburgh, 1887–92 and 1896–7); M. Livingstone, *A Guide to the Public Records of Scotland* (Edinburgh, 1905); J. Maitland Thomson, *The Public Records of Scotland* (Glasgow, 1922); *Historical Atlas of Scotland*, eds. P.G. McNeill and R.G. Nicholson (St Andrews, 1975).

The bibliographies of the works cited here should be consulted for further reading; and the articles mentioned are only a small number of the many to be found in the *Scottish Historical Review*, *Innes Review*, and *Records of the Scottish Church History Society*. This is not a period in which Scotland can be treated in isolation, and it is therefore worth including at least the admirable Fontana series on European history: J.R. Hale, *Renaissance Europe, 1480–1520* (1971), G.R. Elton, *Reformation Europe, 1517–1559* (1963), J.H. Elliott, *Europe Divided, 1559–1598* (1968), and G. Parker, *Europe in Crisis, 1598–1648* (1979); and O. Chadwick's seminal *The Reformation* (London, 1964). For Scotland itself, vols. II and III of the Edinburgh History of Scotland, R.G. Nicholson, *The Later Middle Ages* (1974) and G. Donaldson,

James V – James VII (1965), provide comprehensive coverage. Rosalind Mitchison, *A History of Scotland* (London, 1970) and *Life in Scotland* (London, 1978) compress ideas and information in an impressively readable way. T.C. Smout, *A History of the Scottish People* (London, 1969; paperback 1972), with its emphasis on society rather than politics, was a major event in Scottish historical publishing, and rightly so. *Scottish Society in the Fifteenth Century*, ed. Jennifer M. Brown (now Wormald) (London, 1977) is a collection of essays dealing with all aspects of society, and relevant for the early part of the period. W. Ferguson, *Scotland's Relations with England to 1707* (Edinburgh, 1977) combines vitriolic comment on present historians with perceptive comment on the past. W.C. Dickinson, *Scotland from the Earliest Times to 1603*, revised by A.A.M. Duncan (3rd edn, Oxford, 1977) adds the insight of recent scholarship to a good 'older' history, and is an excellent general survey. B. Webster, *Scotland from the Eleventh Century to 1603* (London, 1975) is a discussion of sources, and far more than that.

Individual studies of the monarchs vary in quality. James III is the subject of a forthcoming book by N.A.T. Macdougall, the acknowledged expert in the field. R.L. Mackie, *James IV* (Edinburgh, 1958) is readable but comparatively lightweight, and James V cries out for a proper study. Most of the 'biographies' and historical novels about Mary queen of Scots are of profit only to their authors, but Antonia Fraser, *Mary Queen of Scots* (London, 1969), although portraying a too sympathetic queen in an unsympathetic country, is certainly worth reading, as is D.H. Willson, *King James VI and I* (New York, 1956), even if to Willson neither James nor Scotland was sympathetic. Maurice Lee Jr has made the study of some of the great political figures of the period very much his own, in *James Stewart, earl of Moray* (New York, 1953) and *John Maitland of Thirlstane* (Princeton, 1959); he has followed these up with a new work – too late, alas, for this book – *Government by Pen* (Chicago and London, 1980), an account of Jame's rule from England through the medium of his leading Scottish councillors. An older but valuable study of James's reign before 1603 is H.G. Stafford, *James VI of Scotland and the Throne of England* (New York, 1940); and there are four articles dealing with Scotland in *James VI and I*, ed. A.G.R. Smith (London, 1973). W.L. Mathieson, *Politics and Religion in Scotland, 1560–1690* (Glasgow, 1902) is a detailed account; D. Nobbs, *England and Scotland, 1560–1707* (London, 1952) a short but interesting essay. Very little on 'constitutional' history exists; the classic – and as yet only – work on parliament is R.S. Rait, *The Parliaments of Scotland* (Glasgow, 1924), highly informative, but in its general thesis of a weak parliament, long overdue for revision. A.L. Brown, 'The Scottish "Establishment" in the Later 15th Century', *Juridical Review* (1978) shows what could and should be done; and A.L. Murray has written a number of very valuable articles, among them 'The Comptroller, 1425–1488' and 'The Lord Clerk Register', both in *Scottish Historical Review (SHR)* LII (1973) and LIII (1974). On the law, R.K. Hannay, *The College of Justice* (Edinburgh, 1933) remains the standard work. J.J. Robertson rescues pre–1532 law and lawyers from their

'Dark Age', in 'The development of the law' in *Scottish Society in the Fifteenth Century*, ed. Brown. G. Donaldson, 'The Legal Profession in Scottish Society in the Sixteenth and Seventeenth Centuries', *Juridical Review* (1976) is an important and fascinating article. A different aspect of justice is discussed by Jenny Wormald, 'Bloodfeud, Kindred and Government in Early Modern Scotland', *Past and Present* 87 (1980). The concept of an 'overmighty' Scottish nobility still lingers on, but a different interpretation is suggested by Jennifer Brown, 'Scottish Politics, 1567–1625' in *James VI and I*, ed. Smith, and in articles dealing with the fourteenth and fifteenth centuries, by A. Grant, 'Earls and Earldoms in late medieval Scotland, c.1310–1460' in *Essays presented to Michael Roberts*, eds. J. Bossy and P. Jupp (Belfast, 1976) and 'The development of the Scottish Peerage', *SHR* LVII (1978), and Jennifer Brown, 'Taming the Magnates?' in *The Scottish Nation*, ed. G. Menzies (London, 1972) and 'The exercise of power' in *Scottish Society in the Fifteenth Century*, ed. Brown.

I.H. Stewart, *The Scottish Coinage* (London, 1955; revised 1967) is an invaluable work on a too-often neglected subject. S.G.E. Lythe, *The Economy of Scotland, 1550–1625, in its European Setting* (Edinburgh, 1960) is a readable and lucid discussion. The only other full-length book is I.F. Grant, *The Social and Economic Developments of Scotland before 1603* (Edinburgh, 1930), a quarry overhung with clouds of gloom. T.M. Devine and S.G.E. Lythe, 'The Economy of Scotland under James VI: a revision article', *SHR* L (1971) and S.A. Burrell, 'Calvinism, Capitalism and the Middle Classes', *Journal of Modern History* 32 (1960) both raise the question of the relevance of Weber's thesis to Scotland, a subject now analysed in a most interesting book – again, unfortunately, published after this book was written – G. Marshall, *Presbyteries and Profits* (Oxford, 1980). The *SHR* devoted one number, XLVIII (April 1969) to Scottish relations with Scandinavia, and the following number (October 1969) contained the second part of one of these articles, James Dow, 'Scottish Trade with Sweden'. The poor law is discussed in the excellent and perceptive article by Rosalind Mitchison, 'The Making of the Old Scottish Poor Law', *Past and Present* 63 (1974). Margaret H.B. Sanderson's book *Scottish Rural Society* is eagerly awaited; meanwhile, her seminal work on the feuing movement on church lands is available in a number of articles, 'The Feuars of Kirklands', *SHR* LII (1973), and 'Some Aspects of the Church in Scottish Society in the Era of the Reformation' and 'Kirkmen and their tenants in the Era of the Reformation', both in *Records of the Scottish Church History Society (RSCHS)* XVII (1970) and XVIII (1972). Also forthcoming is C.J. Larner, *Enemies of God*, the first book on Scottish witchcraft informed by anthropological as well as historical perceptions. For the Highlands, *Munro's Western Isles of Scotland, 1549* has been well edited by R.W. Munro (Edinburgh, 1961). The standard general work remains D. Gregory, *History of the Western Highlands and Isles* (2nd ed., Edinburgh, 1881; reprint 1975), and there is a turgid *History of Argyll* by C.M. MacDonald (Glasgow, 1950); the numerous clan histories range from good to tediously romantic. The Borders are the subject of the excellent book by T.I. Rae, *The Administration of the Scottish Frontier, 1513–1603* (Edinburgh, 1966), while George McDonald Fraser's *The Steel Bonnets* (London, 1971) combines the lively writing familiar to readers of Flashman with an impressive range of information.

The church is the subject of numerous works, too many of which were inspired by the 'historical inevitability' thesis of the triumph of Calvinism, lamentably exemplified, as late as 1961, by J.S. McEwen, *The Faith of John Knox* (London, 1961). As a starting-point, I.B. Cowan's 'Church and Society' in *Scottish Society in the Fifteenth Century*, ed. Brown, is an indispensable discussion of the medieval church. The *Innes Review* is a goldmine which should certainly be explored; among its wealth of articles are D. McRoberts, 'The Scottish Church and Nationalism' and J.A.F. Thomson, 'Innocent VIII and the Scottish Church', both in vol. XIX (1968), and L.J. McFarlane, 'The Primacy of the Scottish Church, 1472–1521' XX (1969). For the Reformation itself, one need look no further back than the publication of two outstanding works, *Essays on the Scottish Reformation*, ed. D. McRoberts (Glasgow, 1962) – essays that range over the whole of the sixteenth century – and G. Donaldson, *The Scottish Reformation* (Cambridge, 1960), a book that is a major achievement both in its own right, and in its visible impact on Reformation scholars who have taken up, expanded, even questioned its arguments. Major contributions in the 'post-Donaldson' era include I.B. Cowan's *Regional Aspects of the Scottish Reformation* (Historical Association Pamphlet, 1978), which opens up a comparatively neglected dimension of the subject, to be further analysed in his forthcoming book on the Reformation. Two articles by M. Lynch, 'The two Edinburgh Town-councils of 1559–60', *SHR* LIV (1975) and 'The "Faithful Brethren of Edinburgh": The Acceptable Face of Protestantism', *Bulletin of the Institute of Historical Research* LI (1978), again anticipate his book on Edinburgh, the first full-length work on a Scottish burgh at the time of the Reformation. The articles by J. Kirk, 'The Influence of Calvinism on the Scottish Reformation', *RSCHS* XVIII (1974) and 'The Polities of the Best Reformed Kirks . . . A Revision Article', *SHR* LIX (1980), along with his introduction to the *Second Book of Discipline*, argue strongly for greater continuity of thought between the early, Knoxian reformers and their Melvillian successors than Donaldson himself saw. D. Shaw is the author of a useful book, *The General Assemblies of the Church of Scotland, 1560–1600* (Edinburgh, 1964), and editor of an equally useful collection of essays, *Reformation and Revolution: Essays presented to the very rev. Hugh Watt* (Edinburgh, 1967). Only in one area has there been no advance. Modern biographies of John Knox, J. Ridley, *John Knox* (Oxford, 1968) and W. Stanford Reid, *Trumpeter of God* (New York, 1974) add little – save in Ridley's case far too many inaccuracies – to the thorough study by P. Hume Brown, *John Knox* (Edinburgh, 1895) and the lively book by Lord Eustace Percy, *John Knox* (London, 1937); and nothing has replaced T. McCrie's *Life of Andrew Melville* (2nd ed., Edinburgh, 1899). But the other works cited here, and the articles in the *Innes Review* and *RSCHS* show how far Reformation scholarship has, since the publication of *The Scottish Reformation*, broken out of the straitjacket of the well-worn theme (which admittedly the Reformers themselves subscribed to) of corruption swept away by purity.

The Reformation cannot be divorced from the wider subject of learning; and more than anyone else, John Durkan has kept the marriage between the two alive and well. His many articles which have opened up the subject of continental influence include the seminal 'Beginnings of Humanism in Scotland', *Innes Review*, IV (1953), 'The Cultural Background in the Sixteenth Century' and 'Education in the Century of the Reformation', both in *Essays on the Reformation*, ed. McRoberts, and more recently, 'Early Humanism and King's College', *Aberdeen University Review* 163 (1980) and 'Giovanni Ferrerio, Gesner and French Affairs', *Bibliothèque d'Humanisme and Renaissance* XLII (1980). He is also the co-author, with J. Kirk, of *The University of Glasgow, 1451–1577* (Glasgow, 1977), a work that notably succeeds in overcoming the remarkable difficulty of making university history 'interesting'. For the other universities: R.G. Cant, *The University of St Andrews* (Edinburgh, 1946), the work of a scholar absolutely at home in his subject; R.S. Rait, *The Universities of Aberdeen* (Aberdeen, 1895); D. Horn, *The University of Edinburgh* (Edinburgh, 1967). On literature, A.M. Kinghorn, *The Chorus of History, 1485–1558* (London, 1971) and G. Kratzman, *Anglo-Scottish Literary Relations, 1430–1550* (Cambridge, 1980) discuss English and Scottish writers. The title of R.D.S. Jack, *The Italian Influence on Scottish Literature* (Edinburgh, 1972) is self-explanatory. Two major poets are the subjects of excellent books: J. MacQueen, *Robert Henryson* (Oxford, 1967) and Priscilla Bawcutt, *Gavin Douglas* (Edinburgh, 1976); and *Bards and Makars*, eds. A.J. Aitken *et al.* (Glasgow, 1977) and *The Scottish Tradition; Essays in honour of R.G Cant*, ed. G.W.S Barrow (Edinburgh, 1974) both contain essential articles. Equally essential for the *speculum principis* tradition is R.J. Lyall, 'Politics and Poetry in Fifteenth and Sixteenth Century Scotland', *Scottish Literary Journal* (1976); and his 'Two of Dunbar's Makars: James Affleck and Sir John the Ross', *Innes Review* XXVII (1976) is a powerful, if necessarily speculative argument for the existence of two late-fifteenth-century lay poets of reputation. A hitherto neglected subject is discussed in the brief but valuable survey, G.G. Simpson, *Scottish Handwriting, 1150–1650* (Edinburgh, 1973). And Scottish apocalyptic thought has recently been given the attention it deserves in A.H. Williamson's courageous and thought-provoking *Scottish National Consciousness in the age of James VI* (Edinburgh, 1979). On architecture, J.G. Dunbar, *The Historic Architecture of Scotland* (London, 1966), S. Cruden, *The Scottish Castle* (Edinburgh, 1960) and G. Hay, *The Architecture of Scottish post-Reformation Churches* (Oxford, 1957) are all valuable and informative, while G. Stell, 'Architecture: the changing needs of society', in *Scottish Society in the Fifteenth Century*, ed. Brown, brings together two disciplines with stimulating effect. M.R. Apted, *The*

Painted Ceilings of Scotland (HMSO, 1966), contains a series of marvellous pictures, though regrettably colour was sacrificed to low price. There is a general survey of Scottish music, H.G. Farmer, *A History of Music in Scotland* (London, n.d.). For this period, the interested student should consult K. Elliott and Helena M. Shire, 'Music of Scotland, 1500–1700', *Musica Britannica* xv; and Shire's *Song, Dance and Poetry of the Court of Scotland under King James VI* (Cambridge, 1969) is a masterly work whose range extends far beyond the reign of James VI. The psalms are discussed by M. Patrick, *Four Centuries of Scottish Psalmody* (London, 1949), and by W. Cowan, 'The Scottish Reformation Psalmody' and A.G. Gilchrist, 'Psalm-versions and French tunes in the Scottish Psalter of 1564', both in *RSCHS* I (1926) and V (1933–5). As music should be listened to, not simply read about, reference is made here to the superb 'Musik fyne: songs and dances of the Scottish Court', Scottish Records no. 33, SR 133.

Appendix: Chronological Table

1468   Marriage of James III and Margaret of Denmark; Orkney (1468) and Shetland (1469) pledged as part of her dowry, and never redeemed.

1471–3 Period of over-ambitious schemes by James III for military conquest of part of Brittany, the county of Saintonge, and the duchy of Gueldres; blocked by parliament, 1473.

1472   Creation of archbishopric of St Andrews.

1474   Major shift in foreign policy, marked by marriage treaty with England; forerunner of Treaty of Perpetual Peace, 1502, and first of series of marriage proposals, none of which materialized until 1503.

1475–6 Successful campaign against John earl of Ross and Lord of the Isles; submission of Lord; forfeiture of earldom.

1479   Imprisonment of king's brothers, Alexander duke of Albany and John earl of Mar; escape of Albany to England; death of Mar. Renewal of Auld Alliance.

1482   Political *coup d'état* at Lauder, led by king's half-uncles, earls of Atholl and Buchan, and earl of Angus − king warded in Edinburgh castle until December. Berwick taken by English army. Failure of usurpation attempt by Albany.

1484   Final forfeiture and flight to France of Albany.

1487   Indult: Innocent VIII's concession whereby king given eight months to nominate to major benefices.

1488   Argyll sacked as chancellor; he, Angus, and other malcontents seized James's heir; rebel army defeated larger royal army at Sauchieburn, and king killed. Accession of James IV.

1492   Treaty with King Hans of Denmark − Norway; renewal of Auld Alliance. Creation of archbishopric of Glasgow.

1493   Final forfeiture of Lord of the Isles and suppression of the Lordship.

1495   Foundation of University of Aberdeen.

1495–7 James IV's ill-conceived support for Perkin Warbeck, pretender to the English throne; unsuccessful raid on northern England, 1496.

1499	Tripartite alliance between kings of France, Denmark, and Scotland.
1502	Scottish force sent to aid King Hans against Norwegian rebellion. 'Treaty of Perpetual Peace' between England and Scotland, with papal confirmation.
1503	Marriage of James IV and Margaret Tudor.
1509	Accession of Henry VIII; worsening relations between England and Scotland. League of Cambrai.
1512	'Holy League': Julius II, Aragon, Venice, England against France; Scotland commanded to join.
1512–13	Attempts by James IV to unite Christendom in crusade against Turks. Renewal of Auld Alliance with Louis XII.
1513	Battle of Flodden: death of king and large number of leading Scotsmen, lay and ecclesiastic. Accession of James V.
1513–28	Minority of James V.
1515–17	First period of regency of John duke of Albany; French influence, exercised through Albany, kept Scotland at peace with England.
1517	Treaty of Rouen: contained provision for marriage of James V to a daughter of Francis I.
1520	Notorious street-fight in Edinburgh between Hamiltons and Douglases: 'Cleanse the Causeway'.
1521–4	Second period of Albany regency: unsuccessful attempts by French to persuade Scots to fight English.
1525	First act against heretical – Lutheran – literature.
1526–8	King held by Archibald Douglas, earl of Angus.
1528	James's escape from Angus, and end of minority. Angus exiled. Burning of Patrick Hamilton for heresy.
1527–36	Negotiations with Charles V, Clement VII, and Francis I for marriage of James V.
1530	Punitive royal action in the borders; hanging of Johnnie Armstrong.
1531	Papal sanction for heavy taxation of church, to finance College of Justice – with paid judges.
1532	Establishment of College of Justice, from former court of session – with unpaid judges.
1535	Further act against heretical literature.
1536–7	James V's visit to France and marriage to Madeleine, daughter of Francis I (January 1537); Madeleine's death (July).
1538	Marriage of James V to Mary of Guise.
1541	Parliament that passed considerable quantity of legislation supporting church and condemning heresy. Failure of James V to turn up to agreed meeting with Henry VIII at York.
1542	Battle of Solway Moss: heavy defeat by English. Death of James V. Accession of week-old daughter, Mary.
1542–61	Minority of Mary.

1543–54   Regency of James Hamilton, earl of Arran and (from 1549) duke of Châtelherault.

1543   Act allowing reading of scripture in vernacular. Failure of Treaty of Greenwich – proposed marriage alliance between Mary and Henry VIII's son Edward.

1544   Beginning of 'Rough Wooing': English devastation of borders and Lothian.

1545   Scottish victory at Ancrum; second devastation of borders.

1546   Burning of George Wishart (March); murder of David Cardinal Beaton by group of Fife lairds (May), who occupied castle of St Andrews.

1547   Fall of St Andrews castle to French force. Battle of Pinkie – victorious English claimed to fight to free Scotland from papal domination.

1548   Treaty of Haddington: Mary to marry Dauphin. Mary sent to France.

1549   First reforming church council, two years after opening session of Council of Trent.

1550   Visit of Mary of Guise to France, with sizeable number of Scottish nobles on the make for French pensions.

1552   Second reforming council; Archbishop Hamilton's *Catechism*.

1554   Arran ousted from the regency by Mary of Guise.

1557   Invitation by small group of Protestant lords to John Knox in Geneva; rescinded. First Band of Lords of the Congregation.

1558   Marriage of Mary and the Dauphin (April). Burning of Walter Myln (April). Parliament's agreement to offer Dauphin the crown matrimonial (November). Death of Mary Tudor and accession of Elizabeth (November).

1559   'Beggars' Summons' (January). Treaty of Cateau-Cambrésis (April); fear of French action against Scottish Protestants. Return of John Knox and riot at Perth; call to arms by Protestants (May). Appointment of Protestant ministers in several burghs, and establishment of kirk session of St Andrews. Regent 'suspended' by Lords of the Congregation (October). Last major reforming council of old church.

1560   English siege of Leith (March). Death of Mary of Guise (June). Treaty of Leith and withdrawal of French and English troops (July). Reformation parliament (August). General Assembly of reformed kirk in being by December. Death of Mary's husband Francis II (December). First Book of Discipline produced.

1561   Mary's return to Scotland (August).

1562   Attempt to finance the new church: the Thirds of Benefices.

1565   Renewed Protestant fears, throughout Europe, of Catholic league involving Scottish queen. Mary's marriage to Henry lord Darnley, and defeat of rebellion led by her Protestant half-brother James earl of Moray – the 'Chaseabout Raid'.

1566	Murder of David Rizzio. Birth of prince James.
1567	Murder of Darnley. Marriage of Mary and James Hepburn, earl of Bothwell. Defeat of Mary and Bothwell at battle of Carberry; Bothwell fled, Mary imprisoned and forced to abdicate in favour of her son, with Moray as regent.
1568	Mary's escape from Lochleven castle, defeat by king's party at battle of Langside, and flight to England.
1570	Assassination of regent Moray.
1572	James Douglas earl of Morton became regent (after short-lived regencies of the earls of Lennox and Mar). Concordat of Leith. Death of John Knox.
1573	Fall of Edinburgh castle — final defeat of remnant of queen's party. Act of Conformity.
1574	Return of Andrew Melville from Geneva. First Poor law.
1577	'Nova Erectio' of Glasgow University, under Melville as principal.
1578	Final version of Second Book of Discipline produced. Fall of Morton.
1579	Arrival from France of James VI's first 'favourite', Esmé Stuart, lord d'Aubigny; created earl of Lennox (1580), then duke (1581). Second Poor Law.
1581	'Negative' Confession of Faith. Thirteen 'model' presbyteries set up. Execution of Morton. Beginning of regular taxation.
1582	'Ruthven Raid': king seized by earls of Gowrie and Mar.
1582–3	Foundation of University of Edinburgh.
1583	King's escape from Ruthven Raiders. Execution of Gowrie, and exile to England of his associates, including some of the Melvillian ministers. Ascendancy of James Stewart, earl of Arran.
1584	The 'Black Acts' (*inter alia*, asserting supremacy of crown in ecclesiastical affairs, denouncing presbyteries) passed.
1585	Fall of Arran; return of exiled lords.
1586	Return of Andrew Melville and other ministers.
1587	Act of Annexation: episcopacy weakened by annexation of temporalities. Shire Election Act. Attempt to introduce justices of the peace. General Band, relating to highlands and borders. Execution of Mary queen of Scots.
1588	Spanish Armada: used by James to negotiate cash from Elizabeth.
1589	Letters from George earl of Huntly to Philip II of Spain intercepted by English. Beginning of feud in north-east Scotland between Huntly and Moray. Marriage of James VI to Anne of Denmark.
1590–7	Period of savage persecution of witches, beginning with North Berwick trials.
1592	Huntly's murder of Moray. The 'Spanish Blanks' — further letters by Huntly to Philip II. The 'Golden Acts' passed.
1593	Foundation of second university at Aberdeen, Marischal College.

1595   Exile of Catholic earls, Huntly and Erroll, and of Francis earl of Bothwell.

1596   Return of Catholic earls; their reconciliation with the kirk. 'Octavians' appointed − committee to manage king's finances; sacked within a year − despite success. 'The constant platt': scheme by Lindsay of Balcarres to improve financial position of ministry. Riot in Edinburgh, turned to advantage of king against ministers.

1597   Anglo-Scottish commission set up to deal with borders.

1597−9   Publication of James VI's *Daemonologie* (1597), *True Law of Free Monarchies* (1598), *Basilikon Doron* (1599).

1600−25   Twenty earls created: majority were men prominent on council − the ruling élite after James's departure for England.

1600   Appointment of three 'parliamentary' bishops: first reversal of eclipse of episcopate. Gowrie conspiracy: survival of king, death of Gowrie and his brother.

1602   Attempt by 'Gentlemen Advanturers of Fife' to colonize Lewis.

1603   Death of Elizabeth. Accession of James to English throne.

1605−6   Further attempts to settle lowlanders in Lewis.

1606   Andrew Melville and seven presbyterian ministers summoned to London; imprisoned. Melville kept in Tower of London until 1611, then in exile until his death, 1622.

1609   Statutes of Iona.

1609−10   Act establishing commissioners of the shires; appointment of JPs.

1610   Restoration of diocesan episcopacy.

1611   Death of George Home, earl of Dunbar, major figure of Scottish government in absence of king; place taken by Alexander Seton, earl of Dunfermline and chancellor.

1612   Opposition in parliament to amount of taxation demanded, led by Michael lord Burleigh.

1617   King's visit to Scotland. Great enthusiasm marred by widespread hostility to his religious policy: the Five Articles of Perth, rejected by general assembly. Parliamentary support for 'constant platt'. Comprehensive act about justices of the peace.

1618   Five Articles passed by general assembly.

1621   Parliament: scene of major struggle to get Five Articles and new form of taxation accepted.

1623   Worst famine year.

1625   Death of James VI.

Index

208